Design Classics
1880-1930

Torsten Bröhan
Thomas Berg

Design Classics
1880-1930

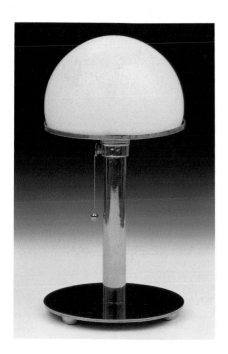

TASCHEN

KÖLN LONDON MADRID NEW YORK PARIS TOKYO

The picture material in this book
comes from the Torsten Bröhan
Archive, Düsseldorf. The objects were
photographed by Angela Bröhan,
Munich, Walter Klein and Horst
Kolberg, Düsseldorf.

Page 2:
Gerrit Thomas Rietveld: »Red-Blue«-
chair, 1918/23

© 2001 TASCHEN GmbH
Hohenzollernring 53, D-50672 Köln
www.taschen.com

© 2001 VG Bild-Kunst, Bonn, for the
works of Josef Albers, Herbert Bayer,
Peter Behrens, Vassilij Kandinsky, Adolf
Loos, Richard Riemerschmid, Gerrit
Rietveld, Herbert Schulze

Edited by Simone Philippi, Cologne
Design: Schnitzler & Wichelhaus
Designagentur, Düsseldorf
English translation: Ishbel Flett,
Frankfurt/Main
French translation: Annie Berthold,
Düsseldorf

Printed in Italy
ISBN 3-8228-6876-0

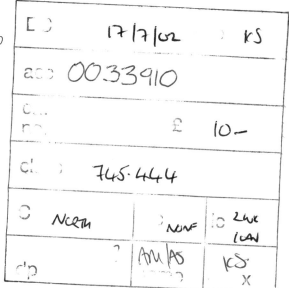

Contents

Inhalt

Sommaire

Design Classics
1880-1930

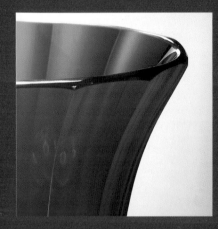

Design is, without a doubt, not only one of the most significant but also one of the most fascinating cultural phenomena of the 20th century. In recent years, the media have increasingly drawn the attention and interest of the public at large to design-related topics. The contributions made by designers to the major German art event in the summer of 1987, »Documenta 8«, and to other similarly spectacular exhibitions, have helped to promote design to the status of an independent art form which is now widely accepted as the equal of painting, sculpture, architecture and photography. This growing interest in design has resulted in the creation of separate design departments in a number of public and private collections and has led to the foundation of several independent design museums. In all these cases, attention has been focused just as closely on contemporary design as on design classics.

This publication outlines the pioneer years of modern design, tracing the development of the design avantgarde between 1880 and 1930. In doing so, it concentrates primarily on design in the German-speaking countries of Europe, where, before the outbreak of the Second World War, the achievements of the Bauhaus and other schools of applied art made what were probably the most significant and interesting contributions, and laid the theoretical foundations for the design development of the 20th century.

Design ist sicher eines der bedeutendsten und faszinierendsten Kulturphänomene im 20. Jahrhundert. In den letzten Jahren ist das Interesse einer breiten Öffentlichkeit an Designthemen durch die Berichterstattung der Medien stark angewachsen. Besonders durch die Beiträge von Designern auf der documenta 8 im Sommer 1987 und anderen spektakulären Ausstellungsereignissen rückte »Design« als eine eigenständige Kunstform neben Malerei, Plastik, Architektur und Fotografie. Diese Designbegeisterung führte dazu, daß eine große Anzahl öffentlicher und privater Sammlungen Designabteilungen gründeten und einige neue eigenständige Designmuseen ins Leben gerufen wurden. Das Interesse der Museumsleute galt dabei zu gleichen Teilen dem zeitgenössischen und dem klassischen Design.

In der hier vorgelegten Publikation soll die Pionierzeit der modernen Designentwicklung, das heißt die Entwicklung der Design-Avantgarde zwischen 1880 und 1930 nachgezeichnet werden. Im Mittelpunkt dieser Darstellung steht dabei das Design im deutschsprachigen Raum. Hier wurden bis zum Ausbruch des Zweiten Weltkrieges insbesondere durch die Leistung des Bauhauses und anderer Kunstschulen die vielleicht wichtigsten und interessantesten Beiträge sowie theoretischen Voraussetzungen für die Designentwicklung des 20. Jahrhunderts erarbeitet.

Le design est certainement l'un des phénomènes culturels les plus importants et les plus fascinants du XXème siècle. L'intérêt du grand public pour ce phénomène s'est considérablement accru ces dernières années grâce aux médias. C'est grâce aussi en particulier aux contributions des designers à la documenta 8 de l'été 1987 et à d'autres événements spectaculaires de ce genre que le «design» est devenu une forme d'art à part entière au même titre que la peinture, les arts plastiques, l'architecture et la photographie. L'engouement grandissant pour la stylique fit qu'un grand nombre de collections privées et publiques s'adjoignirent des sections design et que certaines même créèrent des musées spécialisés. Leur intérêt portait aussi bien sur le design contemporain que sur le design classique.

Nous étudierons ici l'époque héroïque de l'histoire du design, c'est-à-dire le design d'avant-garde de 1880 à 1930, en particulier dans les pays de langue allemande. C'est en effet dans ces pays que, grâce avant tout au Bauhaus et à d'autres écoles d'art, se sont élaborées les créations peut-être les plus intéressantes et les plus importantes ainsi que les conditions théoriques les plus propices à l'évolution du design au XXème siècle.

Christopher Dresser,
1881

Decanter
Glass, silver, ebony
Silverware manufacturers
Hukin & Hèath,
London & Birmingham
Height: 22 cm

Weinkanne
Glas, Silberfassung,
Ebenholz
Silberwarenfabrik
Hukin & Heath,
London & Birmingham
Höhe: 22 cm

Cruche à vin
Verre, monture argent,
bois d'ébène
Manufacture d'objets en
argent Hukin & Heath,
Londres & Birmingham
Hauteur: 22 cm

The origins of modern design history are to be found in 19th-century England. With the rise of industrialisation and the social changes it wrought, the call for a new unity of art and life was voiced here earlier than elsewhere. The leading figures of this movement were the writer, reformer and painter John Ruskin and the painter and social critic William Morris. It was William Morris, in fact, who was the first to make the decisive crossover from fine artist to craftsman and designer. The Arts and Crafts movement founded by Morris attracted many young artists and craftsmen who, in turn, made major contributions to this reformative style. Amongst this group, which included such outstanding designers as Charles Robert Ashbee and Archibald Knox (ill. p. 29), the most important figure was undoubtedly Christopher Dresser. He may be regarded as Europe's very first industrial designer, a forerunner of Peter Behrens. In his designs, Dresser consciously catered to industrial needs, thereby contributing to the aesthetic and technical improvement of industrially produced goods. If we compare his wine decanter (ill. p. 8) of 1881 with the tea maker designed by Herbert Schulze (ill. p. 11), one of today's most talented silversmiths, we realise just how far ahead of his time Dresser's designs actually were – indeed, it is hard to believe that more than a century separates these two designs. For all their subjective differences, the similarity between them may well lie in the designers' mutual

Die Anfänge der modernen Designgeschichte sind bereits im 19. Jahrhundert in England auszumachen. Infolge der beginnenden Industrialisierung und der damit verbundenen sozialen Veränderungen wurde hier früher als anderswo die Forderung nach einer »neuen« Einheit von Kunst und Leben programmatisch gestellt. Die Protagonisten dieser Bewegung waren der Schriftsteller, Sozialreformer und Maler John Ruskin und der Maler und Sozialpolitiker William Morris. Letzterer wagte als erster den entscheidenden Schritt vom bildenden Künstler zum Handwerker und Entwerfer. Die von Morris begründete sogenannte »Arts & Crafts«-Bewegung zog viele junge Künstler und Handwerker an, die ihrerseits wichtige Beiträge zu diesem Reformstil leisteten. Aus diesem Kreis wichtiger Gestalterpersönlichkeiten, zu denen u.a. Charles Robert Ashbee und Archibald Knox (Abb. S. 29) zählten, besaß Christopher Dresser sicher die größte Bedeutung. Er kann vor Peter Behrens als erster europäischer Industriedesigner bezeichnet werden. Dresser machte seine zukunftsweisenden und vorbildlich gestalteten Entwürfe gezielt der Industrie verfügbar und trug damit zur ästhetischen und handwerklichen Verbesserung der seriellen Güterproduktion bei. Wie zukunftsweisend seine Entwürfe waren, kann beim Vergleich seiner 1881 entstandenen Weinkanne (Abb. S. 8) mit der Teemaschine von Herbert Schulze (Abb. S. 11), einem der begabtesten Silberschmiede der Gegenwart, abgelesen werden.

L'histoire du design commence en Angleterre au XIXème siècle. En raison de l'industrialisation et des bouleversements sociaux qui se produisaient, un mouvement étaient prônant une nouvelle «unité» entre l'art et la vie se créa plus tôt qu'ailleurs. Les protagonistes de ce mouvement l'écrivain, réformateur social et peintre John Ruskin et William Morris, peintre et homme politique social. Ce dernier osa faire le pas en devenant artisan et concepteur. Le mouvement Arts and Crafts qu'il créa attira un grand nombre de jeunes artistes et d'artisans qui apportèrent ainsi eux aussi leur tribut à ce style. Parmi les personnalités importantes de ce mouvement – Charles Robert Ashbee et Archibald Knox (ill. p. 29) étaient de ce nombre – Christopher Dresser était certainement la plus marquante. Il peut être considéré avec Peter Behrens comme le premier designer industriel européen. Dresser mit délibérement ses créations très en avance sur leur temps et parfaitement bien conçues à la disposition de l'industrie, contribuant ainsi à l'amélioration esthétique et à la qualité artisanale de la production en série. On peut se rendre compte combien ses créations anticipaient l'avenir en comparant sa cruche à vin datant de 1881 (ill. p. 8) avec la machine à thé de Herbert Schulze (ill. p. 11) un des orfèvres les plus doués de notre époque. Rien ne permet d'imaginer qu'un siècle sépare ces deux objets. Malgré toutes leurs différences individuelles, elles se ressemblent, et cette ressemblance plastique tient probable-

*Herbert Schulze,
1990*

Teamaker
*Silver, glass, ebony
Fachhochschule für
Gestaltung, Düsseldorf
Height: 17.2 cm*

Teemaschine
*Silber, Laborglas,
Ebenholz
Fachhochschule für
Gestaltung, Düsseldorf
Höhe: 17,2 cm*

Machine à thé
*en argent, verre de la-
boratoire, bois d'ébène
Fachhochschule für
Gestaltung, Düsseldorf
Hauteur: 17,2 cm*

quest for a maximum reduction of form in concert with maximum aesthetic effect. The most striking feature of these designs is their simplicity of form in relation to function. Influenced by the English Arts and Crafts movement, the leading Scottish architect Charles Rennie Mackintosh (1864-1928) created a distinctive variation of his own which became known as the Glasgow Style. Like Dresser, Mackintosh adopted certain Oriental influences, as can be seen in the chair he designed for the Chinese Room at Miss Cranston's Ingram Street Tea Rooms in Glasgow (ill. p. 13). The sophisticated purism of Mackintosh's works appealed to the stylistic tastes of the Austrian reform movement. It was this, together with the enthusiasm for Ashbee's Guild of Handicraft and its workshop principles, that led to the foundation of the Wiener Werkstätte (Vienna Workshop) by Josef Hoffmann and his friends in July 1903, which may be regarded as the birth of the Modern Movement in continental Europe. Turn-of-the-century Vienna saw the emergence of a formal syntax based on simple geometric elements such as the circle, square, triangle and octagon.

Man sollte nicht glauben, daß mehr als 100 Jahre zwischen beiden Entwürfen liegen. Der Grund der gestalterischen Ähnlichkeit dürfte bei aller persönlichen Unterschiedlichkeit die Suche nach maximaler Formreduzierung bei höchstmöglicher ästhetischer Wirkung sein. Das Spektakuläre dieser Entwürfe liegt in der Schlichtheit einer gefundenen Urform im Verhältnis zu der gewünschten Funktion. Beeinflußt von der englischen »Arts & Crafts«-Bewegung schuf der bedeutende schottische Architekt Charles Rennie Mackintosh (1864 –1928) eine eigenständige Ausprägung dieses Stils, den sogenannten »Glasgow Style«. Mackintosh verarbeitete, ähnlich wie Dresser, ostasiatische Einflüsse, wie der Stuhl aus dem chinesischen Raum für den Teesalon von Miss Cranston's in der Glasgower Ingram Street belegt (Abb. S. 13). Die gestalterische Ausstrahlung der Werke von Mackintosh mit ihrer raffinierten Puristik kam dem Stilempfinden der österreichischen Erneuerungsbewegung sehr entgegen. Sie führte zusammen mit der Begeisterung für die in England von Ashbee gegründete »Guild of Handicraft« und dem hier praktizierten Werkstättenprinzip schließlich im Juli 1903 zur Gründung der Wiener Werkstätte durch Josef Hoffmann und seine Freunde. Dies war die Geburtsstunde des gestalterischen Aufbruchs in die Moderne auf dem europäischen Kontinent. So entstand in Wien zu Beginn dieses Jahrhunderts eine Formensprache, die sich auf einfache geometrische Grundelemente wie Kreis, Quadrat, Dreieck und Achteck zurückführen ließ.

ment à la recherche de la réduction optimale des formes sans pour autant perdre de vue l'effet le plus esthétique qui soit. Ce qui frappe aussi dans ces deux créations c'est la sobriété d'une forme élémentaire trouvée, par rapport à la fonction recherchée. L'éminent architecte écossais Charles Rennie Mackintosh (1864-1928) créa son propre style à partir du mouvement anglais Arts and Crafts, le «Glasgow Style». A l'instar de Dresser, Mackintosh avait assimilé les influences de l'art asiatique comme en témoigne la chaise de genre chinois conçue pour le salon de thé de Miss Cranston's dans Ingram Street à Glasgow (ill. p. 13). Grâce à la pureté raffinée de leur conception il émanait des œuvres de Makkintosh un attrait qui répondait aux inclinations stylistiques du mouvement réformateur autrichien. Poussés par leur enthousiasme pour la «Guild of Handicraft» fondée en Angleterre par Ashbee et pour le principe du travail en atelier qui y était déjà pratiqué, Josef Hoffmann et ses amis créèrent en juillet 1903 les Ateliers viennois. L'heure du renouveau créateur et du modernisme venait de sonner sur le continent européen. Ainsi à Vienne au début de ce siècle, un nouveau vocabulaire des formes basé sur des figures géométriques tels que cercle, carré, triangle et octogone vit le jour.

Charles Rennie Mackintosh, c. 1905

Cutlery for the Ingram Street Tea Rooms, Glasgow
Metal, silver-plated
Length: 21 cm
(fish knife)

Besteckteile für die Ingram Street Tea Rooms, Glasgow
Metall, versilbert
Länge: 21 cm
(Fischmesser)

Couverts pour les salons de thé d'Ingram Street à Glasgow
Métal argenté
Longueur: 21 cm
(couteau à poisson)

Charles Rennie Mackintosh, 1911

Chair for Ingram Street Tea Rooms
Black-painted maple, horsehair upholstery
Height: 82.5 cm

Stuhl für die Ingram Street Tea Rooms
Ahorn, schwarz lakkiert, Roßhaarbezug
Höhe: 82,5 cm

Chaise pour les salons de thé d'Ingram Street à Glasgow
Erable laqué noir, garniture rembourrée de crins de cheval
Hauteur: 82,5 cm

This highly innovative period in the history of design and the contribution Vienna made to the Modern Movement are clearly illustrated by way of example by the items presented in this publication: Adolf Loos' 1902/04 clock (ill. p. 42), Josef Hoffmann's 1904 chair for the dining room of the Purkersdorf Sanatorium (ill. p. 44) and his German silver dish with lid (ill. p. 50) designed in the same year, or the extraordinarily delicate buckle by Koloman Moser from the same period (ill. p. 47). In the field of glass design, Otto Prutscher was the leading proponent of these design principles (ill. p. 52 and ill. p. 53).

In 1897, six years before the foundation of the Wiener Werkstätte, the Vereinigte Werkstätte für Kunst in Handwerk (United Workshops for Art in Handicraft) were founded in Munich. This blend of art and crafts propagated the unity of artistic design and high-quality craftsmanship at affordable prices. Apart from Munich, another centre of the reform movement in Germany was to be found in Weimar, where Henry van de Velde founded the Sächsische Kunstgewerbeschule (Grand Ducal Saxon School of Arts and Crafts) in 1906. At the time, however, the most important hub of creative innovation was the artists' colony on the Mathildenhöhe in Darmstadt, founded in 1899 by Grand Duke Ernst Ludwig of Hesse.

Diese Zeit des Aufbruchs zu neuen Gestaltungsinhalten und damit Wiens Beitrag zur Moderne wird an vielen hier vorgestellten Objekten nachvollziehbar: Adolf Loos' 1902/04 entworfene Kaminuhr (Abb. S. 42), Josef Hoffmanns 1904 entworfener Stuhl für den Speisesaal des Sanatoriums Purkersdorf (Abb. S. 44) und seine im gleichen Jahr entstandene Deckeldose aus Alpacca (Abb. S. 50), aber auch durch die unerhört delikate Gürtelschnalle von Koloman Moser aus dem gleichen Jahr (Abb. S. 47). Im Glasbereich wurden diese Gestaltungsprinzipien vor allem durch Otto Prutscher umgesetzt (Abb. S. 52 und S. 53).

Bereits sechs Jahre vor Gründung der Wiener Werkstätte, also 1897, wurden in München die »Vereinigten Werkstätten für Kunst im Handwerk« gegründet. Dieser Zusammenschluß propagierte die Einheit von künstlerischem Entwurf und dessen qualitätvoller Ausführung zu sozial verträglichen Preisen. Neben München besaß Deutschland mit dem von Henry van de Velde beeinflußten Weimar – er hatte dort 1906 die Sächsische Kunstgewerbeschule gegründet – ein weiteres Zentrum der Reformbewegung. Die für die Folgezeit wichtigen neuen Impulse gingen jedoch noch stärker von der 1899 von Großherzog Ernst Ludwig von Hessen und bei Rhein ins Leben gerufenen Darmstädter Künstlerkolonie auf der Mathildenhöhe aus.

Ce temps du renouveau de la conception artistique et des formes, et donc du rôle joué par Vienne dans l'avènement du modernisme, sera perceptible dans de nombreux objets exposés ici : la pendule de cheminée d'Adolf Loos créée en 1902/04 (ill. p. 42), la chaise de Josef Hoffmann pour la salle à manger du sanatorium de Purkersdorf datant de 1904 (ill. p. 44) et la même année encore sa boîte à couvercle en argentan (ill. p. 50) sans oublier la boucle de ceinture de Koloman Moser d'une délicatesse inouïe créée la même année (ill. p. 47). Dans le domaine du verre, c'est surtout Otto Prutscher qui a su mettre en pratique ces nouveaux principes de création (ill. p. 52 et p.53).

Six ans déjà avant la création des Ateliers viennois, donc en 1897, les «Münchener Vereinigten Werkstätten für Kunst im Handwerk», les Ateliers réunis munichois, avaient ouvert leurs portes. Ce groupe propagea l'unité de la création artistique et la réalisation de qualité à des prix accessibles. Outre Munich, l'Allemagne possédait un autre centre de renouveau artistique, l'Ecole des Arts décoratifs de Saxe, créée par Henry van de Velde en 1906 à Weimar. Mais c'est de la colonie d'artistes de la colline Sainte-Mathilde à Darmstadt fondée par le grand-duc Ernest Ludovic de Hesse en 1899 qu'allaient venir au cours de la période suivante les impulsions les plus intéressantes en matière de création.

The colony's leading lights, Joseph Maria Olbrich and Peter Behrens, were joined by Patriz Huber, Hans Christiansen, Paul Haustein and Albin Müller, whose design achievements (ill. p. 54 - ill. p. 63) certainly bear comparison with the work of the Wiener Werkstätte in terms of consistent design and sheer expressiveness.

Even though the reform movement at the turn of the century had produced a new style, this was frequently manifested only in the form of expensive one-off items or limited editions of hand-crafted goods. In seeking to imitate the new style, the mass production of goods often resulted in the same mediocre artistic and technical standards which had been the bane of the 19th century. In the face of social change and new technical possibilities, the middle-class craftsmen and artists began to take a stand against the luxurious aesthetic culture of the wealthy elite, favouring in its place the creation of a more broadly based stylistic culture. The most important artistic representative of this new association of artists, architects, craftsmen and industrialists was Peter Behrens. His designs for the German general electrical company Allgemeine Berliner Electricitäts-gesellschaft (AEG) not only gave us the pioneering architecture of his AEG turbine hall, but also heralded the beginnings of an early form of corporate design and corporate identity.

Um die beiden wichtigsten Vertreter der Künstlerkolonie, Joseph Maria Olbrich und Peter Behrens, gruppierten sich Patriz Huber, Hans Christiansen, Paul Haustein und Albin Müller, deren Gestaltungsleistungen (Abb. S. 54 bis S. 63) sich durchaus in ihrer Konsequenz und Aussagekraft mit denen der Wiener Werkstätte messen lassen können.

Auch wenn die Reformbewegung der Jahrhundertwende einen neuen Stil hervorgebracht hatte, so manifestierte sich dieser oft nur in Form kostbarer Einzelanfertigungen oder in der Produktion aufwendiger Kleinserien mit zumeist kunsthandwerklichem Charakter. In der diesem Stil nachempfundenen Massenproduktion von Gebrauchsgütern war jedoch die gleiche minderwertige künstlerische und technische Qualität wie im 19. Jahrhundert anzutreffen. Im Zuge der fortschreitenden gesellschaftlichen Veränderungen und der neuen technischen Möglichkeiten bildete sich aus bürgerlichen Kreisen aller Berufsstände und Künstlern eine Opposition gegen eine luxuriös gestaltete ästhetische Kultur für eine begüterte Elite; man forderte dagegen eine Formkultur auf breiter Basis. Wichtigster künstlerischer Repräsentant dieser neuen, im Werkbund zusammengefaßten Vereinigung von Künstlern, Architekten, Handwerkern und Industriellen war Peter Behrens. Aus seiner künstlerischen Arbeit für die »Allgemeine Berliner Elektricitätsgesellschaft« (AEG) resultierte nicht nur der wegweisende Bau der Turbinenfabrik, sondern auch die Schaffung einer Frühform des »Corporate Design« und der »Corporate Identity«.

Les deux éminents représentants de cette colonie, Joseph Maria Olbrich et Peter Behrens, furent rejoints par Patriz Huber, Hans Christiansen, Paul Haustein et Albin Müller dont les œuvres (ill. p. 54-p. 63) pouvaient se mesurer à celles de la Wiener Werkstätte par leur force d'expression et leur démarche systématique.

Même si le mouvement de renouveau culturel du tournant du siècle a produit un nouveau style, c'était encore souvent sous la forme de réalisations uniques et de valeur ou de petites séries coûteuses fabriquées industriellement avec un caractère artisanal. Mais la production en masse d'objets utilitaires dans ce style présentait le même niveau technique et la même médiocrité artistique qu'au XIXème siècle. Avec les transformations sociales et l'apparition de nouvelles techniques, une opposition commença à se manifester: dans les cercles bourgeois – toutes professions confondues – et chez les artistes, on tirait à boulets rouges sur une culture esthétique tournée vers le luxe et réservée à une élite fortunée, revendiquant au contraire la création d'une culture des formes touchant une plus large fraction de la population. Le représentant le plus marquant sur le plan artistique des architectes, des artistes, des artisans et des industriels regroupés dans le Werkbund était sans conteste Peter Behrens. Son travail artistique pour la «Allgemeine Berliner Elektricitätsgesellschaft» (AEG) n'eut pas seulement pour conséquence la construction très innovatrice de l'usine de turbines mais aussi la création d'une première forme du «Corporate Design» et de la «Corporate Identity».

Two distinct groups began to emerge amongst the members of the Deutscher Werkbund, both representing different attitudes to design in the 20th century: standardisation on the one hand and artistic individuality on the other. Whereas Hermann Muthesius was the spokesman of the first group, van de Velde upheld the other view. The 1914 Werkbund exhibition in Cologne clearly represented both of these design principles: precious luxury glasses produced by the Lötz Witwe glassworks to designs by artists of the Viennese avantgarde could be seen alongside mass-produced glasses by German manufacturers to designs by renowned artists.

The outbreak of the First World War temporarily interrupted this mood of innovation. In 1919, however, when the Bauhaus was established in Weimar by Walter Gropius, it adopted many of the ideas which had already been discussed amongst members of the Werkbund. The teachers and students of the Bauhaus believed in abolishing the distinction between »free« and »applied« art as a basic prerequisite for their future work. For these artists, design was primarily a means of didactic experimentation aimed at contributing towards a more humane environment. The Bauhaus objective of applying aesthetic principles to the production of functional goods is particularly evident in the furniture designs influenced by the Bauhaus artists. The most important representatives of this phenomenon are Marcel Breuer and Ludwig Mies van der Rohe. The standard »types« of tubular steel furniture presented here at their

Unter den Mitgliedern des Werkbundes polarisierten sich zwei Gruppierungen, die die beiden unterschiedlichen Positionen gestalterischen Arbeitens im 20. Jahrhundert vertraten: Standardisierung und Typisierung der Produkte auf der einen Seite, künstlerische Individualität auf der anderen. Während Hermann Muthesius für die erste Gruppe sprach, kämpfte van de Velde auf der anderen Seite. Noch auf der 1914 in Köln veranstalteten Werkbund-Ausstellung waren Gestaltungsbeispiele beider Auffassungen zu sehen: z. B. kostbare Luxusgläser der Glashütte Lötz Witwe nach Künstlerentwürfen der Wiener Avantgarde und seriell ausgeführte Gläser deutscher Hersteller nach Entwürfen namhafter Künstler.

Der Ausbruch des Ersten Weltkrieges führte zu einer vorübergehenden Unterbrechung der Erneuerungsbewegung. Aber bereits 1919 wurden mit der Gründung des Staatlichen Bauhauses in Weimar durch Walter Gropius viele der bereits unter Repräsentanten des Werkbundes diskutierten Ideen wieder aufgenommen. Für das künstlerische Selbstverständnis der am Bauhaus tätigen Lehrer und Schüler war die Aufhebung der Unterscheidung zwischen »freier« und »angewandter« Kunst Grundvoraussetzung zukünftigen Wirkens. Designarbeit war für die Künstler hier zunächst ein Mittel zum didaktischen Experiment mit dem Ziel, zu einer menschenwürdigeren Umwelt beizutragen. Der Anspruch des Bauhauses bei der Umsetzung ästhetischer Vorstellungen für die Produktion von Gebrauchsgütern läßt sich besonders gut bei dem durch Künstler des Bauhauses beeinflußten Möbeldesign emp-

Les membres du Werkbund se scindèrent en deux groupes dont les opinions divergeaient sur la création au XXème siècle : l'un prônait la création de «types» et la standardisation des produits, l'autre l'individualité artistique. Hermann Muthesius parlait au nom du premier groupe, Henry van de Velde au nom du second. Lors de l'exposition du Werkbund en 1914 à Cologne, les deux manières de voir étaient encore représentées : des verres luxueux et coûteux de la Verrerie Lötz Witwe d'après des modèles de l'avant-garde viennoise et des verres fabriqués en série par des fabricants allemands d'après des modèles d'artistes renommés.

Le débút de la Première Guerre mondiale stoppa momentanément le mouvement de renouveau artistique. Mais, dès 1919, avec la fondation du Bauhaus à Weimar par Walter Gropius, bon nombre d'idées déjà discutées parmi les représentants du Werkbund furent finalement reprises. Selon la conception artistique des professeurs et des élèves du Bauhaus, supprimer la distinction entre art «libre» et art «appliqué» était la condition préalable à leurs activités futures. Le travail de design était pour les artistes d'abord un moyen d'expérimentation didactique en vue de participer à la création d'un environnement plus humain. Le Bauhaus avait la prétention de donner une orientation aux idées esthétiques régissant la production d'objets utilitaires, comme l'indique clairement le design de meubles des artistes de l'école, Marcel Breuer et Ludwig Mies van der Rohe étant certainement les représentants les plus éminents de ces desi-

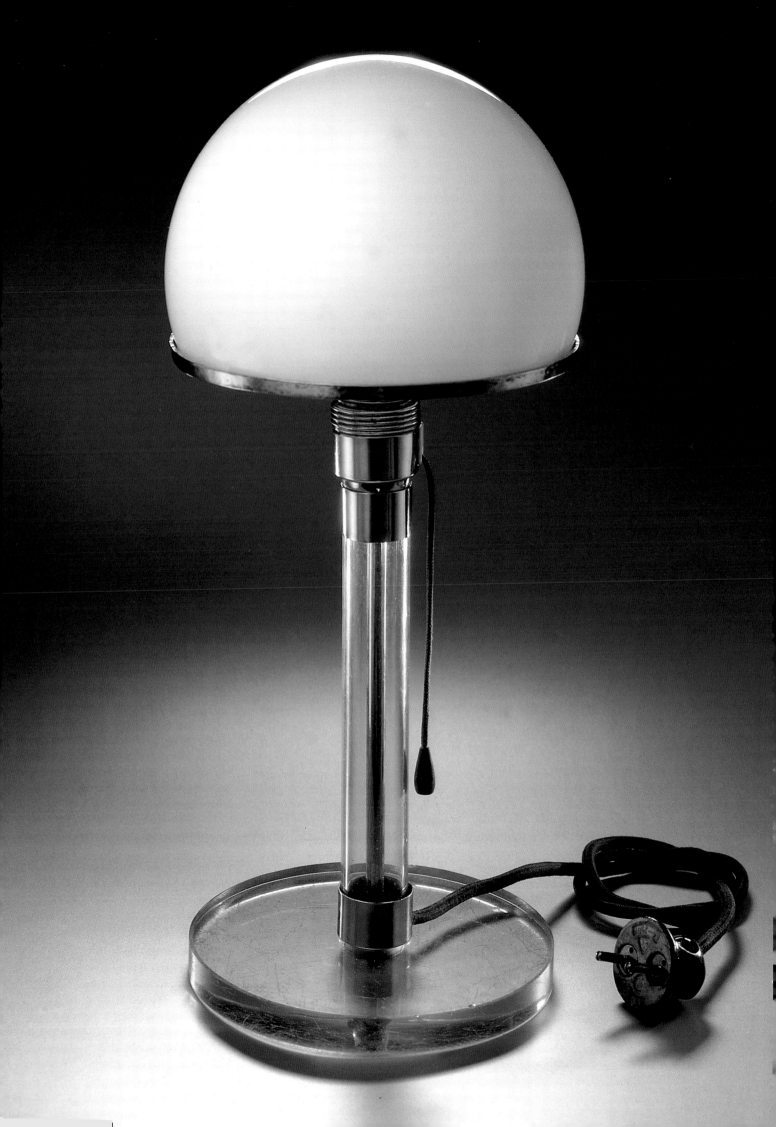

Otto Lindig, c. 1935

Vase
Earthenware, glaze
Ceramic workshop of
Otto Lindig, Dornburg
Height: 17.5 cm

Vase
Steinzeug, Überlauf-
glasur
Keramische Werkstatt
Otto Lindig, Dornburg
Höhe: 17,5 cm

Vase
en grès, vernis
Atelier de céramique
Otto Lindig, Dornburg
Hauteur: 17,5 cm

various stages of development – as prototypes, small artisanal series and industrially mass-produced items (ill. p. 88 - ill. p. 91) – clearly illustrate the design concepts which emerged in the wake of mass production.

The art schools with design ambitions operating at the same time as the Bauhaus include, in particular, the Burg Giebichenstein School of Applied Arts in Halle under the directorship of Paul Thiersch. In contrast to the Bauhaus, a more traditional approach to craftsmanship and workshop production predominated here. Nevertheless, the school did work closely with industrial enterprises – Marguerite Friedlaender's 1930 »Hallesche Form« tea- and coffee-set design for the KPM porcelain manufactury in Berlin (ill. p. 122 and ill. p. 123) proved a major commercial success for the company.

The Bauhaus and the other reformative schools created an intellectual climate which was also supported by a number of design and crafts groups not directly associated with these institutes, both in Germany and abroad. These include such artists as silversmith Emmy Roth (ill. p. 136 and ill. p. 137), Paula Straus (ill. p. 139), and Theodor Wende (ill. p. 134 and ill. p. 135), as well as such architects as Serge Chermayeff (ill. p. 132), Kay Fisker (ill. p. 144), Poul Henningsen (ill. p. 131), Alvar Aalto (ill. p. 130), or J. J. P. Oud (ill. p. 129) whose exemplary works are presented in this publication. This era saw the emergence of an international design style which was soon to gain a foothold in the USA (ill. p. 141).

finden. Als wichtigste Vertreter können Marcel Breuer und Ludwig Mies van der Rohe angeführt werden. Anhand der hier publizierten »Typen« von Stahlrohrmöbeln in ihren verschiedenen Entwicklungsstufen – Prototyp, handwerkliche Kleinserie und industrielle Großproduktion (Abb. S. 88 bis S. 91) – lassen sich die gestalterischen Konzepte nachvollziehen, die die Serienproduktion mit sich brachte.

Zu den parallel zum Bauhaus agierenden Kunstschulen mit Designambitionen zählte insbesondere die von Paul Thiersch geleitete Kunstgewerbeschule Burg Giebichenstein in Halle. Im Gegensatz zum Bauhaus wurden die dort gelehrten und praktizierten Gestaltungsprinzipien durch eine stärker an der Tradition orientierte Auffassung von Handwerk und Werkstattarbeit dominiert. Trotzdem wurde gerade hier eine wichtige Kooperation zwischen entwerfender Schule und einem Industriebetrieb realisiert. Gemeint ist das von Marguerite Friedlaender 1930 für die Staatliche Porzellanmanufaktur (KPM) in Berlin entworfene Tee- und Kaffeeservice »Hallesche Form« (Abb. S. 122 und S. 123), das für die ausführende Firma ein großer wirtschaftlicher Erfolg wurde.

Das Bauhaus und die anderen Reformschulen schufen ein geistiges Klima, das ideell auch von einer Vielzahl von nicht direkt mit diesen Instituten zusammenarbeitenden Gestalter- und Handwerkerkreisen nicht nur in Deutschland, sondern auch im Ausland getragen wurde. Hierzu zählen Künstlerpersönlichkeiten wie die Silberschmiede Emmy Roth (Abb. S. 136 und

gners. Les concepts sur lesquels s'appuyait la production en série peuvent être cernés grâce aux «types» de meubles en tube d'acier exposés ici à divers phases de production: prototype, petite série de type artisanale et fabrication en grand de type industriel (ill. p. 88 - ill. p. 91).

Parmi les écoles d'art de l'époque ayant des prétentions en matière de design comme le Bauhaus, il faut citer celle de Paul Thiersch, la «Kunstgewerbeschule Burg Giebichenstein», l'Ecole des Arts décoratifs de Burg Giebichenstein, installée à Halle. L'établissement enseignait et pratiquait encore, à l'inverse du Bauhaus, une conception traditionnelle de l'artisanat et du travail en atelier. C'est pourtant cette école qui donna l'exemple d'une coopération réussie entre ses élèves créateurs et une entreprise industrielle. Citons le cas du service à thé et à café «Hallesche Form» (ill. p. 122 et p. 123) créé par Marguerite Friedlaender en 1930 pour la KPM de Berlin et qui fut un joli succès commercial pour l'entreprise.

Le Bauhaus et les autres écoles réformatrices créèrent un climat spirituel qui fut soutenu et enrichi par bon nombre d'artisans et de créateurs aussi bien d'Allemagne que de l'étranger bien que n'ayant pas de relations directes avec le Bauhaus et les autres instituts. Parmi ces personnalités, citons l'orfèvre Emmy Roth (ill. p. 136 et p. 137), Paula Straus (ill. p. 139) et Theodor Wende (ill. p. 134 et p. 135), sans oublier les architectes Serge Chermayeff (ill. p. 132), Kay Fisker (ill. p. 144), Poul Henningsen (ill. p. 131), Alvar Aalto (ill. p. 130) et J. J. P. Oud

Marcel Breuer,
1930/31

B 8 Stool
Tubular steel,
chromed,
textile seat
Thonet AG, Germany
Height: 45 cm

Hocker B 8
Stahlrohr,
verchromt,
Stoffbespannung
Thonet AG, Deutsch-
land
Höhe: 45 cm

Tabouret B 8
en tube d'acier
chromé,
garniture de tissu
Thonet AG, Allemagne
Hauteur: 45 cm

Of all the art schools and innovative groups to experiment with new design concepts, the Bauhaus is undisputedly the most important. After the Second World War, the influence of these art schools continued to hold sway; not only in the USA but also in Europe. In 1950/51, the Ulmer Hochschule für Gestaltung (Ulm College of Design) was founded, adopting the concepts of the Bauhaus and adapting them to the changing industrial and social situation. The most intensive realisation of these principles can be found in the collaboration between the Ulmer Hochschule für Gestaltung and the Braun electrical appliances company, which has shaped the development of design right up to the present day to a degree unparalleled in postwar Germany.

S. 137), Paula Straus (Abb. S. 139) und Theodor Wende (Abb. S. 134 und S. 135), aber auch Architekten wie Serge Chermayeff (Abb. S. 132), Kay Fisker (Abb. S. 144), Poul Henningsen (Abb. S. 131), Alvar Aalto (Abb. S. 130) oder J. J. P. Oud (Abb. S. 129), die mit exemplarischen Arbeiten dokumentiert sind. Es entwickelte sich ein internationaler Designstil, der auch in den USA seine Ausprägungen fand (Abb. S. 141).

Von allen Kunstschulen und Erneuerungsgruppierungen, die sich mit neuen Designkonzeptionen beschäftigt haben, ist dem Bauhaus sicher der erste Rang einzuräumen. Nach dem Zweiten Weltkrieg haben sich die Fortwirkungen dieser Kunstschule nicht nur in den USA, sondern auch in Europa niedergeschlagen. In den Jahren 1950/51 wurde mit der Gründung der Ulmer Hochschule für Gestaltung das Ideengut des Bauhauses wieder aufgegriffen und den veränderten Bedingungen von Industrie und Gesellschaft angepaßt. Ihre Prinzipien konnte die Ulmer Hochschule für Gestaltung am ehesten umsetzen, in der Zusammenarbeit mit der Elektrofirma der Brüder Braun deren Unternehmen wie kein anderes im Nachkriegsdeutschland die Entwicklung des Designs bis heute geprägt hat.

(ill. p. 129) dont le travail est illustré ici par quelques exemples. Peu, à peu un style de design international vit le jour, jusqu'en Amérique même où il développa sa propre tendance (ill. p. 141).

De toutes les écoles d'art et des groupes réformateurs qui se sont occupés de design, le Bauhaus mérite sans conteste la première place. Après la Seconde Guerre mondiale, son rayonnement a atteint non seulement les USA mais aussi l'Europe. Avec l'ouverture de l'Ecole de création et de design d'Ulm en 1950/51, les idées du Bauhaus furent reprises et adaptées aux nouvelles conditions économiques et sociales. C'est grâce à sa coopération avec la firme Braun – aucune entreprise allemande de l'après-guerre n'a autant marqué l'évolution du design – que l'école d'Ulm a pu réaliser ses conceptions.

Impulses   *Impulse*   *Impulsiones*

Christopher Dresser,
1885

Decanter
Electroplated nickel
silver
Silverware manufactur-
ers Elkington & Co.,
Birmingham
Height: 21 cm

Weinkanne
Alpacca, versilbert
Silberwarenfabrik
Elkington & Co.,
Birmingham
Höhe: 21 cm

Cruche à vin
Argentan argenté
Manufacture d'argen-
terie Elkington & Co.,
Birmingham
Hauteur: 21 cm

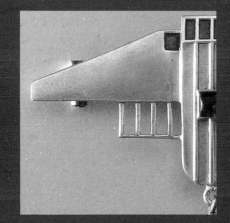

Henry van de Velde, 1895/96

»Bloemenwerft« House, Uccle near Brussels

Haus »Bloemenwerf«, Uccle bei Brüssel

La maison «Bloemenwerf» à Uccle près de Bruxelles

New Concepts for a New Century

The rapid developments of the Industrial Revolution during the course of the 18th and 19th centuries led to revolutionary reforms in the field of arts and crafts around 1900, culminating in the first international exhibition of 1851 in London. This monumental exhibition was intended as a display of human progress exemplified by the machine age. The quality of the craftsmanship on display left much to be desired, however. To the critical observer, the profusion of eclectic historicism and mediocre craftsmanship must surely have provided unequivocal proof that the machine age had numbed all aesthetic sensibilities. The mass production which had become possible as a result of industrialisation and the consequent division of labour had thrown centuries-old traditions of craftsmanship and quality into confusion, resulting in an artistic and aesthetic loss of direction.

Even in the first half of the 19th century, critics and reformers such as John Ruskin, Augustus W.N. Pugin and Owen Jones had called for a new aesthetic honesty which they felt was lacking, especially in architecture and the decorative arts. They called for a return to the ideals of Mediaeval and especially Gothic art. A key figure in the reformation of arts and crafts was William Morris, who had taken the bold and decisive step from fine artist to designer and craftsman, thereby becoming the first to put the new aesthetic concepts into practice. In the workshops of Morris, Marshall, Faulkner & Company, established by Morris in Lon-

Impulse der Jahrhundertwende

Die rasanten Entwicklungen der industriellen Revolution im 18. und 19. Jahrhundert bildeten den Hintergrund der revolutionären kunstgewerblichen Reformen um 1900. Sie erreichten in der ersten Weltausstellung von 1851 in London ihren vorläufigen Höhepunkt. Die monumentale Weltausstellung sollte den Fortschritt der Menschheit durch die Beherrschung der Maschine manifestieren. Sie zeigte jedoch hinsichtlich der künstlerischen Qualität der ausgestellten kunstgewerblichen Waren ein erschreckendes Bild. Auf den kritischen Besucher mußte das Wirrwarr der historistischen Stile in Verbindung mit einer zumeist qualitativ minderwertigen Ausführung so wirken, als wenn die »Maschine« den künstlerischen Geschmack der Menschen verdorben hätte. Die erst durch die Industrialisierung ermöglichte Massenproduktion mit der daraus resultierenden Arbeitsteilung hatte die jahrhundertealte Tradition der handwerklichen Qualität gesprengt und zu einer künstlerischen Orientierungslosigkeit geführt.

Bereits in der ersten Hälfte des 19. Jahrhunderts hatten englische Kunst- und Sozialkritiker, etwa John Ruskin, Augustus W. N. Pugin und Owen Jones eine neue »ästhetische Ehrlichkeit« angemahnt. Diese vermißten sie vor allem in der Architektur und in den »dekorativen Künsten« und sahen sie nur in den Idealen der mittelalterlichen, insbesondere der gotischen Kunst verwirklicht. Die Schlüsselfunktion in der Reformierung des Kunstgewerbes kam William Morris zu, der

Les impulsions novatrices au tournant du siècle

Les progrès rapides de la révolution industrielle aux XVIIIème et XIXème siècles constituent la toile de fond des innovations révolutionnaires dans les arts appliqués vers 1900. Ils atteignent provisoirement leur apogée avec l'Exposition universelle de Londres en 1851, mais cette foire monumentale qui se voulait la manifestation éclatante du progrès humain par la maîtrise de la machine fit piètre figure en ce qui concerne la qualité artistique du mobilier exposé. Le pêle-mêle éclectique des styles aggravé par une fabrication d'une qualité fort médiocre pour la plupart des modèles dut susciter chez le visiteur critique l'impression que la «machine» avait perverti le goût artistique des hommes. La fabrication en masse, rendue enfin possible par la mécanisation de l'industrie, et la division du travail qui s'ensuivit avaient rompu le tandem artisanat-qualité et conduit à l'absence d'orientation artistique.

En Angleterre, dès la première moitié du XIXème siècle, des critiques sociaux et de l'art, tels John Ruskin, Augustus W. N. Pugin et Owen Jones, avaient prêché une nouvelle sincérité esthétique. Selon eux, cette sincérité faisait surtout défaut dans l'architecture et les arts décoratifs et n'était réalisée que dans l'art médiéval, en particulier gothique, et ses idéaux. C'est à William Morris que revint la tâche de rénover les arts décoratifs : lui, le plasticien, devint concepteur et artisan, le premier à transposer les théories de Ruskin sur le plan pratique. Dans les

**Henry van de Velde,
1897/98**

»Cassirer« armchair
Pearwood, corduroy
upholstered
Societé van de Velde &
Co., Brussels
Height: 100 cm

»Cassirer«-
Armlehnstuhl
Birnenholz,
Cordbezug
Societé van de Velde &
Co., Brüssel
Höhe: 100 cm

Fauteuil à accou-
doirs «Cassirer»
en bouleau et
garniture velours
Societé van de Velde &
Co., Bruxelles
Hauteur: 100 cm

don around 1861 together with like-minded artists, goods were made by hand and the use of industrial machinery was rejected on principle. Morris was the first to attempt to design his entire surroundings in accordance with his own artistic concepts, thereby introducing the idea of the ›gesamtkunstwerk‹ (total art work) into the modern reform movement. Influenced at first by Pre-Raphaelite and Neo-Gothic concepts, a distinctive style soon began to emerge – the English Arts & Crafts style.

In the years that followed, guilds and associations of artists and craftsmen soon began to emerge throughout England following Morris' example. One of the most influential of these was the Guild of Handicraft founded by Charles Robert Ashbee in 1888. A particularly outstanding contribution to the English Arts & Crafts style was made by Christopher Dresser, who, strongly influenced by Japanese art, developed a completely new and modern formal syntax for a number of English companies. Unlike Morris, Dresser believed that lasting success could only be achieved through close collaboration with industry. His designs for the metalware manufacturers Hukin & Heath and Elkington & Co. in the 1880s are amongst the most remarkable pioneering achievements in the field of early industrial design.

den entscheidenden Schritt vom bildenden Künstler zum Entwerfer und Handwerker wagte und damit als erster das neue ästhetische Gedankengut in die Realität umsetzte. In den Werkstätten der Firma »Morris, Marshall, Faulkner & Company«, die Morris ab 1861 in London zusammen mit gleichgesinnten Künstlern aufbaute, wurde kunstgewerblicher Bedarf auf rein handwerklicher Basis hergestellt. Die Zuhilfenahme von industriellen Maschinen wurde prinzipiell abgelehnt. Morris unternahm als erster den Versuch, seine gesamte Umgebung nach eigenen künstlerischen Vorstellungen zu gestalten, und führte damit die Idee des Gesamtkunstwerkes in die moderne Reformbewegung ein. Zunächst von präraffaelitischen und neogotischen Einflüssen geprägt, entstand bald ein eigenständiger Stil, der den englischen »Arts & Crafts«-Stil begründete.

In der Folgezeit organisierten sich überall in England Vereinigungen von Künstlern und Handwerkern, die dem Vorbild von Morris folgten. Zu den einflußreichsten gehörte die 1888 von Charles Robert Ashbee gegründete »Guild of Handicraft«. Einen herausragenden Beitrag zum englischen »Arts & Crafts«-Stil leistete Christopher Dresser, der – stark vom japanischen Kunstgewerbe beeinflußt – für zahlreiche englische Firmen eine vollkommen neue und moderne Formensprache entwickelte. Dresser glaubte, im Gegensatz zu Morris, daß nur eine enge Zusammenarbeit mit der Industrie langfristig Erfolg haben könnte. Seine für die maschinelle Produktion ausgelegten Entwürfe aus den 1880er Jahren

ateliers de l'entreprise «Morris, Marshall, Faulkner & Company», construits à Londres en 1861 par Morris et des amis artistes, on fabriquait des objets d'utilisation courante selon des méthodes de production artisanale, toute forme de fabrication industrielle étant rejetée par principe. Morris fut le premier à concevoir l'aménagement de sa maison avec ses propres idées esthétiques, apportant ainsi au mouvement réformateur moderne le principe d'œuvre d'art globale. Imprégnée au départ d'éléments préraphaéliques et néo-gothiques, cette nouvelle esthétique finit par devenir un style à part entière, précurseur direct du style «Arts and Crafts» anglais.

De nombreuses associations d'artistes et d'artisans ne tardèrent pas à se créer un peu partout en Angleterre sur le modèle de celle de Morris. Parmi les plus influentes il y avait notamment l'association de Charles Robert Ashbee baptisée «Guild of Handicraft». Christopher Dresser, fortement influencé par les arts décoratifs japonais, contribua magistralement au mouvement «Arts and Crafts» en créant pour de nombreuses entreprises anglaises un langage des formes inédit et résolument moderne. A l'inverse de Morris, Dresser était convaincu que seule une étroite collaboration avec l'industrie serait un gage de succès à long terme. Ses créations des années 1880 destinées à être fabriquées sur un mode industriel dans les fabriques d'articles métalliques Hukin & Heath et Elkington & Co. comptent parmi les réalisations les plus importantes de cette phase «héroïque» de la stylique industrielle.

The influence of countries outside Europe can also be seen in Liberty & Co., founded in London in 1875 as a department store selling Oriental and East Asian arts and crafts, and producing goods to their own design from 1890 onwards. Some of the more famous designers who worked for Liberty & Co. included Charles F. A. Voyses, Rex Silver and Archibald Knox, whose designs for furniture, textiles, silverware and pewterware dominated the company's range of goods at the turn of the century. In Glasgow, Charles Rennie Mackintosh, the Macdonald sisters and Herbert MacNair formed the »Glasgow Four« group of artists. Mackintosh's designs for the new Glasgow School of Art and Cranston's Tea Rooms created an independent direction within the Arts & Crafts movements which became known as the Glasgow Style. Mackintosh, who never enjoyed the recognition he deserved in Britain, was to achieve his greatest success abroad, most notably in Austria.

On the continent, artistic style initially followed the English example closely. However, the specific regional and national situations and interests soon led to a divergence in styles. In Belgium, the young painter Henry van de Velde, strongly influenced by the theories of Ruskin and Morris, began to concentrate on architecture and the design of everyday objects. In 1894, he designed his first house, the Villa Bloemenwerf in Uccle, near Brussels. His powerful and organically curved designs, strongly abstracted from the floral style of his compatriot Victor Horta, created a completely new style.

für die Metallwarenfabriken Hukin & Heath sowie Elkington & Co. zählen zu den wichtigsten Pionierleistungen auf dem Gebiet des frühen Industriedesigns.

Ebenfalls stark von außereuropäischen Einflüssen geprägt war die Gründung der Firma Liberty & Co. 1875 als Handelshaus für orientalisches und ostasiatisches Kunstgewerbe in London gegründet, produzierte man schon ab den 1890er Jahren kunstgewerbliche Produkte nach eigenen Entwürfen. Zu den bekanntesten Entwerfern der Firma Liberty & Co. zählten Charles F. A. Voysey, Rex Silver und Archibald Knox, deren Entwürfe für Möbel, Textilien für Silber- und Zinnwaren das Programm der Firma um die Jahrhundertwende bestimmten. In Glasgow bildete Charles Rennie Mackintosh zusammen mit den Geschwistern Macdonald und Herbert MacNair die Künstlergemeinschaft der »Glasgow Four«. Seine Entwürfe für die neue »Glasgow School of Art« und die bekannten »Cranston's Tearooms« schufen eine eigenständige Richtung des »Arts & Crafts«-Stils, den sogenannten »Glasgow Style«. Mackintosh, der in England nie die ihm gebührende Wertschätzung genoß, feierte seine größten Erfolge im benachbarten Ausland, vor allem in Österreich.

Die Entwicklung auf dem europäischen Festland orientierte sich zunächst stark an dem englischen Vorbild. Regionale Eigenheiten sowie verschiedene nationale Voraussetzungen und Interessen führten jedoch zu unterschiedlichen Ergebnissen. In Belgien wandte sich der junge Maler Henry

L'entreprise Liberty & Co. fut fortement marquée elle aussi par des influences extra-européennes. Maison de commerce londonienne spécialisée dans les arts décoratifs orientaux et asiatiques depuis 1875, elle se lança dès 1890 dans la fabrication d'objets d'utilisation quotidienne d'après des modèles conçus dans ses ateliers. Parmi les concepteurs les plus connus de l'établissement, il y avait notamment Charles F. A. Voysey, Rex Silver et Archibald Knox dont les créations de meubles, de textiles et d'objets en argent et en cuivre constituaient l'essentiel du programme de la firme vers 1900. A Glasgow, Charles Rennie Mackintosh fonda la communauté d'artistes «Glasgow Four» avec les frères Macdonald et Herbert MacNair. Ses réalisations pour la «Glasgow School of Art», la nouvelle école d'art de la ville, et les célèbres salons de thé «Cranston's Tearooms» créèrent à l'intérieur du style «Arts and Crafts» une tendance particulière, le «Glasgow Style». Mackintosh qui n'obtint jamais l'estime qu'il méritait dans son propre pays fêta ses succès les plus notoires à l'étranger, en particulier en Autriche.

L'évolution qui se produisait sur le continent européen suivait largement le modèle anglais. Mais les particularités tant sur le plan régional que national menaient à des résultats différents. C'est ainsi qu'en Belgique le jeune peintre Henry van de Velde, imprégné des théories de Ruskin et de Morris, se tourna vers l'architecture et la création d'objets utilitaires. En 1894, il fit les plans de sa première maison, la «Villa Bloemenwerf» située à Uccle dans les environs de Bruxelles. Ses créations vi-

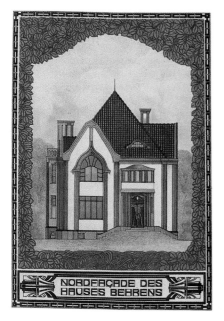

Peter Behrens, 1901

North facade of the house »Peter Behrens« on the Mathildenhöhe in Darmstadt

Nordfassade des Hauses »Peter Behrens«, Darmstadt-Mathildenhöhe

Façade nord de la maison «Peter Behrens», sur la colline à Darmstadt

Van de Velde had enormous influence on the German Jugendstil movement after working for two years in Berlin at Hermann Hirschwald's »Hohenzollern-Kunstgewerbehaus«, and was appointed artistic advisor for industry and crafts of the Grand Duchy of Saxe-Weimar-Eisenach. In 1902, he established an arts and crafts seminar in Weimar, which was expanded to form the Kunstgewerbeschule (School of Applied Arts) of Weimar in 1906/07, where he was director until 1915. In 1919, the school founded by van de Velde became the Bauhaus in Weimar.

In Vienna, a group of young artists, architects and designers rebelled against the established academic system and founded the Vienna Secession in 1897. The leading figures in this movement were Gustav Klimt, Koloman Moser, and the Wagner students Josef Hoffmann and Joseph Maria Olbrich. Their expressed aim was the renewal of art by granting equal status to arts and crafts. In 1899, Hoffmann and Moser were appointed to the teaching staff of the Kunstgewerbeschule in Vienna, which was totally reformed under their influence. In 1903, Hoffmann, Moser and the banker Fritz Waerndorfer founded the Wiener Werkstätte (Vienna Workshops) along the lines of the English guilds. The workshops had a decisive influence on Austrian arts and crafts right up until the 1930s. The early works produced by the metal workshop are a particularly clear manifestation of the design principles of the Wiener Werkstätte: reduced, uncluttered forms, structural simplicity and the use of high-quality materials

van de Velde, stark von den Lehren Ruskins und Morris' geprägt, der Architektur und dem Entwurf von Alltagsgegenständen zu. 1894 entwarf er sein erstes eigenes Wohnhaus, die »Villa Bloemenwerf« in Uccle bei Brüssel. Mit seinen kraftvollen, organisch-geschwungenen Entwürfen, die den floralen Stil seines Landsmannes Victor Horta stark abstrahierten, schuf er einen völlig neuen Stil. Van de Velde übte einen großen Einfluß auf die deutsche Jugendstilbewegung aus. Nachdem er in Berlin zwei Jahre im »Hohenzollern-Kunstgewerbehaus« von Hermann Hirschwald tätig gewesen war, wurde er 1901 zum künstlerischen Berater für Industrie und Kunsthandwerk des Großherzogtums Sachsen-Weimar-Eisenach ernannt. 1902 eröffnete er dann in Weimar ein kunstgewerbliches Seminar, das 1906/07 zur Kunstgewerbeschule Weimar erweitert wurde, der er als Direktor bis 1915 vorstand. 1919 ging aus der von van de Velde gegründeten Kunstgewerbeschule das Staatliche Bauhaus Weimar hervor.

In Wien gründete 1897 eine Gruppe von jungen Künstlern, Architekten und Entwerfern aus Opposition zu der traditionellen Künstlerhausgenossenschaft die Wiener Sezession. Führende Künstlerpersönlichkeiten dieser Bewegung waren Gustav Klimt, Koloman Moser sowie die Wagner-Schüler Josef Hoffmann und Joseph Maria Olbrich. Ihr erklärtes Ziel war die Erneuerung der Kunst durch die Gleichstellung von bildenden und angewandten Künsten. 1899 berief man Hoffmann und Moser als Lehrkräfte an die Wiener Kunstgewerbeschule, die unter ihrer Führung

goureuses aux formes organiques, stylisant le style floral de son compatriote Victor Horta, lui valurent de créer une tendance entièrement nouvelle. Son influence sur le Jugendstil allemand fut immense. Après avoir travaillé deux ans à Berlin au «Hohenzollern-Kunstgewerbehaus» de Hermann Hirschwald, il devint conseiller artistique du grand-duché de Saxe-Weimar-Eisenach pour l'industrie et l'artisanat. Il ouvrit en 1902 à Weimar un cours d'arts décoratifs qui devint en 1906/07 l'Ecole des Arts appliqués de Weimar dont il resta le directeur jusqu'en 1915. Plus tard, en 1919, une autre école allait succéder à cette dernière: le Staatliches Bauhaus de Weimar.

A Vienne, en 1897, un groupe de jeunes artistes, de concepteurs et d'architectes fondait la Sécession de Vienne par opposition à la traditionnelle association d'artistes. Les personnalités les plus marquantes de ce mouvement étaient Gustav Klimt, Koloman Moser ainsi que les élèves de Wagner, Josef Hoffmann et Joseph Maria Olbrich. Leur objectif était de renouveler l'art en fusionnant les arts plastiques et appliqués. Hoffmann et Moser furent appelés en 1899 à enseigner à l'Ecole des Arts décoratifs de Vienne, bientôt réformée de fond en comble sous leur direction. Sur le modèle des «guildes d'artisans» anglaises, Hoffmann, Moser et le banquier Fritz Waerndorfer fondèrent en 1903 les Ateliers viennois dont l'influence prépondérante sur les arts décoratifs autrichiens s'exerça jusque dans les années trente. Ce sont les premières réalisations de l'atelier de métal qui illustrent le mieux les principes de création des Ateliers viennois:

Peter Behrens, 1898

Wine glass
*Glassworks Benedikt
von Poschinger,
Oberzwieselau
Height: 20.6 cm*

Weinglas
*Glashütte Benedikt
von Poschinger,
Oberzwieselau
Höhe: 20,6 cm*

Verre à vin
*Verrerie Benedikt von
Poschinger,
Oberzwieselau
Hauteur: 20,6 cm*

created a simple but expensive elegance.

Alongside Austria, Germany soon became the driving force behind the new movement. In Munich, the »Vereinigten Werkstätten für Kunst im Handwerk« (United Workshops) were founded in 1897. Their most famous members included the artists Richard Riemerschmid, Bruno Paul, Bernhard Pankok, August Endell and Hermann Obrist. In 1898, the »Dresdner Werkstätten für Handwerkskunst« (Dresden Workshops) were founded. The main aim of both these workshops was the propagation and dissemination of high-quality and modern objects. Soon, however, their interest focused no longer on the artisanal techniques of the past, but on the unity of artistic design and high-quality craftsmanship with the aid of industrial machinery. Right from the design stage, mechanical reproduction was to be taken into consideration, permitting the production of beautiful but also inexpensive and therefore commercially viable objects for everyday use.

von Grund auf reformiert wurde. Nach dem Vorbild der englischen Handwerksgilden gründeten Hoffmann, Moser und der Bankier Fritz Waerndorfer 1903 die Wiener Werkstätte, die bis in die 1930er Jahre das österreichische Kunstgewerbe entscheidend prägte. Vor allem die frühen Arbeiten aus der Metallwerkstatt verdeutlichen die spezifischen Gestaltungsprinzipien der Wiener Werkstätte: Reduzierte, klare Formen, konstruktive Einfachheit und die Verwendung edler Materialien führten zu einer schlichten, aber dennoch kostspieligen Eleganz.

Deutschland entwickelte sich parallel zu Österreich schon bald zum eigentlichen Motor der neuen Bewegung. In München wurden 1897 die »Vereinigten Werkstätten für Kunst im Handwerk« ins Leben gerufen. Zu ihren bedeutendsten Mitgliedern zählten die Künstler Richard Riemerschmid, Bruno Paul, Bernhard Pankok, August Endell und Hermann Obrist. 1898 folgte die Gründung der »Dresdner Werkstätten für Handwerkskunst«. Hauptanliegen der beiden Werkstätten war die Propagierung und Verbreitung von qualitätvollem und modernem Kunstgewerbe. Im Mittelpunkt ihrer Interessen stand schon bald nicht mehr die rückwärtsgewandte Besinnung auf handwerkliche Techniken, sondern die Einheit von künstlerischem Entwurf und sorgfältiger Ausführung unter Einbeziehung industrieller Fertigungsmethoden. Bereits im Entwurfsstadium sollten eine spätere mechanische Vervielfältigung berücksichtigt und dadurch die Herstellung formschöner, aber auch kostengünstiger und somit wirtschaftlich

réduction et clarté des formes, simplicité de construction et emploi de matériaux nobles donnant aux modèles une élégance sobre mais très coûteuse.

L'Allemagne s'affirmait avec l'Autriche comme la vraie force motrice du nouveau mouvement. En 1897, à Munich, furent créés les «Vereinigte Werkstätten für Kunst im Handwerk», les Ateliers réunis d'arts décoratifs et appliqués. Parmi les membres fondateurs les plus éminents de ce groupe figuraient Richard Riemerschmid, Bruno Paul, Bernhard Pankok, August Endell et Hermann Obrist. En 1898, c'était au tour des «Dresdner Werkstätten für Handwerkskunst», les Ateliers réunis de Dresde, d'ouvrir leurs portes. Le programme des deux groupes était de faire connaître et de propager un art artisanal moderne et de qualité. Bientôt cependant leur préoccupation majeure ne fut plus de faire appel aux techniques artisanales du passé mais de réaliser la synthèse entre projet artistique et réalisation de qualité selon des procédés industriels. Dès le stade de la conception, il s'agissait de prendre en considération la reproduction mécanique ultérieure, ce qui permettrait la fabrication d'objets utilitaires plus beaux de forme mais dont le coût inférieur et le succès commercial seraient assurés.

In addition to Munich, Dresden and Weimar, Darmstadt also became a centre of the German reform movement with the establishment of the Mathildenhöhe artists' colony in 1899 under the patronage of Grand Duke Ernst Ludwig of Hessen. In Darmstadt the influence of Vienna and Munich merged in two leading artist figures – Joseph Maria Olbrich and Peter Behrens – creating a synthesis which culminated in the 1901 exhibition »Ein Dokument Deutscher Kunst« (A Document of German Art), widely regarded as the apex of the German Jugendstil movement. The outward appearance of the early Darmstadt artists' colony was also shaped by Patriz Huber, Hans Christiansen, Paul Haustein and Albin Müller. A typical feature of the Darmstadt style was the consistency with which the principle of the »Gesamtkunstwerk« (total work of art) was pursued down to the last detail in the interior design of the houses.

erfolgreicher Gebrauchsgegenstände ermöglicht werden.

Neben München, Dresden und Weimar entstand 1899 unter dem Patronat des Großherzogs Ernst Ludwig von Hessen und bei Rhein die Darmstädter Künstlerkolonie auf der Mathildenhöhe als ein weiterer Ort der deutschen Reformbewegung. In Darmstadt verbanden sich Wiener und Münchner Einflüsse in Form zweier führender Künstlerpersönlichkeiten – Joseph Maria Olbrich und Peter Behrens – zu einer Synthese, die 1901 mit der Ausstellung »Ein Dokument Deutscher Kunst« den Höhepunkt der deutschen Jugendstilbewegung ausmachte. Das Erscheinungsbild der frühen Darmstädter Künstlerkolonie wurde außer von Olbrich und Behrens im wesentlichen von Patriz Huber, Hans Christiansen, Paul Haustein und Albin Müller geprägt. Typisch für den Darmstädter Stil war die Konsequenz in der Gestaltung der Innenräume, die bis in das letzte Detail dem Prinzip des Gesamtkunstwerkes unterlag.

En dehors de Munich, Dresde et Weimar, une autre colonie d'artistes s'affirmait elle aussi comme un centre du mouvement réformateur allemand: celle de la colline Sainte-Mathilde à Darmstadt dans la vallée du Rhin, placée sous le patronage du grand-duc Ernest Ludovic de Hesse. Le groupe réalisa la synthèse des tendances munichoises et dresdoises en la personne de deux personnalités de premier plan: Joseph Maria Olbrich et Peter Behrens. En 1901, l'exposition du groupe «Un document d'art allemand» constitua l'apogée du Jugendstil allemand. Outre Olbrich et Behrens déjà cités, Patriz Huber, Hans Christiansen, Paul Haustein et Albin Müller forgèrent eux aussi l'image et le style de ce groupe dont la caractéristique essentielle était l'aménagement parfaitement homogène des intérieurs, dicté jusque dans les moindres détails par le principe d'œuvre d'art globale.

Christopher Dresser's designs for English silverware manufacturers in the 1880s are the earliest documents of successful collaboration between an independent designer and industry. The absolute reduction of his forms to their structural necessities strongly suggests that Dresser had studied Japanese arts and crafts in some depth. By contrast, Archibald Knox's designs for Liberty & Co. are inspired by Celtic motifs.

Die Entwürfe von Christopher Dresser für englische Silberwarenproduzenten aus den 1880er Jahren sind die frühesten Dokumente einer erfolgreichen Zusammenarbeit zwischen einem unabhängigen »Designer« und der Industrie. Die absolute Reduktion seiner Formen auf ihre konstruktiven Notwendigkeiten läßt sich nur durch Dressers intensive Auseinandersetzung mit dem japanischen Kunstgewerbe erklären. Dagegen ließ sich Archibald Knox bei seinen Entwürfen für Liberty & Co. stark von keltischen Motiven inspirieren.

Les créations de Christopher Dresser des années 1880 pour des fabricants d'objets en argent sont les documents les plus anciens qui existent sur la collaboration réussie d'un «designer» indépendant et de l'industrie. La réduction absolue des formes à leurs nécessités constructives ne s'explique que par l'étude intensive que fit Dresser des arts décoratifs japonais. Quant aux créations d'Archibald Knox pour Liberty & Co. elles sont inspirées de motifs décoratifs celtiques.

Christopher Dresser, 1887

Toast rack
Metal, silver-plated
Silverware manufacturers Hukin & Heath, London & Birmingham
Height: 13.5 cm

Toastständer
Metall, versilbert
Silberwarenfabrik Hukin & Heath, London & Birmingham
Höhe: 13,5 cm

Porte-toast
Métal argenté
Manufacture d'objets en argent Hukin & Heath, Londres & Birmingham
Hauteur: 13,5 cm

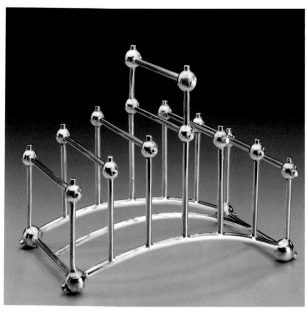

**Christopher Dresser,
c. 1880**

Toast rack
Metal, silver-plated
Silverware manufactur-
ers Hukin & Heath,
London & Birmingham
Height: 12.5 cm

Toastständer
Metall, versilbert
Silberwarenfabrik
Hukin & Heath,
London & Birmingham
Höhe: 12,5 cm

Porte-toast
Métal argenté
Manufacture d'objets
en argent
Hukin & Heath,
Londres & Birmingham
Hauteur: 12,5 cm

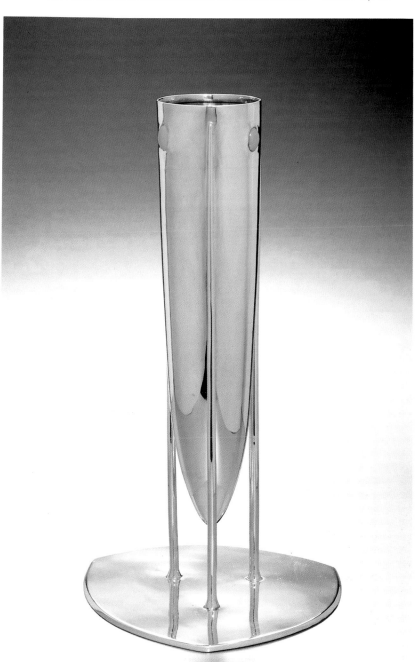

**Archibald Knox,
1902**

Vase
Silver, turquoise
cabochons
Liberty & Co., London
Height: 19 cm

Vase
Silber, Türkiscabochons
Liberty & Co., London
Höhe: 19 cm

Vase
Argent et cabochons
turquoise
Liberty & Co., Londres
Hauteur: 19 cm

**Archibald Knox,
1903**

Spoon
Silver, enamel
Liberty & Co., London
Length: 18.7 cm

Löffel
Silber, Email
Liberty & Co., London
Länge: 18,7 cm

Cuillère
Argent, émail
Liberty & Co., Londres
Longueur: 18,7 cm

Henry van de Velde designed the entire interior furnishings for his »Bloemenwerf« house in Uccle, near Brussels, in 1895/96. The so-called »Bloemenwerf« chair, originally designed for the dining room of the house, is one of the few ground-breaking chair designs to have been created in the 19th century. The book case illustrated here was produced from 1898 on by the Societé van de Velde & Co. in various sizes. The example shown here was probably purchased in 1900 at the 8th Vienna Secession Exhibition.

Für sein Haus »Bloemenwerf« in Uccle bei Brüssel entwarf Henry van de Velde 1895/96 die gesamte Inneneinrichtung. Der sogenannte »Bloemenwerf«-Stuhl, ursprünglich für das Eßzimmer des Hauses entworfen, zählt zu den wenigen wegweisenden Stuhlentwürfen der Designgeschichte, die noch im ausgehenden 19. Jahrhundert entstanden. Der abgebildete Bücherschrank ist ab 1898 in verschieden langen Versionen von der Societé van de Velde & Co. ausgeführt worden. Das hier gezeigte Möbel wurde vermutlich 1900 auf der VIII. Wiener Sezessionsausstellung erworben.

Henry van de Velde, 1895/96

Dining room,
Bloemenwerf House,
Uccle, near Brussels

Speisezimmer,
Haus Bloemenwerf,
Uccle bei Brüssel

Salle à manger
de la maison
»Bloemenwerf« à
Uccle près de Bruxelles

Henry van de Velde, 1895

**»Bloemenwerf«
chairs**
Bubinga frame,
rush seat
Société van de Velde
& Co., Brussels
Height: 99 cm
(armchair)

**Satz »Bloemen-
werf«-Stühle**
Bubingaholz,
Strohgeflecht
Société van de Velde
& Co., Brüssel
Höhe: 99 cm
(Armlehnstuhl)

**Série de chaises
»Bloemenwerf«**
Bois de bubinga et
cannage
Société van de Velde
& Co., Bruxelles
Hauteur : 99 cm
(fauteuil à accoudoirs)

Henry van de Velde conçoit en 1895/96
l'ensemble de l'aménagement intérieur
de sa maison «Bloemenwerf» à Uccle
près de Bruxelles. Sa chaise appelée
«Bloemenwerf», destinée à la salle à manger, fait partie des quelques créations de
chaises très modernes de l'histoire du design qui sont créées encore à la fin du XI-
Xème siècle. La bibliothèque est commer-
cialisée à partir de 1898 dans des versions et des longueurs différentes par la
Société van de Velde & Co. Le meuble
présenté ici a été acheté probablement
en 1900 à la 8ème Exposition de la Sécession viennoise.

**Henry van de Velde,
1899**

*Study, Munich Seces-
sion Exhibition 1899*

*Arbeitszimmer,
Münchner Sezessions-
ausstellung 1899*

*Bureau de travail, Ex-
position de la Séces-
sion munichoise 1899*

**Henry van de Velde,
1898/99**

Bookcase
*Oak, glass panels
Société van de Velde
& Co., Brussels
Width: 237 cm*

Bücherschrank
*Eiche, Türfüllungen
aus Glas
Société van de Velde
& Co., Brüssel
Breite: 237 cm*

Bibliothèque
*Chêne et panneaux en
verre
Société van de Velde
& Co., Bruxelles
Largeur : 237 cm*

It was probably while he was still in Berlin that Henry van de Velde was commissioned to produce designs for the Westerwald pottery industry at Höhr-Grenzhausen. The contract may well have been awarded in connection with the 1902 Düsseldorf industrial exhibition, where his pottery designs were presented to the public for the first time. Van de Velde's forms, together with his experimental glazing, give his ceramics an Oriental touch.

Vermutlich noch zu seiner Berliner Zeit erhielt Henry van de Velde den Auftrag, für die Westerwälder Steinzeugindustrie in Höhr-Grenzhausen als Entwerfer tätig zu werden. Der Auftrag stand wahrscheinlich im Zusammenhang mit der Düsseldorfer Industrieausstellung von 1902, auf der die nach seinem Entwurf ausgeführten Steinzeugwaren zum ersten Mal der Öffentlichkeit vorgestellt wurden. Die Formen van de Veldes in Verbindung mit den experimentellen Überlaufglasuren geben den Keramiken eine ostasiatische Prägung.

Il est probable que Henry van de Velde ait reçu encore à Berlin une commande des ateliers de poterie de Höhr-Grenzhausen. Cette commande avait peut-être un rapport avec l'Exposition industrielle de Düsseldorf en 1902 où pour la première fois des créations à lui sont présentées au public. Les formes ainsi que les vernis expérimentaux utilisés donnent un air asiatique à ses céramiques.

32

Henry van de Velde, 1902

Vase
Stoneware, red/violet salt glaze
Art-Pottery
Reinhold Hanke, Höhr
Height: 91 cm

Bodenvase
Steinzeug, rot-violette Salzglasur
Steinzeugfabrik & Kunsttöpferei
Reinhold Hanke, Höhr
Höhe: 91 cm

Vase
en grès et vernis rouge violet
Poteries
Reinhold Hanke, Höhr
Hauteur : 91 cm

**Henry van de Velde,
1902/03**

Vase
Fine stoneware, blue
glaze, painted dark
blue
Art-Pottery
Reinhold Hanke,
Höhr
Height: 22 cm

Vase
Feinsteinzeug, blaue
Glasur, dunkelblaue
Bemalung
Steinzeugfabrik &
Kunsttöpferei Reinhold
Hanke, Höhr
Höhe: 22 cm

Vase
Grès fin, vernis bleu et
peinture bleu foncé
Poteries
Reinhold Hanke,
Höhr
Hauteur: 22 cm

33

**Henry van de Velde,
1902**

Vase
Stoneware,
yellow/grey salt glaze
Art-Pottery
Reinhold Hanke,
Höhr
Height: 20 cm

Vase
Steinzeug, gelb-graue
Salzglasur
Steinzeugfabrik &
Kunsttöpferei
Reinhold Hanke,
Höhr
Höhe: 20 cm

Vase
en grès et vernis gris-
jaune
Poteries
Reinhold Hanke,
Höhr
Hauteur: 20 cm

In 1902, Henry van de Velde was appointed artistic advisor to Grand Duke Ernst Ludwig of Saxe-Weimar. The same year, he designed a set of silver tableware as a wedding gift from the State of Saxe-Weimar to the Grand Ducal couple. This cutlery design was produced in series by the silverware manufacturers Koch & Bergfeld. During his Weimar period, van de Velde's design style became increasingly functional, with a strongly curved line and an emphasis on structural features.

1902 folgte Henry van de Velde der Berufung zum künstlerischen Berater des Großherzogs Ernst Ludwig von Sachsen-Weimar-Eisenach. Noch im gleichen Jahr entwarf er ein silbernes Tafelgeschirr, das als Hochzeitsgeschenk des Landes Sachsen-Weimar für das großherzogliche Paar diente. Das dazugehörige Besteck wurde später von der Silberwarenfabrik Koch & Bergfeld in Serie produziert. Während van de Veldes Weimarer Zeit versachlichte sich sein Entwurfsstil zunehmend: Neben die geschwungene Linie trat die Betonung der Konstruktion.

En 1902 Henry van de Velde prend ses fonctions de conseiller artistique du grand-duc Ernest Ludovic de Saxe-Weimar-Eisenach. Il crée cette année-là un service de table en argent que le Land de Saxe-Weimar offre en cadeau de mariage au couple grand-ducal. Les couverts seront fabriqués plus tard en série par la fabrique Koch & Bergfeld. Pendant son séjour à Weimar, le style de van de Velde devient plus fonctionnel: l'accent mis sur la construction côtoie la ligne courbe.

**Henry van de Velde,
c. 1898**

Tray
*Bronze, silver-plated,
wooden core
Bronzecasters
Walter Elkan, Berlin
Width: 71 cm*

Tablett
*Bronze, versilbert,
Holzkern
Bronzegießerei
Walter Elkan, Berlin
Breite: 71 cm*

Plateau
*Bronze argenté et bois
Fonderie Walter Elkan,
Berlin
Largeur: 71 cm*

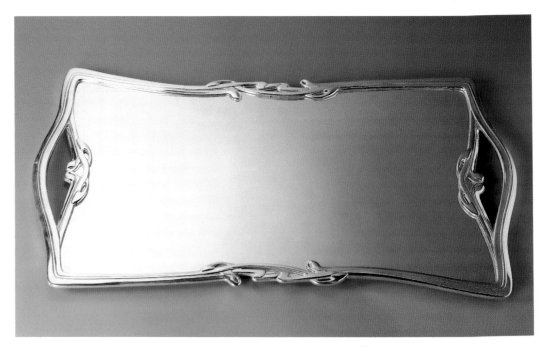

*Die stamp on tray,
Henry van de Velde
monogram*

*Prägestempel auf dem
Tablett, Monogramm
Henry van de Velde*

*Poinçon sur le plateau,
monogramme de Henry van de Velde*

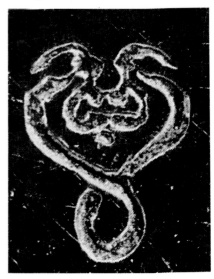

Henry van de Velde, 1902/03

Snail fork, caviar knife, oyster fork
Silver, tortoiseshell
Silverware manufacturers Koch & Bergfeld,
Bremen
Length: 20 cm
(caviar knife)

Schneckengabel, Kaviarmesser, Austerngabel
Silber, Schildpatt
Silberwarenfabrik
Koch & Bergfeld,
Bremen
Länge: 20 cm
(Kaviarmesser)

Fourchette à escargot, à huître et couteau à caviar
en argent et écaille
Manufacture d'objets
en argent
Koch & Bergfeld,
Brême
Longueur: 20 cm
(couteau à caviar)

Henry van de Velde, 1904/05

Chair
Beechwood, woven
cane
Furniture manufacturers Scheidemantel,
Weimar
Height: 95.5 cm

Stuhl
Buche, Rohrgeflecht
Hofmöbelfabrik
Scheidemantel,
Weimar
Höhe: 95,5 cm

Chaise
en hêtre et cannage
Manufacture de
meubles
Scheidemantel,
Weimar
Hauteur: 95,5 cm

Jan Eisenloeffel,
1901/02

Bowl
Silver, enamel
Amstelhoeck metal-
works,
Amsterdam
Width: 28 cm

Schale
Silber, Email
Firma Amstelhoeck,
Metallwerkstatt,
Amsterdam
Breite: 28 cm

Coupe
en argent et émail
Entreprise
Amstelhoeck,
atelier de métaux,
Amsterdam
Largeur : 28 cm

Jan Eisenloeffel,
1902

Kettle and stand
Brass, iron
Eisenloeffel workshop,
Overveen near Haar-
lem
Height: 87 cm

Wasserkessel auf
Ständer
Messing, Eisen
Werkstatt Eisenloeffel,
Overveen bei Haarlem
Höhe: 87 cm

Bouilloire sur sup-
port
Laiton et fer
Atelier Eisenloeffel,
Overveen près de
Haarlem
Hauteur: 87 cm

Jan Eisenloeffel,
1902

Teapot and rechaud
Copper, bone
Eisenloeffel workshop,
Overveen, near
Haarlem
Height: 29 cm

Teekanne auf
Rechaud
Kupfer, Bein
Werkstatt Eisenloeffel,
Overveen bei Haarlem
Höhe: 29 cm

Théière sur réchaud
en cuivre et pied
Atelier Eisenloeffel,
Overveen près de
Haarlem
Hauteur: 29 cm

At the 1st International Arts and Crafts Exhibition in Turin in 1902, the modern metalware designs by the Dutch Jan Eisenloeffel attracted considerable attention. Following his apprenticeship as a goldsmith and silversmith and after training with Fabergé in St. Petersburg for some time, Eisenloeffel took charge of the newly founded metalwork department of the Amstelhoeck company in Amsterdam, before becoming self-employed in 1902. Structural sobriety is the predominant feature of his designs for coloured metals. Eisenloeffel's work was marketed by the Dutch company »De Woning« and the »Vereinigte Werkstätten München« (United Workshops) in Munich.

Auf der 1. Internationalen Kunstgewerbe-ausstellung von 1902 in Turin erhielten die modernen Metallwarenentwürfe des Holländers Jan Eisenloeffel große Anerkennung. Nach einer Lehre als Gold- und Silberschmied und einem längeren Praktikum bei Fabergé in St. Petersburg übernahm Eisenloeffel zunächst die Leitung der neugegründeten Metallabteilung der Firma Amstelhoeck in Amsterdam, bevor er sich 1902 selbständig machte. Vor allem seine Entwürfe für Buntmetalle zeichnen sich durch ihre konstruktive Sachlichkeit aus. Eisenloeffels Arbeiten wurden von der holländischen Firma »De Woning« und den »Vereinigten Werkstätten München« vertrieben.

Au cours de la 1ère Exposition des Arts décoratifs de Turin en 1902, les créations en métal du Hollandais Jan Eisenloeffel sont remarquées et appréciées pour leur modernité. Après un apprentissage comme orfèvre et un long stage chez Fabergé à Saint-Pétersbourg, il prend tout d'abord la direction de la section «objets en métal» nouvellement créée chez le fabricant hollandais Amstelhoeck, puis se met à son compte. Ses objets réalisés dans des métaux colorés se caractérisent par leur sobriété. Les créations d'Eisenloeffel sont commercialisées par la maison hollandaise «De Woning» et par les «Vereinigte Werkstätten München».

**Jan Eisenloeffel,
1902**

Coffee and tea set
Brass, ebony
Eisenloeffel workshop,
Overveen near
Haarlem
Height: 26 cm
(teapot on rechaud)

**Kaffee- und
Teeservice**
Messing, Ebenholz
Werkstatt Eisenloeffel,
Overveen bei Haarlem
Höhe: 26 cm (Teekanne auf Rechaud)

**Service à café et à
thé**
Laiton et bois d'ébène
Atelier Eisenloeffel,
Overveen près de
Haarlem
Hauteur : 26 cm
(théière sur réchaud)

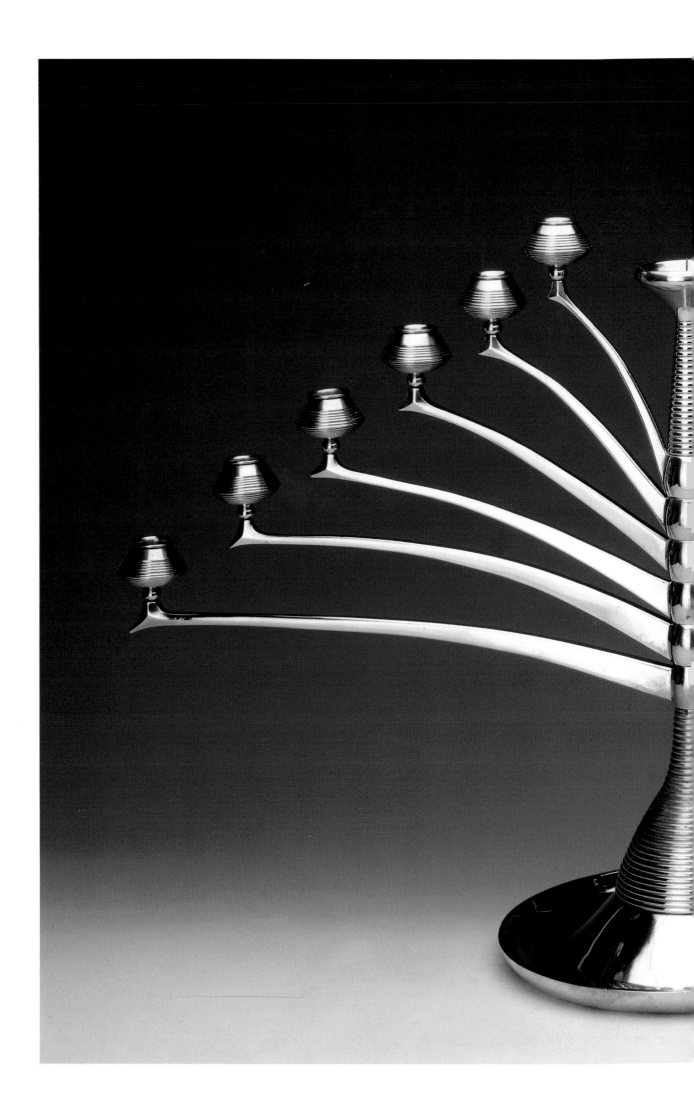

Bruno Paul,
1901

Candle holder
Brass
Metalware
manufacturers
Seifert & Co.,
Dresden-Löbtau
Height: 44 cm

Kerzenleuchter
Messing
Metallwarenfabrik
Seifert & Co.,
Dresden-Löbtau
Höhe: 44 cm

Bougeoir
en laiton
Usine d'articles
métalliques
Seifert & Co.,
Dresden-Löbtau
Hauteur: 44 cm

In Germany, Munich became the fore-
most centre of artists seeking to reform
the fields of art, architecture and crafts.
In 1896, the art and literature periodical
»Jugend«, from which the German version of Art Nouveau derived its name –
»Jugendstil« – was published for the first
time. In the following year, the »Vereinigte Werkstätten für Kunst im Handwerk
München« (Munich United Workshops)
was founded, fproducing and manufacturing innovative designs. Its more famous co-founders included Richard
Riemerschmid and Bruno Paul, both of
whom were to make decisive contributions to the development of modern design in their capacity as directors of leading German schools of applied arts.

München wurde innerhalb Deutschlands
zum ersten Zentrum derjenigen bildenden Künstler, die Kunst, Architektur und
Kunstgewerbe reformieren wollten. 1896
erschien hier erstmals die Kunst- und
Literaturzeitschrift »Jugend«, die dem
»Jugendstil« seinen Namen gab. 1897
wurden die »Vereinigten Werkstätten für
Kunst im Handwerk München« gegründet, die die Produktion und die Herstellung von fortschrittlichen kunstgewerblichen Entwürfen übernahmen. Zu ihren
bekanntesten Gründungsmitgliedern
zählten Richard Riemerschmid und Bruno
Paul, die später als Direktoren von führenden deutschen Kunstgewerbeschulen für
die Entwicklung des modernen Designs
von entscheidender Bedeutung waren.

En Allemagne, Munich devient le premier
centre d'artistes désireux de réformer
l'art, l'architecture et les arts décoratifs.
En 1896 paraît le premier numéro de la
revue littéraire et artistique «Jugend» qui
donne son nom au Jugendstil. L'année
suivante les «Vereinigte Werkstätten für
Kunst im Handwerk München», Ateliers
réunis de Munich, commencent la fabrication d'objets au design progressistes
design Parmi les membres fondateurs les
plus connus, signalons Richard Riemerschmid et Bruno Paul qui joueront plus
tard un rôle décisif dans le développement du design en tant que directeurs
d'écoles d'arts décoratifs renommées.

**Richard
Riemerschmid, 1900**

Wine glass
Glassworks Benedikt
von Poschinger,
Oberzwieselau
Height: 10.9 cm

Weinglas
Glashütte Benedikt
von Poschinger,
Oberzwieselau
Höhe: 10,9 cm

Verre à vin
Verrerie Benedikt
von Poschinger,
Oberzwieselau
Hauteur: 10,9 cm

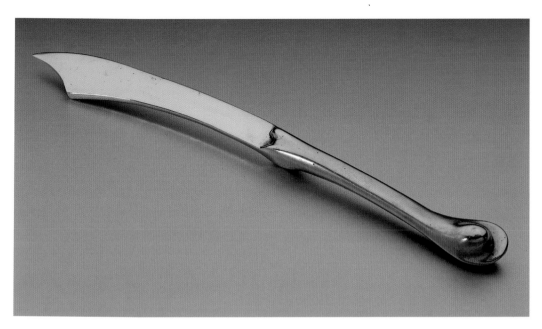

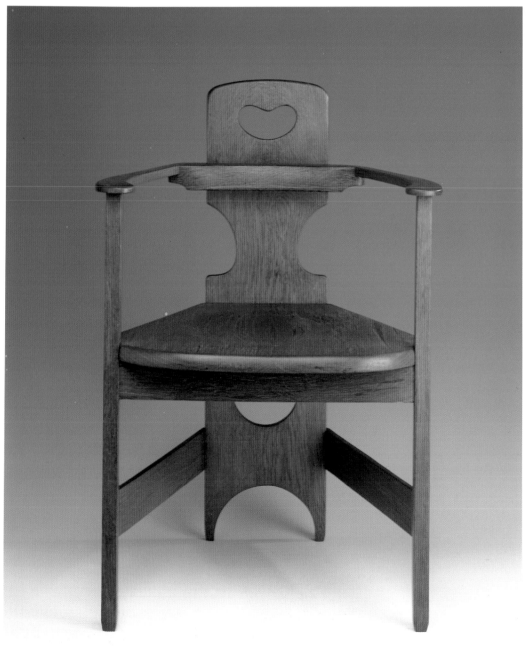

**Richard Riemer-
schmid, 1898/99**

Paperknife
Brass
Vereinigte Werkstätten
für Kunst im
Handwerk, Munich
Length: 24.5 cm

Brieföffner
Messing
Vereinigte Werkstätten
für Kunst im
Handwerk, München
Länge: 24,5 cm

Coupe-papier
en laiton
Vereinigte Werkstätten
für Kunst im
Handwerk, Munich
Longueur: 24,5 cm

**Richard Riemer-
schmid, 1900**

Armchair
Oak
Cabinetmakers
Fleischauer's Söhne,
Nuremberg
Height: 84 cm

Armlehnstuhl
Mooreiche
Kunstschreinerei
Fleischauer's Söhne,
Nürnberg
Höhe: 84 cm

Fauteuil à accoudoirs
en chêne
Ebénisterie d'art
Fleischauer's Söhne,
Nürnberg
Hauteur: 84 cm

Otto Wagner and his student Adolf Loos created an architectural and design syntax derived entirely from functional requirements. They rejected the concept of ornamentation for its own sake. Wagner's design for the Austrian Post Office Savings Bank in Vienna, built in 1904/06, is surely the most consistent example of the functionalist tendencies of the Modern Movement in Vienna.

Otto Wagner und sein Schüler Adolf Loos suchten in ihren Architektur- und Objektentwürfen nach einer Formensprache, die sich allein aus der jeweiligen Funktion ergeben sollte. Das rein schmückend eingesetzte Ornament lehnten sie ab. Der Entwurf Wagners für das 1904/06 erbaute Österreichische Postsparkassenamt verwirklichte am konsequentesten die funktionalen Sachlichkeitstendenzen der Wiener Moderne.

Otto Wagner et son élève Adolf Loos cherchent dans leurs créations architecturales et d'objets un langage des formes qui doit résulter uniquement de leur fonction respective et refusent systématiquement l'ornement purement décoratif. L'aménagement de la Caisse d'épargne de la poste autrichienne par Wagner en 1904/06 est un modèle du genre : les tendances fonctionnelles des modernistes viennois y sont réalisées avec la plus grande logique.

Adolf Loos,
1902/04

Clock
Brass, bevelled glass
Johann Heeg, Vienna
Height: 48.2 cm

Pendeluhr
Messing,
facettiertes Glas
Johann Heeg, Wien
Höhe: 48,2 cm

Pendule
en laiton et
verre à facettes.
Johann Heeg, Vienne
Hauteur: 48,2 cm

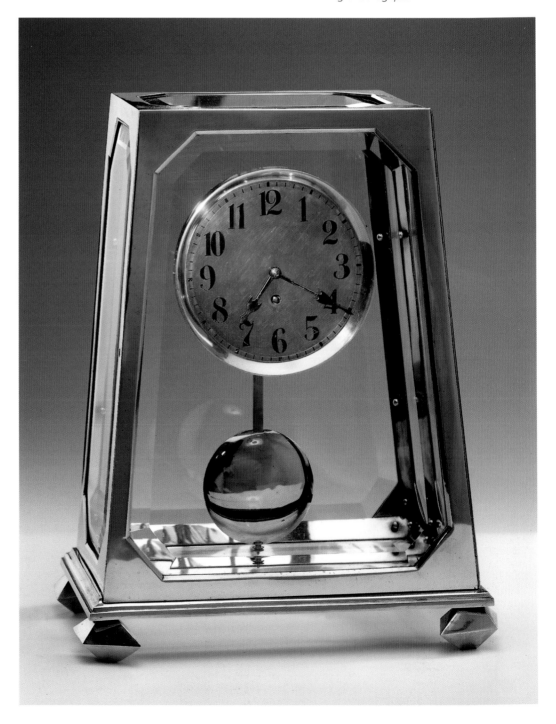

**Otto Wagner,
1905/06**

Meeting room, Aus-
trian Post Office
Savings Bank, Vienna

Sitzungssaal der Öster-
reichischen Postspar-
kasse in Wien

Salle de réunion de la
Caisse d'épargne autri-
chienne à Vienne

**Otto Wagner,
1905/06**

**Armchair for Aus-
trian Post Office
Savings Bank,
Vienna (modified)**
Bentwood, alumin-
ium, woven cane
Furniture
manufacturers
Jakob & Josef Kohn,
Vienna
Height: 78.5 cm

**Armlehnstuhl für
die Österreichische
Postsparkasse
(Variante)**
Bugholz, Aluminium,
Rohrgeflecht
Möbelfabrik
Jakob & Josef Kohn,
Wien
Höhe: 78,5 cm

**Fauteuil à accou-
doirs pour la Caisse
d'épargne autri-
chienne (variante)**
Bois de hêtre
courbé, aluminium,
cannage
Fabrique de meubles
Jakob & Josef Kohn,
Vienne
Hauteur: 78,5 cm

Josef Hoffmann,
1904/05

Dining room of Pur-
kersdorf Sanatorium
near Vienna

Speisesaal des Sanato-
riums Purkersdorf bei
Wien

Salle à manger du sa-
natorium de Purkers-
dorf près de Vienne

Josef Hoffmann,
1904

Dining room chair
for Purkersdorf
Sanatorium
Bentwood, plywood,
leather
Furniture
manufacturers
Jakob & Josef Kohn,
Vienna
Height: 99 cm

Stuhl für den Speise-
saal des Sanatori-
ums Purkersdorf
Bugholz, Sperrholz,
Lederbezug
Möbelfabrik
Jakob & Josef Kohn,
Wien
Höhe: 99 cm

Chaise pour la salle
à manger du sanato-
rium de Purkersdorf
en bois courbé, contre-
plaqué et garniture de
cuir
Fabrique de meubles
Jakob & Josef Kohn,
Vienne
Hauteur: 99 cm

Carl Witzmann,
1904/05

Display cabinet
Blackstained oak,
marble, glass
Cabinetmaker
Karl Vogel, Wien
Height: 179.5 cm

Vitrinenschrank
Eiche, schwarz ge-
beizt, Marmor, Glas
Möbeltischler
Karl Vogel, Wien
Höhe: 179,5 cm

Vitrine
Chêne teinté noir, mar-
bre et verre
Menuisier
Karl Vogel, Vienne
Hauteur: 179, 5 cm

In 1904, Josef Hoffmann was commissioned to design the Purkersdorf Sanatorium near Vienna. The interior fittings and furnishings were produced by the Wiener Werkstätte (Vienna Workshop) on the basis of designs by Hoffmann and Koloman Moser, with the sole exception of the bentwood chairs for the dining room, which were manufactured in quantity by the furniture factory of Jakob & Josef Kohn. A typical feature of Hoffmann's mass-produced furniture designs is the use of spherical components to link the legs of the chairs with the seats.

1904 erhielt Josef Hoffmann den Auftrag für die Planung des Sanatoriums Purkersdorf bei Wien. Der Innenausbau wurde nach Entwürfen Hoffmanns und Koloman Mosers von der Wiener Werkstätte übernommen. Nur die in größeren Stückzahlen benötigten Bugholzstühle für den Speisesaal wurden bei der Möbelfabrik Jakob & Josef Kohn in Auftrag gegeben. Typisch für die seriellen Möbelentwürfe Hoffmanns sind die Kugelelemente, die Stuhlbeine und Sitzfläche miteinander verbinden.

Josef Hoffmann est chargé en 1904 du projet de sanatorium à Purkersdorf près de Vienne. L'aménagement intérieur est réalisé par les Ateliers viennois sur une conception de Hoffmann et de Koloman Moser. Seules les chaises en bois courbé de la salle à manger sont fabriquées par la fabrique de meubles Jakob & Josef Kohn en raison de leur nombre élevé. Les meubles de série de Hoffmann se caractérisent par leurs éléments sphériques, les pieds de chaise et les sièges.

Carl Witzmann, 1904/05

Sideboard
Black-stained oak, marble, glass
Cabinetmaker
Karl Vogel, Vienna
Height: 179.5 cm

Anrichte
Eiche, schwarz gebeizt, Marmor, Glas
Möbeltischler
Karl Vogel, Wien
Höhe: 179,5 cm

Bahut
en chêne teinté noir, marbre et verre
Menuisier
Karl Vogel, Vienne
Hauteur: 179,5 cm

Koloman Moser's imaginative and modernistic design approach had a considerable influence on applied arts in the early years of the Vienna Secession. In collaboration with the Viennese glass dealers Bakalowits & Söhne, a series of liqueur glasses of different heights were created and exhibited in 1900 at the 8th Vienna Secession Exhibition, where they were displayed on a buffet decorated with »The Miraculous Draught of Fishes«. A typical feature of Moser's jewellery designs is his use of animal motifs in conjunction with simple silver settings intended to emphasise the artistry of the design rather than the material value.

Der phantasievolle und zugleich moderne Entwurfsstil Koloman Mosers übte einen großen Einfluß auf das Kunstgewerbe der frühen Wiener Sezessionszeit aus. In Zusammenarbeit mit dem Wiener Glaswarenhandel Bakalowits & Söhne entstanden die unterschiedlich hohen Likörgläser, die 1900 auf der VIII. Wiener Sezessionsausstellung auf dem Buffet »Der reiche Fischzug« dekoriert waren. Typisch für Mosers Schmuckentwürfe ist die Verwendung von Tiermotiven in Verbindung mit einfachen Silberfassungen, die nicht den Materialwert, sondern den künstlerischen Entwurf hervorheben sollten.

Le style de création de Koloman Moser alliant modernité et imagination exerça une grande influence sur les arts décoratifs de la Sécession viennoise à ses débuts. De sa collaboration avec le commerce de verrerie Bakalowits & Söhne de Vienne date la série de verres à liqueur présentée sur le buffet «Der reiche Fischzug» (la pêche abondante) de la 8ème Exposition de la Sécession viennoise. Les créations de bijoux de Moser se caractérisent par l'emploi de motifs animaliers dans des montures en argent très simples dont le but n'est pas de souligner la valeur du matériau mais de mettre en valeur la conception artistique.

46

Koloman Moser, 1900

Sideboard
»Der reiche Fischzug«,
8th Vienna Secession Exhibition 1900

Buffet
»Der reiche Fischzug«
VIII. Wiener Sezessionsausstellung 1900

Buffet
»Der reiche Fischzug«
8ème Exposition de la Sécession viennoise 1900

Koloman Moser, 1900

Two liqueur glasses
E. Bakalowits & Söhne, Vienna (distributors)
Height: 32 cm/16.5 cm

Zwei Likörgläser
E. Bakalowits & Söhne, Wien (Vertrieb)
Höhe: 32 cm/16,5 cm

Verres à liqueur
E. Bakalowits & Söhne, Vienne (édition)
Hauteur: 32 cm/16,5 cm

Koloman Moser,
c. 1904

Buckle
Silver, opals, ruby
Wiener Werkstätte,
goldsmith Anton Pribil
Width: 6 cm

Gürtelschnalle
Silber, Opale, Rubin
Wiener Werkstätte,
Goldschmied
Anton Pribil
Breite: 6 cm

Boucle de ceinture
en argent, opale et
rubis
Wiener Werkstätte,
orfèvre Anton Pribil
Largeur: 6 cm

Koloman Moser,
1901

Sherry decanter
Glass, metal,
silver-plated
E. Bakalowits & Söhne,
Vienna (distributors)
Height: 24 cm

Sherrykaraffe
Glas, Metallfassung,
versilbert
E. Bakalowits & Söhne,
Wien (Vertrieb)
Höhe: 24 cm

Carafe à sherry
en verre, monture en
métal argenté
E. Bakalowits & Söhne,
Vienne (édition)
Hauteur: 24 cm

In 1903, Josef Hoffmann, Koloman Moser and the banker Fritz Waerndorfer founded the Wiener Werkstätte (Vienna Workshop). That same year, a silversmith workshop was established, producing designs by Hoffmann and Moser, and later by other artists of the Wiener Werkstätte. The metalwork from the early phase of the Wiener Werkstätte is characterised by its puristic, architectural design, which appears to anticipate the formal developments of the 1920s.

1903 gründeten Josef Hoffmann, Koloman Moser und der Bankier Fritz Waerndorfer die Wiener Werkstätte. Noch im gleichen Jahr wurde eine voll funktionsfähige Silberschmiedewerkstatt eingerichtet, in der die Entwürfe von Hoffmann und Moser und später auch die von anderen Künstlern der Wiener Werkstätte ausgeführt wurden. Die Metallarbeiten aus der Frühphase der Wiener Werkstätte zeichnen sich durch ihre puristische, architektonische Gestaltung aus, die die Formentwicklung der 20er Jahre vorwegzunehmen scheint.

En 1903, Josef Hoffmann, Koloman Moser et le banquier Fritz Waerndorfer fondent les Ateliers viennois. La même année, ils ouvrent un atelier d'orfèvrerie parfaitement équipé où sont réalisées les créations de Hoffmann, de Moser ainsi que plus tard celles des artistes qui travailleront aux Ateliers. Les travaux des Ateliers viennois de la première période se distinguent par leur design puriste et architectonique qui semble anticiper l'évolution des formes au XXème siècle.

48

Josef Hoffmann, 1903/04

Teapot
Silver, ebony
Wiener Werkstätte,
silversmith Adolf Ebrich
Height: 15 cm

Teekanne
Silber, Ebenholz
Wiener Werkstätte,
Silberschmied
Adolf Ebrich
Höhe: 15 cm

Théière
en argent et bois
d'ébène
Wiener Werkstätte,
orfèvre Adolf Ebrich
Hauteur: 15 cm

Josef Hoffmann,
c. 1904

Dish
Silver, lapis lazuli
cabochons
Wiener Werkstätte
Width: 15 cm

Schale
Silber, Lapislazuli-
Cabochons
Wiener Werkstätte
Breite: 15 cm

Coupe
en argent et cabo-
chons de lapis-lazuli
Wiener Werkstätte
Largeur: 15 cm

Josef Hoffmann,
c. 1904

Dish with lid
Silver
Wiener Werkstätte,
silversmith
Josef Wagner
Width: 15 cm

Deckeldose
Silber
Wiener Werkstätte,
Silberschmied
Josef Wagner
Breite: 15 cm

Boîte à couvercle
en argent
Wiener Werkstätte,
orfèvre Josef Wagner
Largeur: 15 cm

Hallmarking of
illustrated teapot,
Wiener Werkstätte,
silver workshop

Punzierung der
abgebildeten
Teekanne, Wiener
Werkstätte, Silber-
schmiedewerkstatt

Ciselure de la théière
représentée,
Wiener Werkstätte,
atelier d'orfèvrerie

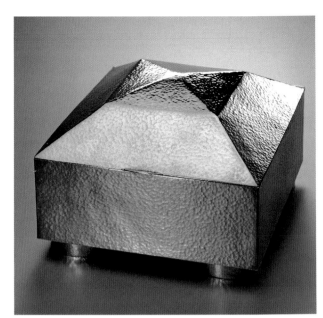

**Josef Hoffmann,
1909**

Dish with lid
German silver
Wiener Werkstätte
Height: 10.7 cm

Deckeldose
Alpacca
Wiener Werkstätte
Höhe: 10,7 cm

Boîte à couvercle
en argentan
Wiener Werkstätte
Hauteur : 10,7 cm

**Josef Hoffmann,
1905**

Menagerie
Silver, red coral, glass
Wiener Werkstätte,
silversmith Josef Czech
Height: 17.5 cm

Menage
Silber, rote Koralle,
Glas
Wiener Werkstätte,
Silberschmied
Josef Czech
Höhe: 17,5 cm

Huilier
en argent, corail
rouge et verre
Wiener Werkstätte,
orfèvre Josef Czech
Hauteur: 17,5 cm

Josef Hoffmann,
c. 1905

Dish with lid
German silver
Wiener Werkstätte
Height: 13 cm

Deckeldose
Alpacca
Wiener Werkstätte
Höhe: 13 cm

Boîte à couvercle
Argentan
Wiener Werkstätte
Hauteur : 13 cm

Josef Hoffmann,
c. 1910

Vase
Brass
Wiener Werkstätte
Height: 16.5 cm

Vase
Messing
Wiener Werkstätte
Höhe: 16,5 cm

Vase
Laiton
Wiener Werkstätte
Hauteur : 16,5 cm

Otto Prutscher, 1908

*Various crystal glasses,
Kunstschau Vienna
1908*

*Verschiedene
Kristallgläser,
Kunstschau Wien 1908*

*Verres de cristal,
Kunstschau Vienne
1908*

**Otto Prutscher,
c. 1907**

Champagne glass
*Glass, blue decor,
geometric cut
Glassworks
Adolf
Meyr's Neffe,
Winterberg
Height: 20.3 cm*

Sektschale
*Glas, blauer Überfang,
quadratischer Schliff-
dekor
Glashütte
Adolf
Meyr's Neffe,
Winterberg
Höhe: 20,3 cm*

Coupe à champagne
*Verre avec couche
supérieure bleue et
décor en taille carrée
Verrerie Adolf Meyr's
Neffe, Winterberg
Hauteur: 20,3 cm*

In 1907, Hoffmann's student Otto Prutscher was appointed head of the open-drawing department of the School of Applied Arts in Vienna. In addition to teaching, he also worked as an architect and designer. His glassware designs, produced by the glassworks Adolf Meyr's Neffe and Lötz Witwe, possess an almost architectonic clarity of form. His glassware designs were also marketed by the Wiener Werkstätte (Vienna Workshop), where Prutscher was a member of the artistic staff from 1907/08.

Der Hoffmann-Schüler Otto Prutscher wurde 1907 Leiter des offenen Zeichensaales an der Wiener Kunstgewerbeschule. Parallel zu seiner Lehrtätigkeit arbeitet er als Architekt und Entwerfer. Seine von den Glashütten Adolf Meyr's Neffe und Lötz Witwe ausgeführten Glasentwürfe zeichnen sich durch ihre klare, architektonische Formgebung aus. Vertrieben wurden die Gläser u.a. von der Wiener Werkstätte, als deren künstlerischer Mitarbeiter Prutscher ab 1907/08 tätig war.

En 1907 Otto Prutscher, un élève de Hoffmann, prend la direction de la salle de dessin ouverte de l'Ecole des arts décoratifs de Vienne. Parallèlement à ses activités professorales, il est concepteur et architecte. Ses créations en verre réalisées par la verrerie Adolf Meyr's Neffe et Lötz Witwe se caractérisent par leur plastique claire et architectonique. Les verres sont commercialisés entre autres par les Wiener Werkstätte dont Prutscher est le collaborateur artistique à partir de 1907/08.

53

Otto Prutscher, 1908

Rosebowl
Glass, black enamel and gold decor
Glassworks Lötz Witwe, Klostermühle
Height: 9 cm

Blumenschale
Glas, schwarzer Email- und Golddekor
Glashütte Lötz Witwe, Klostermühle
Höhe: 9 cm

Coupe à fleurs
Verre avec décor doré et en émail
Verrerie Lötz Witwe, Klostermühle
Hauteur: 9 cm

Otto Prutscher, 1910/11

Liqueur set
Clear glass, stained yellow
Glassworks Adolf Meyr's Neffe, Winterberg
Height: 21.5 cm
(decanter)

Likörservice
Farbloses Glas mit Gelbbeize
Glashütte Adolf Meyr's Neffe, Winterberg
Höhe: 21,5 cm
(Karaffe)

Service à liqueur
Verre blanc teinté de jaune
Verrerie Adolf Meyr's Neffe, Winterberg
Hauteur : 21,5 cm
(Carafe)

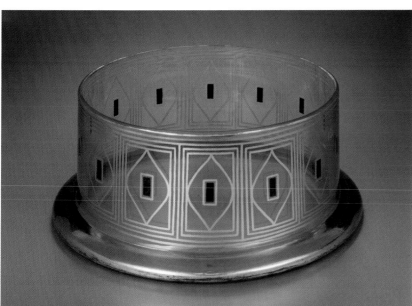

Joseph Maria Olbrich, 1902

*Hessian Room,
1st International
Crafts Exhibition,
Turin 1902*

*Hessisches Zimmer,
1. Internationale
Kunstgewerbeaus-
stellung, Turin 1902*

*Pièce hessoise, 1ère Ex-
position internationale
de l'Art décoratif mo-
derne à Turin 1902*

Joseph Maria Olbrich, c. 1902

Bookcase	**Bibliotheksschrank**	**Bibliothèque**
Stained oak	*Eiche, dunkel gebeizt*	*en chêne foncé*
Furniture manufac-	*Hofmöbelfabrik Julius*	*Manufacture de meu-*
turers Julius Glückert,	*Glückert, Darmstadt*	*bles Julius Glückert,*
Darmstadt	*Höhe: 214,5 cm*	*Darmstadt*
Height: 214.5 cm		*Hauteur : 214,5 cm*

In 1899, Joseph Maria Olbrich was called from Vienna to Darmstadt by Grand Duke Ernst Ludwig of Hesse to establish an artists' colony along with six other artists, in a bid to revitalise and promote the arts and crafts in Hesse. For the »Hessian Room« exhibited in 1902 at the 1st International Crafts Exhibition in Turin, Olbrich designed the bookcase produced by the Darmstadt-based furniture maker Julius Glückert.

1899 wurde Joseph Maria Olbrich vom Großherzog Ernst Ludwig von Hessen und bei Rhein aus Wien nach Darmstadt berufen, um dort zusammen mit sechs weiteren Künstlern eine Künstlerkolonie zu gründen, die das hessische Handwerk und die dortige Kunstindustrie beleben und fördern sollte. Für das »Hessische Zimmer«, das 1902 auf der 1. Internationalen Kunstgewerbeausstellung in Turin ausgestellt wurde, entwarf Olbrich den Bibliotheksschrank, der von der Darmstädter Hofmöbelfabrik Julius Glückert ausgeführt wurde.

Joseph Maria Olbrich est appelé en 1899 à Darmstadt par le grand-duc Ernest Ludovic de Hesse, qui le charge de fonder une colonie d'artistes dans le but de revitaliser et d'encourager l'artisanat et l'industrie de l'art de la Hesse. Il la montera avec six autres collègues. C'est pour «Das Hessische Zimmer» («La pièce hessoise»), exposée à Turin en 1902 à la 1ère Exposition internationale de l'Art décoratif moderne, qu'Olbrich conçoit la bibliothèque, réalisée par la manufacture de meubles Julius Glückert de Darmstadt.

Joseph Maria Olbrich, c. 1902

Candle holder
Pewter
Metalware
manufacturers
Eduard Hueck,
Lüdenscheid
Height: 36 cm

Kerzenleuchter
Zinn
Metallwarenfabrik
Eduard Hueck,
Lüdenscheid
Höhe: 36 cm

Bougeoir
Etain
Usine d'articles métalliques
Eduard Hueck,
Lüdenscheid
Hauteur: 36 cm

Peter Behrens, 1901

Dining room of the
house »Peter Behrens«
on the
Mathildenhöhe in
Darmstadt

Speisezimmer, Haus
»Peter Behrens«,
Darm-
stadt, Mathildenhöhe

Salle à manger
de la maison «Peter
Behrens», Darmstadt,
Mathildenhöhe

**Peter Behrens,
1900/01**

Set of goblets
Clear glass, ruby glass
Rheinische Glashütte
AG, Cologne-Ehrenfeld
Height: 21.5 cm
(champagne glass)

Satz Kelchgläser
Farbloses Glas,
Rubinglas
Rheinische Glashütte
AG, Köln-Ehrenfeld
Höhe: 21,5 cm
(Sektschale)

Série de coupes
en verre blanc et verre
rouge rubis
Verrerie Rheinische
Glashütte,
Köln-Ehrenfeld
Hauteur : 21,5 cm
(coupe à champagne)

Apart from Joseph Maria Olbrich, the most famous co-founder of the Darmstadt artists' colony was Peter Behrens. His architectural debut, the »Peter Behrens House« on the Mathildenhöhe, was an idealised »Gesamtkunstwerk« (total art work) with extravagant interior fittings – such as the sets of goblets illustrated here – which brought him adulation and vehement criticism in equal measure. Like Henry van de Velde, Behrens also worked as a designer for the Westerwald pottery in Höhr-Grenzhausen.

Neben Joseph Maria Olbrich war Peter Behrens das bekannteste Gründungsmitglied der Darmstädter Künstlerkolonie. Mit seinem architektonischen Erstlingswerk, dem »Haus Peter Behrens« auf der Mathildenhöhe, schuf er ein idealisiertes Gesamtkunstwerk, das durch die extravaganten Details der Inneneinrichtung, wie den hier abgebildeten Kelchglassatz, große Bewunderung, aber auch starke Kritik hervorrief. Wie Henry van de Velde war auch Behrens als Entwerfer für die Westerwälder Steinzeugindustrie in Höhr-Grenzhausen tätig.

Outre Joseph Maria Olbrich, Peter Behrens est le co-fondateur le plus célèbre de la colonie d'artistes de Darmstadt. Sa première réalisation architectonique, la maison «Peter Behrens», sur la colline Sainte-Mathilde est une œuvre d'art globale idéalisée qui suscite autant l'admiration la plus grande que la critique la plus sévère pour son aménagement intérieur aux détails extravagants tels que les verres à pied exposés ici. A l'instar d'Henry van de Velde, Behrens travaille lui aussi comme concepteur pour les ateliers de poteries Westerwälder de Höhr-Grenzhausen.

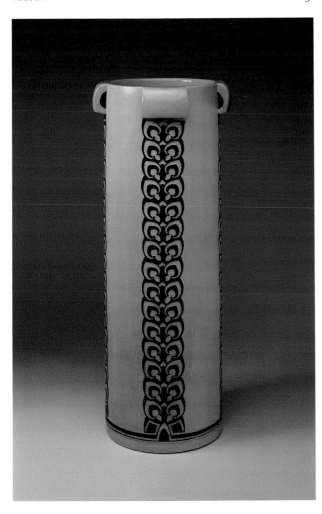

Peter Behrens,
c. 1904

Umbrella stand	**Schirmständer**	**Porte-parapluies**
Stoneware, grey salt glaze, painted blue Pottery Reinhold Merkelbach, Grenzhausen Height: 59 cm	Steinzeug, graue Salzglasur, blau bemalt Steinzeugfabrik Reinhold Merkelbach, Grenzhausen Höhe: 59 cm	en grès, vernis gris, peinture bleue Poteries Reinhold Merkelbach, Grenzhausen Hauteur: 59 cm

Peter Behrens,
c. 1903

Dish with lid	**Deckeldose**	**Boîte à couvercle**
Fine stoneware, green glaze, painted red Pottery Reinhold Hanke, Höhr Height: 20 cm	Feinsteinzeug, grüne Glasur, rot bemalt Steinzeugfabrik & Kunsttöpferei Reinhold Hanke, Höhr Höhe: 20 cm	en grès fin, vernis vert, peinture rouge Poteries Reinhold Hanke, Höhr Hauteur: 20 cm

Patriz Huber, 1901/02

Matchbox
Silver, green agate
cabochons
Silverware manufac-
turers Martin Mayer,
Mainz
Width: 4.5 cm

Zündholzdose
Silber, grüne Achat-
Cabochons
Silberwarenfabrik
Martin Mayer, Mainz
Breite: 4,5 cm

Boîte d'allumettes
en argent et cabo-
chons d'agate verte
Manufacture d'objets
en argent
Martin Mayer, Mayence
Largeur : 4,5 cm

Patriz Huber, 1901/02

Two brooches
Silver, turquoise/lapis
lazuli cabochons
Jewellery makers
Theodor Fahrner,
Pforzheim
Length: 2.5 cm/3.2 cm

Zwei Broschen
Silber, Türkis-/Lapisla-
zuli-Cabochon
Schmuckwarenfabrik
Theodor Fahrner,
Pforzheim
Länge: 2,5 cm/3,2 cm

Deux broches
en argent, cabochons
de turquoise et de
lapis-lazuli
Joaillerie Theodor
Fahrner,
Pforzheim
Longueur:
2,5 cm/3,2 cm

Patriz Huber, the youngest co-founder of the Darmstadt artists' colony, was called there at the age of 21, and made a name for himself as an interior designer and applied artist. His jewellery and silverware designs indicate a considerable capacity for abstraction. Paul Haustein, who worked in Darmstadt from 1903, was already one of the second generation of the artists' colony. In recognition of his particular talent in the field of metalware design, as evidenced in his Darmstadt designs, he was appointed to the teaching staff of the Stuttgarter Kunstgewerbeschule (School of Applied Arts) where he taught in the metalwork department.

Patriz Huber, im Alter von 21 Jahren als jüngstes Gründungsmitglied an die Darmstädter Künstlerkolonie berufen, wurde hauptsächlich als Innenarchitekt und Entwerfer für Kunstgewerbe bekannt. Seine Schmuck- und Silberwarenentwürfe zeichnen sich durch ihre abstrakte Oberflächengestaltung aus. Paul Haustein, ab 1903 in Darmstadt tätig, gehörte bereits zur zweiten Generation der Künstlerkolonie. Seinem besonderen Talent für die Gestaltung von Metallwaren entsprechend, das sich schon in seinen Darmstädter Entwürfen ausdrückte, erhielt er 1905 einen Lehrauftrag für Metallkunst an der Stuttgarter Kunstgewerbeschule.

Patriz Huber, avec ses 21 ans le plus jeune membre fondateur de la colonie d'artistes de Darmstadt, se fait connaître essentiellement comme architecte décorateur et concepteur dans le domaine des arts décoratifs. Ses créations de bijoux et d'objets en argent se distinguent par la conception abstraite des surfaces. Paul Haustein, à Darmstadt dès 1903, appartient déjà à la deuxième génération d'artistes de la colonie. Son talent particulier pour le modelage des métaux, visible déjà dans ses créations de l'époque de Darmstadt, lui vaut d'être appelé à diriger la section «art du métal» de l'Ecole des Arts décoratifs de Stuttgart en 1905.

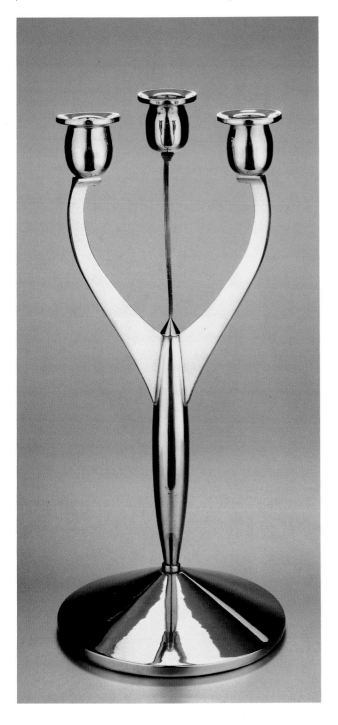

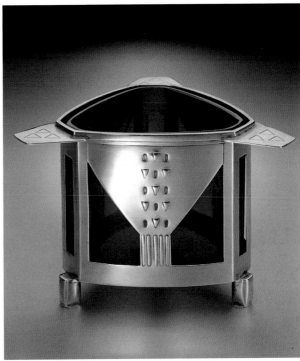

**Paul Haustein,
c. 1904**

Candle holder
Brass
Metalware
manufacturers
Georg Pöschmann,
Dresden
Height: 35.5 cm

Kerzenleuchter
Messing
Metallwarenfabrik
Georg Pöschmann,
Dresden
Höhe: 35,5 cm

Bougeoir
en laiton
Usine d'articles
métalliques
Georg Pöschmann,
Dresde
Hauteur: 35,5 cm

**Paul Haustein,
c. 1904**

Sweetmeat dish
Silver, blue glass
Silverware manufacturers Ernst Ludwig
Vietor, Darmstadt
Height: 8.8 cm

Konfektschale
Silber, blauer
Glaseinsatz
Silberwarenfabrik
Ernst Ludwig Vietor,
Darmstadt
Höhe: 8,8 cm

Coupe à confiserie
en argent et verre bleu
Manufacture d'objets
en argent Ernst Ludwig
Vietor, Darmstadt
Hauteur: 8,8 cm

In 1906, the architect and designer Albin Müller, until then professor at the Kunstgewerbeschule (School of Applied Arts) in Magdeburg, was called to the Darmstadt artists' colony. On the death of Joseph Maria Olbrich (1908), he took over the leading role within the artists' colony, profoundly influencing its later phase up to 1914 with his many-facetted oeuvre. Many of his designs were created in close collaboration with the respective manufacturing companies.

1906 wurde der Architekt und Entwerfer für Kunstgewerbe Albin Müller, bis dahin Professor an der Magdeburger Kunstgewerbeschule, an die Darmstädter Künstlerkolonie berufen. Nach dem Tod von Joseph Maria Olbrich (1908) übernahm er die führende Rolle innerhalb der Künstlerkolonie und prägte mit seinem überaus vielseitigen Werk ihre Spätphase bis 1914. Seine zahlreichen Entwürfe entstanden in enger Kooperation mit den jeweils ausführenden Firmen.

En 1906 Albin Müller, architecte et concepteur dans le domaine des arts décoratifs, jusque-là enseignant à l'Ecole des Arts décoratifs de Magdebourg, est invité à venir travailler à Darmstadt. Après la mort de Josef Maria Olbrich en 1908, il exerce un rôle directeur sur la colonie dont les activités jusqu'en 1914 sont marquées par son œuvre extrêmement variée. Ses nombreuses créations sont réalisées en collaboration étroite avec les fabricants.

**Albin Müller,
c. 1903**

Teapot and rechaud
Copper, brass
Metalware
manufacturers
Eduard Hueck,
Lüdenscheid
Height: 33.5 cm

**Teekanne auf
Rechaud**
Kupfer, Messing
Metallwarenfabrik
Eduard Hueck,
Lüdenscheid
Höhe: 33,5 cm

Théière sur réchaud
en cuivre et laiton
Usine d'articles
métalliques
Eduard Hueck,
Lüdenscheid
Hauteur: 33,5 cm

Albin Müller,
c. 1908

Coffee set
Porcelain, green under-
glaze decoration
Porcelain factory Bur-
gau,
Ferdinand Selle
Height: 26.5 cm
(coffee pot)

Kaffeeservice
Porzellan, grüne Unter-
glasurbemalung
Porzellan-Manufaktur
Burgau,
Ferdinand Selle
Höhe: 26,5 cm
(Kaffeekanne)

Service à café
en porcelaine et pein-
ture verte sous vernis
Manufacture de
porcelaine Burgau,
Ferdinand Selle
Hauteur: 26,5 cm
(cafetière)

61

Albin Müller,
c. 1908

White wine glass
Facet-cut glass
Crystal manufacturers
Benedikt von
Poschinger,
Oberzwieselau
Height: 20.5 cm

Weißweinglas
Glas, facettiert
geschliffen
Kristallglasfabrik
Benedikt von
Poschinger,
Oberzwieselau
Höhe: 20,5 cm

Verre à vin blanc
Verre taillé en facettes
Cristallerie Benedikt
von Poschinger,
Oberzwieselau
Hauteur: 20,5 cm

Albin Müller,
c. 1905

Punch bowl
Pewter, green glass
Metalware manufac-
turers Eduard Hueck,
Lüdenscheid
Height: 36.5 cm

Bowle
Zinn, grüner
Glaseinsatz
Metallwarenfabrik
Eduard Hueck,
Lüdenscheid
Höhe: 36,5 cm

Bol
en étain et applica-
tions de verre de
couleur verte
Usine d'articles métalli-
ques Eduard Hueck,
Lüdenscheid
Hauteur: 36,5 cm

Albin Müller,
c. 1905/06

Table clock	**Tischuhr**	**Pendule de table**
Patina-covered brass, serpentine	Messing, patiniert, Serpentinstein	Laiton patiné et serpentine
Fürstl. Stollbergsches Hüttenamt, Ilsenburg am Harz and Sächsische Serpentin-Stein-Gesellschaft, Zöblitz	Fürstl. Stollbergsches Hüttenamt Ilsenburg am Harz; Sächsische Serpentin-Stein-Gesellschaft, Zöblitz	Fürstl. Stollbergsches Hüttenamt, Ilsenburg am Harz Sächsische Serpentin-Stein-Gesellschaft, Zöblitz
Height: 31.5 cm	Höhe: 31,5 cm	Hauteur: 31,5 cm

Albin Müller,
c. 1905

Table clock	**Tischuhr**	**Pendule de table**
Inlaid serpentine	Serpentinstein, mehrfarbig eingelegt	avec serpentine en diverses couleurs
Sächsische Serpentin-Stein-Gesellschaft, Zöblitz	Sächsische Serpentin-Stein-Gesellschaft, Zöblitz	Sächsische Serpentin-Stein-Gesellschaft, Zöblitz
Height: 39 cm	Höhe: 39 cm	Hauteur: 39 cm

62

Before he was called to the artists' colony in Darmstadt in 1911, Emanuel Josef Margold was assistant to Josef Hoffmann in the department of architecture at the Kunstgewerbeschule (School of Applied Arts) in Vienna. While in Vienna, he enjoyed considerable success as a designer. From 1912, he designed packaging, window displays and shop fittings for the Hermann Bahlsen biscuit factory in Hanover. His designs were typical of the Austrian decorative style of the day.

Vor seiner Berufung (1911) an die Künstlerkolonie Darmstadt war Emanuel Josef Margold Assistent von Josef Hoffmann in der Architekturklasse der Wiener Kunstgewerbeschule. Bereits in Wien hatte er sich mit großem Erfolg dem Entwurf von Kunstgewerbe gewidmet. Ab 1912 war er als Entwerfer für die Keksfabrik Hermann Bahlsen in Hannover tätig, für die er neben Verpackungen auch Schaufensterentwürfe und Ladeneinrichtungen gestaltete. Seine Entwürfe waren ganz dem zeitgenössischen österreichischen Dekorationsstil verpflichtet.

Avant d'être appelé à la colonie d'artistes de Darmstadt en 1911, Emanuel Josef Margold est l'assistant de Josef Hoffmann pour la classe d'architecture de l'Ecole d'Arts décoratifs de Vienne. Déjà à cette époque, il se consacre avec succès à la création dans le domaine des arts décoratifs. A partir de 1912, il travaille comme concepteur pour la biscuiterie Hermann Bahlsen de Hanovre, créant des emballages et se chargeant de la décoration des vitrines et des intérieurs de magasins. Ses créations se voulaient conformes au style décoratif autrichien de l'époque.

Emanuel Josef Margold, 1914

Biscuit box
Polychrome printed sheet metal
Made for H. Bahlsen biscuit factory, Hanover
Width: 19.1 cm

Keksdose
Blech, polychrom bedruckt
Hergestellt für die Keksfabrik H. Bahlsen, Hannover
Breite: 19,1 cm

Boîte à biscuits
en tôle, impression polychrome
Fabriquée par la biscuiterie H. Bahlsen, Hanovre
Hauteur: 19,1 cm

Emanuel Josef Margold, 1913/14

Advertisement for H. Bahlsen's biscuit factory

Reklame für die Keksfabrik H. Bahlsen

Réclame pour la biscuiterie H. Bahlsen

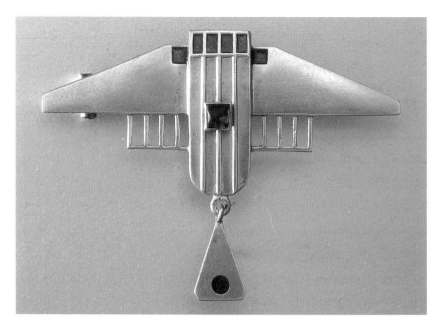

64

**Max Benirschke,
1906/07**

Necklace
*Silver, river pearls,
blue opaque enamel
Jewellery makers
Theodor Fahrner,
Pforzheim
Length: 9 cm
(pendant)*

Collier
*Silber, Flußperlen, blau-
es Opakemail
Schmuckwarenfabrik
Theodor Fahrner,
Pforzheim
Länge: 9 cm
(Anhänger)*

Collier
*en argent, perles et
émail opaque bleu
Joaillerie
Theodor Fahrner,
Pforzheim
Longueur: 9 cm
(pendentif)*

**Georg Kleemann,
1903/04**

Brooch
*Silver, enamel,
amethyst
Jewellery makers
Victor Mayer, Mainz
Width: 4 cm*

Brosche
*Silber, Email, Amethyst
Schmuckwarenfabrik
Victor Mayer, Mainz
Breite: 4 cm*

Broche
*en argent, émail et
améthyste
Joaillerie Victor Mayer,
Mayence
Largeur: 4 cm*

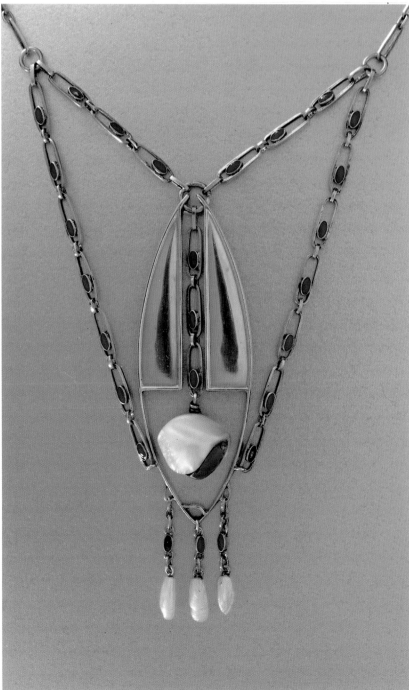

Even before the turn of the century, the jewellery industry in Pforzheim had already begun to adopt the new »Jugendstil«. Affordable modern fashion jewellery designs by renowned artists soon became a major commercial factor, enhancing the image of the predominantly profit-oriented jewellery manufacturers. From around 1900, the floral style of the Pforzheim jewellery production began to change in favour of a more abstractly geometric style under the influence of the Darmstadt artists.

Die Pforzheimer Schmuckwarenindustrie setzte bereits vor der Jahrhundertwende in Teilen ihrer Produktion auf den »Jugendstil«. Moderner, von bekannten Künstlern entworfener, preisgünstiger Modeschmuck wurde schon bald zu einem wichtigen Wirtschaftsfaktor und stärkte gleichzeitig das Image der hauptsächlich am Profit orientierten Schmuckfabrikanten. Ab ca. 1900 wandelte sich, stark von den Entwürfen der Darmstädter Künstlerkolonie beeinflußt, der florale Stil der Pforzheimer Schmuckwarenproduktion zugunsten einer abstrakt-geometrischen Formgestaltung.

Le XIXème siècle ne touche pas encore à sa fin que l'industrie du bijou de Pforzheim fabrique une partie de ses modèles dans le «Jugendstil». Les bijoux modernes meilleur marché, créés par des artistes connus, deviennent bientôt un facteur économique important et renforcent en même temps la renommée des fabricants de bijoux intéressés principalement par le profit. A partir de 1900, le style floral de la bijouterie pforzheimaise, très influencée par les créations des artistes de Darmstadt, prend des formes plus géométriques et abstraites.

65

Ferdinand Morawe, 1902/03

Pendant
Gilded silver, sapphire cabochons
Jewellery makers Theodor Fahrner, Pforzheim
Length: 8.5 cm

Anhänger
Silber, vergoldet, Saphir-Cabochons
Schmuckwarenfabrik Theodor Fahrner, Pforzheim
Länge: 8,5 cm

Pendentif
en argent doré et cabochons de saphir
Joaillerie Theodor Fahrner, Pforzheim
Longueur: 8,5 cm

Franz Boeres, 1904/05

Pendant	**Anhänger**	**Pendentif**
Silver, enamel, river pearls	Silber, Email, Flußperlen	Argent, émail et perles
Jewellery makers Theodor Fahrner, Pforzheim	Schmuckwarenfabrik Theodor Fahrner, Pforzheim	Joaillerie Theodory Fahrner, Pforzheim
Length: 5 cm	Länge: 5 cm	Longueur: 5 cm

Starting with his series of so-called »Prairie Houses«, the American architect Frank Lloyd Wright developed an interior-design style oriented entirely towards the forms of his own architecture, thereby elevating his buildings to the status of a »Gesamtkunstwerk« (total art work). In his designs, Wright combined features of the English Arts and Crafts movement with profoundly American influences and his own penchant for Japanese form. His geometrically structured furnishings have a distinctive uncluttered simplicity.

Der amerikanische Architekt Frank Lloyd Wright entwickelte, ausgehend von seinen sogenannten »Präriehäusern«, einen Einrichtungsstil, der sich völlig an den Formen seiner eigenen Architektur orientierte und seine Bauten zu Gesamtkunstwerken erhob. Wright verband in seinen Entwürfen englische Arts & Crafts-Vorbilder mit uramerikanischen Einflüssen und seiner Vorliebe für japanische Formen. Seine geometrisch konstruierten Möbel zeichnen sich durch ihre sachliche Einfachheit aus.

L'architecte américain Frank Lloyd Wright crée à partir de sa «maison-prairie» un style d'ameublement imprégné de ses concepts architecturaux et faisant de ses constructions des œuvres d'art globales. Wright associe le style anglais Arts and Crafts avec des éléments indigènes américains et des formes japonaises. Ses meubles construits géométriquement se caractérisent par leur sobriété.

Frank Lloyd Wright, 1904

Chair for the Larkin Company canteen, Buffalo/NY
Stained oak, leather
Height: 102 cm

Stuhl für die Kantine des Verwaltungsgebäudes der Larkin Company, Buffalo/NY
Eiche, dunkel gebeizt, Lederbezug
Höhe: 102 cm

Chaise pour la cantine de l'administration de la Larkin Company, Buffalo/NY.
Chêne foncé et garniture de cuir
Hauteur: 102 cm

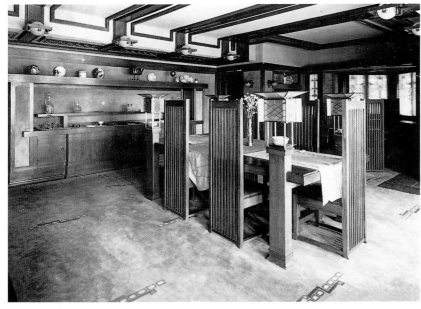

**Frank Lloyd Wright,
1906/09**

*Frederich C. Robie
House dining room,
Chicago/Ill.*

*Speisezimmer im Fre-
derick C. Robie House,
Chicago/Ill.*

*Salle à manger de la
Frederick C. Robie
House, Chicago/Ill.*

**Frank Lloyd Wright,
1908**

**Chair from the Isa-
bel Roberts House,
River Forest, Ill.**
*Poplar, leather
Height: 100 cm*

**Stuhl aus dem Isabel
Roberts House, Ri-
ver Forest/Ill.**
*Pappel, Lederbezug
Höhe: 100 cm*

**Chaise de l'Isabel
Roberts House,
River Forest/Ill.**
*Peuplier, garniture de
cuir
Hauteur: 100 cm*

**Frank Lloyd Wright,
1902**

**Chair from the Fran-
cis W. Little House,
Peoria/Ill.**
*Oak, leather
Height: 101 cm*

**Stuhl aus dem Fran-
cis W. Little House,
Peoria/Ill.**
*Eiche, Lederbezug
Höhe: 101 cm*

**Chaise de la Francis
W. Little House,
Peoria/Ill.**
*Chéne, garniture de
cuir
Hauteur: 101 cm*

Werkbund

The Werkbund: Vanguard of Industrial Design

Even though the reform movement which emerged at the turn of the century had created a new style, rejecting the eclectic historicism of the 19th century, much of the work created in the new style was produced in the form of one-offs or in expensive limited editions by traditional artisanal methods, and was thus undoubtedly of high design quality and craftsmanship. Industrial production, however, was soon churning out masses of anonymous, low-quality Jugendstil products which differed from those of the 19th century only in their use of new stylistic quotations. The sole exceptions to this rule were to be found where independent design artists and industrial producers worked in close cooperation.

In 1906, the 3rd Exhibition of German Arts and Crafts (III. Deutsche Kunstgewerbeausstellung) in Dresden clearly indicated that Jugendstil in Germany no longer possessed its former significance. The language of form had altered increasingly in favour of a more stringent expression emphasising the function of the objects. For the first time, the concept and organisation of the exhibition had been placed entirely in the hands of the participating artists and architects. Only those products were exhibited which had been created as the result of a positive cooperation between the designing artist and the producer. It differed from previous exhibitions in that it presented not only luxury craftsmanship, but also affordable industrially produced goods of exemplary design and execution.

Werkbund: Wegbereiter des industriellen Designs

Die Reformbewegung der Jahrhundertwende hatte zwar einen neuen Stil geschaffen und damit eine Abkehr von den historisierenden Stilimitationen des 19. Jahrhunderts bewirkt, doch waren die meisten Arbeiten des neuen Stils als kostbare Einzelanfertigungen oder in teuren Kleinserien auf rein kunsthandwerklicher Basis hergestellt worden. Gestalterische Qualität und handwerkliche Perfektion hatten sich in diesem Rahmen zweifellos durchgesetzt. Dagegen waren die schon bald von der Industrie in Massen produzierten, anonymen Jugendstilerzeugnisse lediglich mit neuen Stilzitaten ausgestattete Dekorwaren, die in ihrer minderwertigen Qualität noch ganz in der Tradition des 19. Jahrhunderts standen. Ausnahmen waren nur dort zu beobachten, wo unabhängig entwerfende Künstler und industrielle Produzenten eng zusammenarbeiteten.

Schon die III. Deutsche Kunstgewerbeausstellung von 1906 in Dresden zeigte, daß der Jugendstil in Deutschland seine ursprüngliche Bedeutung verloren hatte. Die Formensprache hatte sich zunehmend zugunsten einer strengeren, die Funktion der Objekte betonenden Ausdrucksweise gewandelt. Erstmalig lagen Konzeption und Organisation der Ausstellung ausschließlich bei den beteiligten Künstlern und Architekten. Ausgestellt wurden nur solche Erzeugnisse, die aus einer positiven Kooperation zwischen entwerfenden Künstlern und Herstellern hervorgegangen waren. Gezeigt wurde nicht – wie sonst üblich – ausschließlich Lu-

Le Werkbund, précurseur du design industriel

Le mouvement réformateur avait créé vers 1900 un style nouveau, abandonnant ainsi les imitations éclectiques du XIXème siècle. La plupart des objets réalisés dans le nouveau style restaient malgré tout des pièces uniques de valeur ou étaient fabriquées en petite série à un prix élevé. Il n'empêche que la qualité créatrice et la perfection artisanale avaient réussi à s'imposer. En revanche, ce que l'industrie commençait à produire en masse dans le Jugendstil n'était que des objets décoratifs anonymes, ornés de nouveaux motifs stylistiques, bien dans la tradition du XIXème siècle par leur qualité fort médiocre. Les seules exceptions qu'on pouvait observer résultaient de la collaboration étroite entre artistes indépendants et fabricants industriels.

Dès la 3ème Exposition des Arts appliqués de Dresde en 1906, il fut clair que le Jugendstil avait perdu de son importance initiale. Le langage des formes avait évolué en un style plus sévère, soulignant la fonction de l'objet. Pour la première fois, la conception et l'organisation de l'exposition étaient entièrement entre les mains des artistes et des architectes exposants. Seuls les produits qui étaient le résultat d'une collaboration fructueuse entre concepteurs et réalisateurs étaient exposés. Cette fois, l'exposition ne montrait pas seulement des modèles de luxe mais aussi des modèles bon marché qui, pour être fabriqués industriellement, n'en devaient pas moins être parfaits tant au niveau de la conception que de la réalisation. L'objectif

Founder members of the Deutscher Werkbund

Die Gründungsmitglieder des Deutschen Werkbundes

Les membres fondateurs du Werkbund allemand

The express aim of the exhibition was the promotion of exemplary standards of design in the fields of architecture, crafts and industry in the service of a new social and aesthetic quality of life.

The innovative concept of the Dresden exhibition set the standards for the Deutscher Werkbund (DWB), which was founded the following year. Its formation in October 1907 was the result of increasing animosity between the organisers and supporters of the Dresden exhibition amongst the commercial associations and the more conservatively-minded guilds of craftsmen, who felt threatened by their exclusion from the exhibition organisation. The founding members of the Deutscher Werkbund were 12 renowned artists, architects and craftsmen and 12 companies and workshops committed to its ideals. In 1908, the first rules of association of the Deutscher Werkbund defined the aims of the new organisation as follows: »The purpose of the association is the refinement of commercial work in collaboration between art, industry and craftsmanship through education, propaganda and unanimity on decisive issues«.

Within the space of just one year, Werkbund membership had risen to some 500 and by 1915 there were almost 2000 members. The Werkbund grouped not only artists, architects, craftsmen, workshops and industrial producers, but also representatives of commerce and industry, art theoreticians, experts, publicists and publishers. From 1912 onwards, the Werkbund began publishing its popular annuals with illustrations and texts report-

xuskunstgewerbe, sondern auch preiswertes, da maschinell hergestelltes »Industriekunstgewerbe«, das jedoch in Entwurf und Ausführung vorbildlich sein mußte. Erklärtes Ziel war die mustergültige Gestaltung von Architektur, Kunstgewerbe und Industrieprodukten im Dienst einer neuen sozialen und ästhetischen Lebensqualität.

Das neuartige Konzept der Dresdner Ausstellung war Anlaß und zugleich Vorbild für den im Jahr darauf gegründeten Deutschen Werkbund (DWB). Seine Gründung im Oktober 1907 resultierte aus der zunehmenden Anfeindung der Organisatoren und Befürworter des Dresdner Modells von seiten der Wirtschaftsverbände und der eher konservativen Kunstgewerbevereine, die sich durch ihren Ausschluß von der Ausstellungsorganisation bedroht fühlten. Als Gründungsmitglieder fungierten zwölf prominente Künstler, Architekten und Kunstgewerbler sowie zwölf engagierte Firmen und Werkstätten. Die erste Satzung des DWB definierte 1908 die Zielsetzung der neuen Organisation: »Der Zweck des Bundes ist die Veredlung der gewerblichen Arbeit im Zusammenwirken von Kunst, Industrie und Handwerk durch Erziehung, Propaganda und geschlossene Stellungnahme zu einschlägigen Fragen.«

Innerhalb nur eines Jahres wuchs die Mitgliederzahl des Deutschen Werkbundes auf knapp 500; 1915 waren es schon fast 2000. In ihm organisiert waren nicht nur Künstler, Architekten, Kunsthandwerker, kunstgewerbliche Werkstätten und industrielle Produzenten, sondern auch Wirtschaftsvertreter,

était d'élaborer une forme d'architecture, d'arts appliqués et de produits industriels au service d'une qualité de vie sociale et esthétique entièrement nouvelle.

Le concept inédit de l'exposition de Dresde fut à la fois l'origine et le modèle du Werkbund allemand (Union des artistes décorateurs), créé un an plus tard. L'hostilité croissante dont les organisateurs de l'exposition et les préconisateurs de ce concept étaient l'objet de la part des syndicats et des associations d'artistes plus conservatrices, qui se sentaient menacés par leur exclusion de l'organisation de l'exposition, fut à l'origine de la fondation du Deutscher Werkbund en octobre 1907. Au nombre des membres fondateurs figuraient douze artistes et architectes célèbres ainsi que douze représentants de grandes firmes et ateliers d'arts décoratifs. Les premiers statuts du Werkbund établis en 1908 définissaient ainsi le programme de l'organisation: «Le but du Werkbund est l'amélioration du travail professionnel avec le concours de l'art, de l'industrie et de l'artisanat par l'éducation, la propagande et l'unanimité sur les points décisifs.»

En un an seulement, le nombre des membres du Deutscher Werkbund atteignit presque les 500 et en 1915, il était de 2000 environ. L'organisation ne comptait pas seulement des artistes, des architectes, des artisans, des ateliers d'arts décoratifs et des fabricants industriels, elle accueillait aussi des représentants de l'économie, des théoriciens de l'art, des experts, des journalistes politiques et des éditeurs.

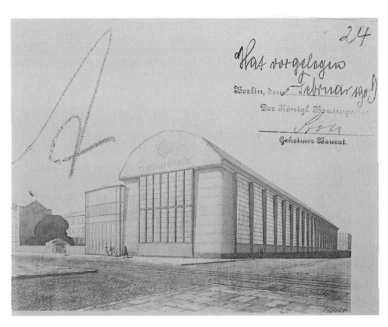

Peter Behrens, 1908

Design for the AEG turbine hall in Berlin-Moabit

Entwurf für die Turbinenhalle der AEG in Berlin-Moabit

Ebauche de l'usine de turbines d'AEG à Berlin-Moabit

ing the results of their work and providing new artistic inspiration. The annual also included a list of the addresses and fields of work of its members in a bid to encourage cooperation between them. Moreover, the Werkbund organised member participation in national and international arts and crafts exhibitions. In 1912, the Austrian and Hungarian Werkbund were founded along the lines of the Deutscher Werkbund and, in 1913, the Czech and Swiss Werkbund followed. The initial highlights of the Werkbund work were displayed at the Werkbund exhibition of 1914 in Cologne.

The new relationship between art and industry was exemplified by Peter Behrens' work for the German electrical company Allgemeine Berliner Elektricitätsgesellschaft (AEG), where he had been appointed artistic adviser in 1907, shortly before the foundation of the Werkbund. Behrens' work for the electrical company ranged from planning the factory halls and administrative buildings to redesigning a considerable proportion of the product range and developing a uniform modern company typography. The cooperation between Behrens and AEG was to remain unique as a collaboration of art with industry. Behrens created a corporate identity for AEG long before such a concept became taken for granted amongst designers and entrepreneurs.

Although the Werkbund focused primarily on cooperation with industry, artisanal craftsmanship was not excluded. However, the divergent interests of industry and artisanal crafts-

Kunsttheoretiker, Sachverständige, Publizisten und Verleger. Ab 1912 erschienen die weit verbreiteten Jahrbücher des DWB, die anhand von reichem Bild- und Textmaterial die Ergebnisse der Werkbundarbeit verbreiteten und auch neue künstlerische Anregungen vermittelten. Adressverzeichnisse informierten über Anschriften und Arbeitsgebiete seiner Mitglieder und förderten so die Zusammenarbeit zwischen diesen. Darüber hinaus organisierte der DWB die Beteiligung seiner Mitglieder an nationalen und internationalen Kunst- und Gewerbeausstellungen. Nach seinem Vorbild formierten sich 1912 der Österreichische und Ungarische Werkbund, 1913 der Tschechische und Schweizer Werkbund. Einen vorläufigen Höhepunkt erreichte die Werkbundarbeit mit der Kölner Werkbundausstellung von 1914.

Vorbildlich für das neue Verhältnis von Kunst und Industrie wurde die Zusammenarbeit von Peter Behrens mit der »Allgemeinen Berliner Elektricitätsgesellschaft« (AEG), die 1907 noch kurz vor Gründung des DWB durch die Berufung Behrens' zum künstlerischen Beirat der AEG begonnen hatte. Behrens plante Fabrik- und Verwaltungsgebäude, gestaltete große Teile der Produktpalette neu und entwickelte eine einheitlich moderne Firmentypographie.

Obwohl der Deutsche Werkbund den Schwerpunkt seiner Arbeit auf die Zusammenarbeit mit der Industrie legte, wurde das Handwerk nicht ausgeschlossen. Der unterschiedliche Anspruch von Industrie und Handwerk führte jedoch zu einer häufig geführ-

A partir de 1912, elle édita un annuaire largement diffusé sous la forme d'une riche iconographie accompagnée de commentaires pour présenter les résultats de ses recherches et proposer de nouvelles idées artistiques. En outre, une liste publiait l'adresse et la spécialité de ses membres, encourageant ainsi ceux-ci à collaborer entre eux. Le Werkbund organisait aussi la participation de ses membres à des expositions nationales ou internationales. D'autres associations similaires au modèle allemand se créèrent à leur tour : en 1912, le Werkbund autrichien et hongrois et en 1913, le Werkbund suisse et tchèque. Un événement considérable pour le Werkbund allemand fut la grande exposition de Cologne de 1914 qui présentait la synthèse de ses travaux et de ses recherches.

La collaboration entre Peter Behrens et la «Allgemeine Berliner Elektricitätsgesellschaft» (AEG), qui avait débuté peu de temps avant la création du Werkbund par la nomination de Behrens comme conseiller artistique de la firme, fut l'exemple même des nouvelles relations entre l'art et l'industrie. Behrens édifia pour AEG des bâtiments industriels modernes, créa une grande partie de sa nouvelle production et la première marque distinctive uniforme. Ce modèle d'association entre l'art et l'industrie reste unique par son ampleur. Behrens avait créé pour la firme une «Corporate Identity» bien longtemps avant que cette notion ne devienne évidente pour les designers et les entrepreneurs.

Bien que la collaboration avec l'industrie fût un élément essentiel de son tra-

manship led to recurrent debates on matters of principle: while industrial design demanded standardisation and forms which had to be reoriented towards function and mechanical reproducibility, many artists feared that such a trend was bound to destroy artistic individuality. The debate on standardisation and individuality came to a head in 1914 with a conflict – known as the »Werkbundstreit« – that almost spelt the end of the Werkbund.

The horrors of the first fully mechanised war had a sobering effect on the hitherto euphoric attitude towards machinery and temporarily clipped the wings of the Werkbund ideals. The cataclysm of the war affected the Werkbund during a phase in which it looked likely to disband anyway. The unbridgeable gap between standardisation and individuality, the egotism of the industrialists seeking to cater for national interests and, finally, the increasingly politicised ideals of the Werkbund members were all factors which threatened its continued existence. The Werkbund idea, with its positive and negative, artistic and commercial experiences, forms the link between Jugendstil and the functional Modernism of the 20s and early 30s. Without the theoretical and practical basis created by the Werkbund, the development of modern industrial design as we know it would not have been possible.

ten Grundsatzdiskussion: Der industrielle Entwurf verlangte nach Typisierung und nach Formen, die sich sowohl an Funktion als auch an maschineller Produzierbarkeit zu orientieren hatten. Viele Künstler fürchteten, daß dieser Weg nur auf Kosten der künstlerischen Individualität beschritten werden könnte. Der Gegensatz von Typ und Individualität führte 1914 im sogenannten »Werkbundstreit« beinahe zum Auseinanderbrechen des Deutschen Werkbundes.

Der Erste Weltkrieg mit seinen menschenverachtenden Materialschlachten relativierte die euphorische Einstellung gegenüber der Maschine und führte zu einer vorübergehenden Ernüchterung der Werkbundideale. Die Zäsur durch den Weltkrieg traf den DWB ohnehin in einer Phase, in der sein Ende zu befürchten war. Der unüberbrückbare Gegensatz von Typ und Individualität, die Egoismen der an nationalen Interessen orientierten Wirtschaftsvertreter und die zunehmende Politisierung im Gedankengut der Werkbundleute bedrohten seinen Weiterbestand. Die Werkbundidee mit den daraus resultierenden positiven wie negativen künstlerischen und wirtschaftlichen Erfahrungen stellt das Bindeglied zwischen Jugendstil und der funktionalen Moderne der 20er und frühen 30er Jahre dar. Ohne die vom Werkbund geschaffenen theoretischen und praktischen Grundlagen wäre die Entwicklung des modernen Industriedesigns sicher nicht möglich gewesen.

vail, le Werkbund ne négligea pas pour autant l'artisanat. Mais les nécessités divergentes de l'industrie et de l'artisanat provoquèrent souvent une discussion de principe : la création industrielle demandait un modèle type et des formes tenant compte tant de la fonction que du travail de production mécanisé. Bon nombre d'artistes craignaient que cela ne se fasse au détriment de l'individualité artistique. La contradiction entre «type» et individualité provoqua en 1914 la fameuse «querelle du Werkbund» qui mena celui-ci au bord de l'éclatement.

La Première Guerre mondiale et son immense boucherie mécanisée mirent un frein à la confiance euphorique envers la machine, entraînant un refroidissement momentané des idéaux du Werkbund. La cassure engendrée par la guerre touchait de toute façon l'association à un moment crucial où elle était menacée d'éclatement. La contradiction insoluble entre forme type et individualité, les égoïsmes nationaux des représentants de l'économie allemande ainsi que la politisation croissante des idées du Werkbund menaçaient l'existence même de ce dernier. Ces idées et les expériences qui s'en suivirent, positives comme négatives, artistiques comme économiques, constituent le lien entre le Jugendstil et le modernisme fonctionnel des années vingt et trente. Sans les fondements théoriques et pratiques établis par le Werkbund, le design industriel n'aurait pu se développer.

Peter Behrens, c. 1910

Brochure advertising
AEG kettles

Werbeprospekt für
Tee- und Wasserkessel
der AEG

Prospectus publicitaire
pour les bouilloires
d'AEG

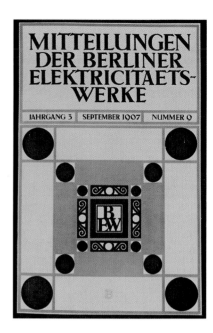

Peter Behrens, 1907

»Mitteilungen der
Berliner Elektricitaets-
werke« (Informations
from the Berlin electric
power company)

»Mitteilungen der
Berliner Elektricitaets-
werke«

«Mitteilungen der
Berliner Elektricitaets-
werke» (Informations
de la compagnie d'é-
lectricité de Berlin)

**Peter Behrens,
1909**

Electric kettle
Brass
AEG, Berlin
Height: 20.5 cm

**Elektrischer Heiß-
wasserkessel**
Messing
AEG, Berlin
Höhe: 20,5 cm

Bouilloire électrique
en laiton
AEG, Berlin
Hauteur: 20,5 cm

From 1907 onwards, Peter Behrens was responsible for the entire corporate image of the German general electrical company Allgemeine Berliner Elektricitäts-gesellschaft (AEG). He developed a uniform formal language for the company's electrical products, combining the highest aesthetic standards with the requirements of industrial production. In this respect, Behrens may be regarded as the most consistent proponent of the ideals expounded by the Deutscher Werkbund.

Ab 1907 war Peter Behrens für das gesamte äußere Erscheinungsbild der »Allgemeinen Berliner Elektricitäts-Gesellschaft« (AEG) verantwortlich. Für die Elektrowaren des Konzerns entwickelte er eine einheitliche Formensprache, die trotz höchster ästhetischer Ansprüche den produktionstechnischen Bedingungen einer industriellen Fertigung gerecht wurde. Behrens verwirklichte damit am konsequentesten die Ideale des Deutschen Werkbundes.

Peter Behrens est responsable de l'image de marque de la «Allgemeine Berliner Elektricitäts-Gesellschaft» (AEG) à partir de 1907. Il développe pour les appareils électriques de la firme un langage formel unique qui malgré ses exigences esthétiques élevées tenait compte des exigences techniques d'une fabrication de type industriel. Behrens est celui qui réalisa de la manière la plus systématique les idéaux du Deutscher Werkbund.

Peter Behrens,
1909

Electric kettle
Brass
AEG, Berlin
Height: 19.5 cm

Elektrischer Heiß-
wasserkessel
Messing
AEG, Berlin
Höhe: 19,5 cm

Bouilloire électrique
en laiton
AEG, Berlin
Hauteur: 19,5 cm

Peter Behrens,
c. 1930

»Synchron« electric
clock
Brass, sheet metal
AEG, Berlin
Diameter: 25.3 cm

»Synchron«-
Netzanschluß-Uhr
Messing, Blech
AEG, Berlin
Durchmesser: 25,3 cm

«Synchron» –
pendule électrique
en laiton et fer blanc
AEG, Berlin
Diamètre: 25,3 cm

Josef Hoffmann, 1914

Austrian House, Werkbund exhibition Cologne 1914

Österreichisches Haus, Werkbundausstellung Köln 1914

Maison autrichienne, Exposition du Werkbund à Cologne en 1914

At the 1914 Werkbund exhibition in Cologne, the Austrian Werkbund (founded in 1912 along the lines of the Deutscher Werkbund) had its own pavilion. Some of its members presented glasses produced by the Lötz Witwe glassworks and others. The clear-cut architectonic decors in conjunction with complex and sophisticated processes are typical of the Austrian style before 1914.

Josef Hoffmann, 1911

Tumbler
Glass, matt etching, painted bronzite decor
J. & L. Lobmeyr, Vienna
Height: 10.3 cm

Becher
Glas, matt geätzt, gemalter Bronzitdekor
J. & L. Lobmeyr, Wien
Höhe: 10,3 cm

Gobelet
en verre dépoli et décor de bronzite peint
J. & L. Lobmeyr, Vienne
Hauteur : 10,3 cm

Auf der Kölner Werkbundausstellung (1914) war der 1912 nach Vorbild des DWB gegründete Österreichische Werkbund mit einem eigenen Haus vertreten. Aus diesem Anlaß wurden einige seiner Mitglieder mit dem Entwurf von Gläsern beauftragt, die u.a. von der Glashütte Lötz Witwe produziert wurden. Die strengen, architektonischen Dekore in Verbindung mit der aufwendigen und kostspieligen Verarbeitung sind typisch für das Erscheinungsbild des österreichischen Kunstgewerbes vor dem Ersten Weltkrieg.

L'Union des artistes autrichiens (le Werkbund autrichien), créée en 1912 sur le modèle du Werkbund allemand (DWB), présente à l'exposition du Werkbund en 1914 à Cologne sa propre maison. A cette occasion, quelques artistes membres sont chargés de la conception de verres, produits en particulier par la verrerie Lötz Witwe. Les sobres décors architectoniques associés à un façonnage compliqué et coûteux sont caractéristiques des arts appliqués autrichiens avant la Première Guerre mondiale.

Michael Powolny, 1914

Vase
Glass, white underlay, blue striate
Glassworks
Lötz Witwe, Klostermühle
Height: 17 cm

Vase
Glas, weißer Unterfang, aufgelegte blaue Fäden
Glashütte Lötz Witwe, Klostermühle
Höhe: 17 cm

Vase
en verre, couche inférieure blanche et fils bleus
Verrerie Lötz Witwe, Klostermühle
Hauteur: 17 cm

Carl Witzmann, 1913

Vase
Glass, black overlay, cut decor
Glassworks Lötz Witwe, Klostermühle
Height: 11.2 cm

Vase
Glas, schwarzer Überfang, geschliffener Dekor
Glashütte Lötz Witwe, Klostermühle
Höhe: 11,2 cm

Vase
en verre, couche supérieure noire et décor taillé
Verrerie Lötz Witwe, Klostermühle
Hauteur: 11,2 cm

Bauhaus & Burg
Giebichenstein

**Henry van de Velde,
1910/11**

*Hochschule für Bilden-
de Kunst, Weimar;
from 1919 administra-
tive and studio build-
ing of the Staatliches
Bauhaus Weimar*

*Hochschule für
Bildende Kunst,
Weimar; ab 1919 Ver-
waltungs- und Atelier-
gebäude des Staat-
lichen Bauhauses
Weimar*

*Ecole supérieure des
Arts plastiques de
Weimar; à partir de
1919, bâtiments admi-
nistratifs et ateliers du
Bauhaus.*

79

Art-School Reform: The Bauhaus and Burg Giebichenstein

Alongside the traditional academies and art schools teaching the fundamental principles of the fine arts – painting, sculpture and architecture – the late 19th century saw the emergence of schools of applied arts focusing instead on the conception and, increasingly, execution of design. Although this duality of fine arts and applied arts was at times overcome, the art-school system continued to predominate. It was only the advent of the First World War and the resulting widespread acceptance of utopian socialist ideals that led to an intellectual and practical reorientation in art education from 1916/17.

A major innovative influence in the field of art-school reform came with the foundation of the Bauhaus in Weimar in 1919. Under the directorship of Walter Gropius, the Grand Ducal Saxon Academy of Arts and the Grand Ducal Saxon School of Arts and Crafts founded by Henry van de Velde in 1906 were united under the name of the »Staatliches Bauhaus in Weimar«. In the 1919 Bauhaus manifesto, Gropius outlined the programme of the new school as follows:

Kunstschulreform: Bauhaus und Burg Giebichenstein

Neben den traditionellen Kunstakademien und -schulen, die für die Vermittlung der bildenden Künste, Malerei, Plastik und Architektur zuständig waren, hatten sich gegen Ende des 19. Jahrhunderts – meist im Zusammenhang mit Gründungen von Kunstgewerbemuseen – die Kunstgewerbeschulen etabliert. Hier standen der Entwurf und zunehmend auch die Ausführung von kunstgewerblichen Arbeiten im Mittelpunkt. Diese Dualität von bildenden und angewandten Künsten war zwar in einigen Fällen durchbrochen worden, beherrschte aber weitgehend das Kunstschulsystem. Erst die Auswirkungen des Ersten Weltkrieges und die in seiner Folge verstärkt aufgekommenen sozialistischen Gesellschaftsutopien führten ab 1916/17 auch in der Kunstpädagogik zu einer geistigen und praktischen Neuorientierung.

Bahnbrechend auf dem Gebiet der Kunstschulreform war die Gründung des Bauhauses in Weimar 1919. Unter der Führung von Walter Gropius wurden die Großherzoglich Sächsische Hochschule für bildende Kunst und die 1906 von Henry van de Velde gegründete Sächsische Kunstgewerbeschule unter der Bezeichnung »Staatliches Bauhaus in Weimar« vereint. Im Bauhausmanifest (1919) fomulierte Gropius das Programm der neuen Schule:

La réforme de l'Ecole des Arts décoratifs : Bauhaus et Burg Giebichenstein

A côté des académies et des écoles des beaux-arts traditionnelles qui enseignaient les arts plastiques – peinture, sculpture, architecture – diverses écoles d'arts décoratifs s'étaient créées vers la fin du XIXème siècle, le plus souvent en relation avec des créations de musées d'arts décoratifs. L'enseignement qui y était diffusé portait sur la conception et de plus en plus aussi sur la réalisation de travaux d'arts décoratifs. Ce système bipolaire arts plastiques/arts appliqués avait réussi dans quelques cas à s'effacer mais dominait encore largement l'enseignement de l'art. Il fallut les séquelles de la Première Guerre mondiale et la manifestation croissante des utopies socialistes pour qu'à partir de 1916/17 une nouvelle orientation se produise aussi dans dans l'enseignement de l'art tant sur le plan intellectuel que sur plan pratique.

La création du Bauhaus à Weimar en 1919 avait ouvert la voie à la réforme des écoles d'art. Sous la direction de Walter Gropius, l'Académie des Beaux-Arts du grand-duché de Saxe et l'Ecole des Arts décoratifs créée par Henry van de Velde en 1906 fusionnèrent sous le titre de «Staatliches Bauhaus in Weimar». Dans le manifeste du Bauhaus (1919), Gropius précisait le programme de la nouvelle école :

»The aim of the Bauhaus is the uniform work of art – the great building – in which there is no distinction between monumental and decorative art«. The »new building of the future« was to be erected by artists and craftsmen together on equal terms. The distinction between fine arts and applied arts was thus dissolved and arts and crafts united under the umbrella of architecture.

The workshop system became the basis of the Bauhaus teaching programme: professors were now masters, students were apprentices, and seminars or classes were workshops. After the obligatory basic course, Bauhaus students served an apprenticeship in the school's own workshops. Alongside the existing workshops for sculpture, weaving and printing, new workshops were established for carpentry, wood carving, metalwork, glassmaking and stage design. The artistic direction of the workshops was the responsibility of the ›form master‹, assisted by a ›craft master‹ responsible for the practical training in techniques of craftsmanship. Gropius was able to gain a number of leading European avantgarde artists as ›form masters‹: in 1919, the painter and art teacher Johannes Itten, the painter Lyonel Feininger and the sculptor Gerhard Marcks; in 1920, the painter Georg Muche; in 1921, the painters Paul Klee, Oskar Schlemmer and Lothar Schreyer; in 1922, the painter Wassily Kandinsky.

»Ziel des Bauhauses ist das Einheitskunstwerk – der große Bau –, in dem es keine Grenze gibt zwischen monumentaler und dekorativer Kunst.« Der »neue Bau der Zukunft« sollte von Künstlern und Handwerkern gemeinsam und gleichberechtigt errichtet werden. Die Trennung von bildenden und angewandten Künsten wurde somit aufgehoben, die Kunst und das Handwerk unter dem Dach der Architektur vereint.

Zum strukturellen Träger des Lehrprogramms am Bauhaus wurde das Werkstattsystem: Professoren wurden zu Meistern, Studenten zu Lehrlingen und Seminare bzw. Klassen zu Werkstätten. Nach dem obligatorischen »Vorkurs« absolvierten die Bauhausschüler in den schulinternen Werkstätten eine handwerkliche Lehre. Neben den bereits vorhandenen Werkstätten für Bildhauerei, Weberei und Druckerei wurden neue Werkstätten für Tischler, Holzbildhauer-, Metall-, Glas- und Bühnenarbeit eingerichtet. Die künstlerische Leitung der Werkstätten oblag den sogenannten Formmeistern, denen jeweils ein für die handwerkliche Ausbildung zuständiger Werkmeister zur Seite gestellt war. Als Formmeister gewann Gropius in kurzer Zeit einen Kreis führender europäischer Avantgarde-Künstler: 1919 den Maler und Kunstpädagogen Johannes Itten, den Maler Lyonel Feininger und den Bildhauer Gerhard Marcks, 1920 den Maler Georg Muche, 1921 die Maler Paul Klee, Oskar Schlemmer und Lothar Schreyer, schließlich 1922 den Maler Wassily Kandinsky.

«...le but du Bauhaus est d'ériger l'œuvre d'art qui sera tout en un – la grande construction – dans laquelle il n'y aura pas de frontière entre art monumental et art décoratif». La «nouvelle construction de l'avenir» devrait être érigée en commun et sans distinction par des artistes et des artisans. Elle ferait voler en éclats le mur séparant arts plastiques et arts appliqués, l'art et l'artisanat seraient réunis sous le toit commun de l'architecture.

La charpente du programme d'enseignement au Bauhaus était l'atelier: les professeurs devinrent des maîtres-artisans, les étudiants des apprentis et les classes des ateliers. Après le cours préliminaire obligatoire, les élèves du Bauhaus suivaient une formation d'artisans dans les ateliers de l'école. Outre les ateliers de sculpture, de tissage et d'imprimerie déjà existants, on en ouvrit d'autres : menuiserie, sculpture sur bois, métal, verre et théâtre. La direction artistique des ateliers était attribuée à des maîtres de la forme assistés de maîtres artisans chargés de la formation artisanale. Gropius réussit en peu de temps à attirer à l'école comme maîtres de la forme toute une série d'artistes avant-gardistes de renom: en 1919, le peintre et pédagogue Johannes Itten, le peintre Lyonel Feininger et le sculpteur Gerhard Marcks; en 1920 c'était le tour du peintre Georg Muche, en 1921 de Paul Klee, d'Oskar Schlemmer et de Lothar Schreyer, en 1922 de Wassily Kandinsky.

81

Apart from Gropius, the most influential figure of the early Bauhaus days in Weimar was Johannes Itten. It was he who developed the basic course where Bauhaus students were taught the elementary principles and techniques of art in a completely new way. At the same time, he was responsible for almost all the workshops as ›form master‹. In 1923, Itten left the Bauhaus because he wanted no part in the collaboration with industry sought by Gropius which would involve a restructuring of the workshops and the teaching programme. Whereas Gropius had evoked the unity of arts and crafts during the expressionistic early phase of the Bauhaus, still under the impact of the war years, by 1922 he was evoking the new unity of art and technology. The Bauhaus workshops were no longer to be mere teaching workshops creating individual craftsmanship, but were to be transformed into productive workshops creating prototypes for industry.

Gropius found a suitable successor for Itten in the Hungarian artist László Moholy-Nagy, who was able to give the Bauhaus fresh inspiration. In 1923, Moholy-Nagy took over the basic course and the metal workshop at the Bauhaus in Weimar. Under his auspices, the metal workshop evolved from an artisanal silversmith workshop

Itten war neben Gropius die bestimmende Gestalt am frühen Weimarer Bauhaus. Er entwickelte die »Vorlehre«, mit der den Bauhausschülern auf völlig neue Weise die elementarsten Prinzipien und Techniken der Kunst vermittelt wurden. Daneben war er anfangs als Formmeister für die Leitung fast aller Werkstätten zuständig. 1923 verließ Itten das Bauhaus, weil er die von Gropius angestrebte Kooperation mit der Industrie und die in diesem Zusammenhang geforderte Umstrukturierung der Werkstätten und des Lehrprogramms nicht mittragen wollte. Hatte Gropius in der expressionistischen Frühphase des Bauhauses, noch unter dem Eindruck der Kriegsjahre, die Einheit von Kunst und Handwerk beschworen, so forderte er spätestens ab 1922 die neue Einheit von Kunst und Technik. Die Bauhauswerkstätten sollten nicht länger in Form bloßer Lehrwerkstätten individuelles Kunsthandwerk herstellen, sondern durch zielgerichtete Aufgaben in Produktivwerkstätten umgewandelt werden, in denen Prototypen für die Industrie entstehen sollten.

In der Person des ungarischen Künstlers László Moholy-Nagy fand Gropius einen geeigneten Nachfolger für Itten, der in der Lage war, dem Bauhaus neue Impulse zu geben. 1923 übernahm Moholy-Nagy die Leitung des Vorkurses und der Metallwerkstatt am

Itten fut avec Gropius la figure la plus marquante de la première phase du Bauhaus. Il institua l'enseignement préliminaire au cours duquel les élèves acquéraient d'une manière entièrement nouvelle des connaissances sur les principes et les techniques les plus élémentaires. Au début, Itten fut également responsable en tant que maître de la forme de la direction de presque tous les ateliers. Mais, en 1923, il quitta le Bauhaus, ne voulant pas porter la responsabilité de la restructuration des ateliers et de l'enseignement que la coopération avec l'industrie visée par Gropius rendait nécessaire. Si, au cours de la phase expressionniste du Bauhaus, Gropius, encore sous le coup des années de guerre, s'était donné pour but de réaliser l'unité de l'art et de l'artisanat, il prôna au plus tard en 1922 l'unité de l'art et de la technique. Les ateliers du Bauhaus devaient cesser sans tarder d'être de simples ateliers d'artisanat individuel et devenir des ateliers de production où des prototypes seraient élaborés pour l'industrie.

Gropius chercha pour succéder à Itten un artiste capable de donner une nouvelle impulsion au Bauhaus et qu'il trouva en la personne du Hongrois László Moholy-Nagy. En 1923, Moholy-Nagy prit la direction du cours préliminaire et de l'atelier de métal. C'est sous sa direction que d'orfèvrerie artisanale cet

Joost Schmidt, 1923

Poster for the »Bau-
haus Exhibition, Wei-
mar 1923«

Plakat für die »Bau-
haus Ausstellung
Weimar 1923«

Affiche pour «l'exposi-
tion du Bauhaus à
Weimar en 1923»

to a design workshop for metal industrial products, setting examples for
changes in the other workshops as
well. Even before Moholy-Nagy took
over the basic course, Josef Albers had
introduced the workshop apprenticeship as a follow-up to the basic course
in order to prepare Bauhaus students
for the practical work in the workshops right from the start of their
studies. In addition to regular visits to
artisanal and industrial enterprises, experimentation with materials was a
focal point of their studies.

The first major Bauhaus exhibition held
in the summer of 1923 clearly indicated the changes which had taken
place in the workshops. The expressive
style of the early Bauhaus, dominated
by artistic individuality and romantic
notions of craftsmanship, had been
transformed under the influence of
the Dutch »De Stijl« movement and
Russian Constructivism into an objective collective form of expression, combining the form and colour theories of
Paul Klee and Wassily Kandinsky to create a uniform Bauhaus style. On this
basis, the workshops had produced
functionally oriented standard types of
everyday objects, whose design was
predominantly based on cubist geometric components.

Weimarer Bauhaus. Unter seiner Leitung entwickelte sich – exemplarisch
auch für die Veränderungen in den anderen Werkstätten – die Metallwerkstatt von einer kunsthandwerklichen
Silberschmiede zu einer Entwurfswerkstatt für Industrieprodukte aus Metall.
Bereits kurz vor der Übernahme der
Vorlehre durch Moholy-Nagy war am
Bauhaus unter der Leitung Josef
Albers' die Werklehre eingeführt worden, die als Ergänzung zur Vorlehre
die Bauhausschüler bereits ab dem
ersten Studienjahr auf die praktische
Arbeit in den Werkstätten vorbereiten
sollte. Neben dem regelmäßigen Besuch von Handwerks- und Industrie-
betrieben stand hier das spielerische
Experimentieren mit Werkstoffen im
Mittelpunkt des Studiums.

Bereits die erste große Bauhaus-Aus-
stellung im Sommer 1923 verdeutlich-
te den Wandel der Werkstattarbeit.
Der expressive, von künstlerischer Individualität und handwerklicher Roman-
tik dominierte uneinheitliche Stil des
frühen Bauhauses hatte sich, nicht zu-
letzt unter den Einflüssen der holländischen »De Stijl«-Bewegung und des
russischen Konstruktivismus, zu einem
sachlichen, kollektiven Gestaltungsaus-
druck gewandelt. Er vereinte die von
Paul Klee und Wassily Kandinsky in der
Form- bzw. Farbenlehre entwickelten
Grundformen und -farben zu einer einheitlichen »Bauhaussprache«. Auf dieser Basis waren in den Werkstätten
funktionsorientierte Typen von Gebrauchsgeräten entstanden, deren
Gestaltung weitgehend auf kubisch
zusammengesetzten, geometrischen
Elementen beruhte.

atelier se transforma en un atelier de
conception de produits industriels en
métal, ce qui se produira aussi pour les
autres ateliers. Juste avant la reprise du
cours préliminaire par Moholy-Nagy, Josef Albers avait ajouté la théorie du travail manuel et une formation artisanale
au cours préliminaire pour préparer les
élèves de première année au futur travail d'apprentissage en atelier. Outre
les visites d'usines et d'entreprises artisanales, des exercices expérimentaux
sur divers matériaux étaient une autre
partie essentielle de l'enseignement.

La première grande exposition du Bauhaus pendant l'été 1923 avait déjà
montré une évolution dans le travail
d'atelier. Le style du Bauhaus de la première période, varié, expressif, dominé
par la recherche individuelle et le ro-
mantisme artisanal, s'était transformé
en une expression créatrice collective,
sobre, influencée par le mouvement
«De Stijl» et le constructivisme russe.
Ce «langage Bauhaus» unique était la
synthèse des théories des formes et
des couleurs élémentaires développées
par Paul Klee et Wassily Kandinsky.
C'est sur cette base que furent créés
au Bauhaus des types d'objets fonc-
tionnels, formés à partir d'éléments
géométriques et surtout de forme cubi-
que.

In 1924/25, the changing political climate in nationalist-dominated Thuringia led to the closure of the Bauhaus
in Weimar. This might have been the
end of the Bauhaus concept, had it
not been for the fact that the socialist
city authorities of Dessau offered the
Bauhaus the opportunity of continuing
its work there. As there were no suitable premises available for the Bauhaus on a permanent basis, the city
authorities provided financial support
for the construction of new buildings
to plans drawn up by Walter Gropius
and the doors could be opened in De-
cember 1926. The construction of the
school complex, comprising a workshop building, student hall of
residence and four separate houses for
the Bauhaus masters in addition to the
school building itself, gave Gropius
and the Bauhaus the opportunity of
implementing their new building and
lifestyle concepts on a large scale for
the very first time. The Bauhaus workshops were included in the building
project right from the start. For
example, the carpentry workshop,
headed by Marcel Breuer from April
1925 onwards, was responsible for
furnishing the entire building. Breuer's
tubular steel furniture, developed in
collaboration with the local Junkers
works, caused a sensation. The metal
workshop produced lamps to designs
by Marianne Brandt and Max Krajewski, and the wall painting workshop
was in charge of wall decoration,
while the printing workshop produced
the signs throughout the school.

1924/25 führte die veränderte politi-
sche Situation in Thüringen zur Schlie-
ßung des Weimarer Bauhauses. Daß
dies jedoch nicht das Ende der
Bauhausidee bedeutete, war dem An-
gebot der Stadt Dessau zu verdanken,
die der Bauhausleitung die Möglichkeit
eröffnete, in Dessau an ihre Arbeit an-
zuknüpfen. Da hier noch keine geeigneten Gebäude für die dauerhafte Un-
terbringung des Bauhauses vorhanden
waren, stellte die Stadt die finanziellen
Mittel für die Errichtung von Neubau-
ten nach Plänen von Walter Gropius
zur Verfügung, die bereits im Dezem-
ber 1926 eingeweiht werden konnten.
Mit dem Bau des Schulkomplexes, der
neben dem eigentlichen Schulgebäude
auch ein Atelierhaus (Studentenwohn-
heim) und vier separate Wohnhäuser
für die Bauhausmeister umfaßte, er-
gab sich für Gropius und das Bauhaus
zum ersten Mal die Gelegenheit, ihre
Vorstellungen vom »Neuen Bauen und
Wohnen« in einem großen Rahmen zu
verwirklichen. Die Bauhauswerkstätten
wurden von Anfang an in das Baupro-
jekt einbezogen. So war die Tischlerwerkstatt, die ab April 1925 unter der
Leitung von Marcel Breuer stand, für
die gesamte Möblierung der Gebäude
zuständig. Ganz besonderes Aufsehen
erregten die Möbel aus gebogenem
Stahlrohr, die Breuer in Zusammenarbeit mit den örtlichen Junkers-
Werken entwickelt hatte. Die Metallwerkstatt übernahm die Ausführung
der Beleuchtungskörper nach Entwurf
von Marianne Brandt und Max Krajewski. Der Werkstatt für Wandmalerei
oblag die farbige Gestaltung der
Wandflächen. Die Druckwerkstatt sorg-
te für die Ausschilderung der Räumlich-
keiten.

En 1924/25, la situation politique venait de changer en Thuringe et le Bauhaus de Weimar dut fermer ses portes.
Que ceci n'ait pas signifié la mort de
l'idée du «Bauhaus», c'est grâce à la ville de Dessau qui proposa à la direction
d'accueillir l'école. Aucun bâtiment de
la ville ne pouvant abriter le Bauhaus à
long terme, la municipalité débloqua
des crédits pour construire les édifices
nécessaires sur des plans de Walter Gropius, et, en 1926, l'école ouvrait ses
portes. Pour Gropius et le Bauhaus, c'é-
tait la première occasion de réaliser l'i-
dée de «construction nouvelle et
d'habitat nouveau» à grande échelle:
le complexe scolaire était composé du
bâtiment de l'école, d'une aile pour les
ateliers (logements des étudiants) et de
quatre maisons de maître. Les ateliers
de l'école furent mis immédiatement à
contribution dans le projet de construction : la menuiserie, par exemple, dirigée à partir d'avril 1925 par Marcel
Breuer, fut chargée de créer le mobilier
de l'école. Les meubles en tubes d'acier
fabriqués en collaboration avec les usines Junkers locales provoquèrent de
nombreuses réactions. L'atelier du métal se chargea de l'éclairage (les lampes
étaient de Marianne Brandt et de Max
Krajewski). La décoration des murs pro-
venait ole l'atelier de peinture murale
et les pancartes indiquant l'emplace-
ment des salles étaient réalisées par l'a-
telier d'imprimerie.

*Walter Gropius,
1925/26*

School complex,
Bauhaus Dessau

Schulkomplex
Bauhaus Dessau

Le bâtiment du
Bauhaus de Dessau

The early years in Dessau involved considerable reforms in the teaching plan and many staff changes. The reforms aimed to orient the workshops more clearly towards the productive work demanded by Gropius. This resulted in the division of the workshops into teaching and production, as already defined in the 1925 curriculum. In order to exploit the productive work commercially, a limited company – the Bauhaus GmbH – was founded that same year to organise the sale of Bauhaus products and grant production licences. There were staff changes in the leadership of the workshops. By 1925, four of the seven departments were headed by the so-called ›young masters‹ or journeymen who had successfully completed their apprenticeships at the Bauhaus in Weimar: Marcel Breuer was in charge of carpentry, Hinnerk Scheper wall painting, Joost Schmidt the sculpture workshop and Herbert Bayer the printmaking and advertising workshop; in 1927, Gunta Stölzl took over the weaving workshop. The young masters combined the artistic and artisanal training they had received at the Bauhaus in Weimar and thus represented the new type of artist combining the unity of art and technology which Gropius aimed for. Under their auspices, the workshops of the Bauhaus in Dessau created a new functional and logically based design concept for everyday objects, textiles and typography, which was to revolutionise modern industrial design.

Die frühe Dessauer Zeit war geprägt durch Reformen im Lehrplan und personelle Veränderungen im Lehrkörper. Ziel der Reformen war die stärkere Ausrichtung der Werkstätten an der von Gropius geforderten Produktivarbeit. Hieraus resultierte die bereits 1925 im Lehrplan festgeschriebene Teilung der Werkstattarbeit in Lehr- und Produktivbetrieb. Um die Ergebnisse der Produktivarbeit auch kommerziell auszuwerten, wurde im gleichen Jahr die schon in Weimar geplante Bauhaus-GmbH gegründet, die den Verkauf von Bauhausprodukten und die Vergabe von Herstellungslizenzen organisieren sollte. Die personellen Veränderungen betrafen die Leitung der Werkstätten. Vier der insgesamt sieben Abteilungen wurden schon ab 1925 von den sogenannten »Jungmeistern« geleitet, die ihre Ausbildung am Bauhaus Weimar erfolgreich abgeschlossen hatten: Marcel Breuer leitete die Tischlerei, Hinnerk Scheper die Wandmalerei, Joost Schmidt die plastische Werkstatt und Herbert Bayer die Werkstatt für Druck und Reklame; Gunta Stölzl übernahm 1927 die Leitung der Weberei. Die Jungmeister verband ihre sowohl künstlerische als auch handwerkliche Ausbildung, die sie am Weimarer Bauhaus erhalten hatten. Sie repräsentierten den neuen Typus von Künstler, der die von Gropius angestrebte Einheit von Kunst und Technik in sich vereinte. Unter ihrer Leitung erarbeiteten die Werkstätten am Dessauer Bauhaus eine neue, auf funktionalen und logischen Überlegungen basierende Formgebung und Gestaltung von Gebrauchsgeräten, Textilien und Typographie, die das moderne Industriedesign revolutionierten.

La première période du Bauhaus de Dessau fut marquée par des réformes scolaires et des changements de professeurs. En procédant à ces modifications, Gropius visait à faire des ateliers des établissements de production. La répartition du travail d'atelier en enseignement et en production, déjà fixée dans le plan d'études de 1925, fut désormais pratiquée. Au cours de la même année, Gropius fonda une SARL, prévue déjà du temps de Weimar, afin d'assurer l'exploitation financière des produits du Bauhaus. Quatre des sept sections furent dirigées dès 1925 par d'anciens élèves, les «jeunes maîtres», qui avaient suivi avec succès l'enseignement du Bauhaus : Marcel Breuer dirigeait la menuiserie, Hinnerk Scheper l'atelier de peinture murale, Joost Schmidt l'atelier de sculpture et Herbert Bayer celui de l'imprimerie et de la réclame; Gunta Stölzl reprit la direction de l'atelier de tissage en 1927. Les jeunes maîtres étaient unis par la formation artistique et artisanale qu'ils avaient reçue au Bauhaus de Weimar. Ils représentaient cette génération d'artistes qui avait assimilé l'idée de Gropius sur l'unité de l'art et de la technique. C'est sous leur direction que les ateliers du Bauhaus de Dessau élaborèrent des nouveautés – objets utilitaires, textiles et typographie – qui allaient révolutionner le design industriel et dont la conception s'appuyait sur des réflexions logiques et fonctionnelles.

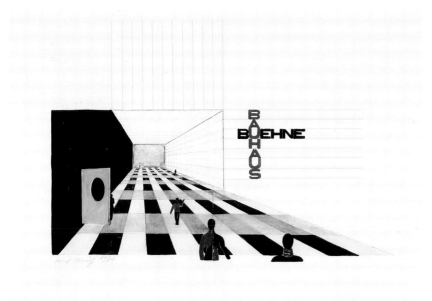

Kurt Schmidt, 1924

Poster design for
Bauhaus theatre

Plakatentwurf für die
Bauhausbühne

Projet d'affiche pour le
théâtre du Bauhaus

In the summer semester of 1927, an independent department of architecture was established under the direction of the Swiss architect Hannes Meyer. With the exception of the printmaking and advertising workshop and the stagecraft workshop, which remained independent divisions, all the other workshops were now amalgamated under the designation »interior design« and placed under the architecture workshop. Klee and Kandinsky, who had not been form masters since 1925 and 1927 respectively, took over the new seminar for sculpture and painting in which Bauhaus students were given the opportunity of a purely artistic training for the first time.

In February 1928, when the Bauhaus was at its height, Gropius unexpectedly resigned as director of the school. Together with Gropius, Moholy-Nagy, Marcel Breuer and Herbert Bayer also left the Bauhaus in Dessau. Under the directorship of Hannes Meyer (April 1928 – July 1930) and Ludwig Mies van der Rohe (August 1930 – July 1933), who succeeded Gropius, the teaching and workshop concept became increasingly biased towards architecture, resulting in a more theoretical and academic form of study at the Bauhaus.

Zum Sommersemester 1927 kam es nun endlich auch zur Einrichtung einer selbständigen Architekturabteilung unter der Leitung des Schweizer Architekten Hannes Meyer. Mit Ausnahme der Druck- und Reklamewerkstatt sowie der Bühnenwerkstatt, die als selbständige Bereiche bestehenblieben, wurden nun alle anderen Werkstätten unter der Bezeichnung »Inneneinrichtung« versammelt und der »Architektur« unterstellt. Klee und Kandinsky, die ab 1925 bzw. 1927 nicht mehr als Formmeister tätig waren, übernahmen das neu gebildete »Seminar für freie plastische und malerische Gestaltung«, in dem den Bauhausschülern zum ersten Mal eine rein künstlerische Ausbildung ermöglicht wurde.

Völlig überraschend erklärte Gropius im Februar 1928 – zu einem Zeitpunkt, als sich das Bauhaus auf dem Höhepunkt seiner Entwicklung befand – seinen Rücktritt als Direktor der Schule. Zusammen mit Gropius verließen auch Moholy-Nagy, Marcel Breuer und Herbert Bayer das Dessauer Bauhaus. Unter den Nachfolgern von Gropius im Direktorenamt, Hannes Meyer (April 1928 – Juli 1930) und Ludwig Mies van der Rohe (August 1930 – Juli 1933), kam es dann zu einer immer stärker werdenden Ausrichtung des Lehr- und Werkstättenbetriebs auf die Architektur. Eine zunehmende Theoretisierung und Verschulung des Studiums am Bauhaus waren die Folge.

Au cours de l'été 1927, une section d'architecture autonome fut enfin organisée sous la direction de l'architecte suisse Hannes Meyer. A l'exception des ateliers d'imprimerie et réclame et de théâtre qui restèrent autonomes, toutes les autres sections furent réunies sous la dénomination «décoration intérieure» et subordonnées à l'architecture. Klee et Kandinsky qui – l'un en 1925, l'autre en 1927 – furent déchargés de leur fonction de maîtres de la forme prirent la direction d'une nouvelle section : le «séminaire de création plastique et picturale libre» au cours duquel les élèves pouvaient acquérir pour la première fois au Bauhaus une formation purement artistique.

Quand, en février 1928, à la surprise de tous, Gropius fit savoir son intention de démissionner de son poste de directeur, le Bauhaus se trouvait à son apogée. Moholy-Nagy, Marcel Breuer et Herbert Bayer démissionnèrent en même temps que lui. Sous le mandat des successeurs de Gropius à la tête de l'établissement, – Hannes Meyer d'avril 1928 à juillet 1930 et Ludwig Mies van der Rohe d'août 1930 à juillet 1933 – l'architecture prit peu à peu le pas sur l'enseignement et le travail en atelier. Les études commencèrent à prendre un caractère plus scolaire et théorique.

Marcel Breuer, 1923

Poster design for
Bauhaus theatre

Plakatentwurf für die
Bauhausbühne

Projet d'affiche pour le
théâtre du Bauhaus

A certain degree of rivalry existed between the Bauhaus and the Burg Giebichenstein School of Applied Arts run by the architect Paul Thiersch in Halle. Thiersch had become director of what was, at the time, an insignificant school in Halle in 1915 and had gradually transformed it into a modern institute of applied arts. By adding specialist courses for architecture and interior design, applied arts for women, sculpture, painting and graphic arts, and by establishing two teaching workshops – one for enamelling and one for fine metalwork – Thiersch succeeded in having his teaching institute recognised in 1918 as a fully fledged school of applied arts. In 1919/20, further workshops were established for woodwork, book binding, fabric printing and wallpaper, textiles and ceramics. By restructuring the teaching workshops to create production workshops from the summer of 1920 onwards, and moving away from the concept of a traditional school of applied arts, Thiersch actually anticipated the direction the Bauhaus in Weimar was to take.

From this point onwards, the workshops were divided into teaching, contract work, and production for the school's own use. Regular participation at trade fairs and the creation of a marketing and distribution network ensured sales of the workshop products and established the school's reputation. When the workshops moved into the building of Burg Giebichenstein in 1921/22, it was renamed »Werkstätten der Stadt Halle, Staatlich-städtische Kunstgewerbeschule Burg Giebichenstein« (City of Halle Workshops,

In einer gewissen Konkurrenzsituation zum Bauhaus stand die von dem Architekten Paul Thiersch geleitete Kunstgewerbeschule der Burg Giebichenstein in Halle an der Saale. Thiersch hatte 1915 die Leitung der bis dahin eher unbedeutenden Handwerkerschule der Stadt Halle übernommen und sie in mehreren Stufen zu einer modernen Kunstgewerbeanstalt reformiert: Durch die Angliederung von Fachklassen für Architektur- und Raumgestaltung, kunstgewerbliche Frauenarbeit, Bildhauerei, Malerei und Grafik und durch den Aufbau von zwei Lehrwerkstätten – eine für Emailkunst und eine für Feinmetall – erreichte Thiersch 1918 die von ihm angestrebte Anerkennung seiner Lehranstalt als Kunstgewerbeschule. 1919/20 wurden weitere Werkstätten für Holzbearbeitung, Buchbinderei, Stoff- und Tapetendruck, Textilarbeit und Keramik eingerichtet. Mit der Umstrukturierung der Lehrwerkstätten in Produktionswerkstätten ab Sommer 1920 nahm Thiersch die Entwicklungen am Weimarer Bauhaus vorweg und löste sich damit vom Konzept einer traditionellen Kunstgewerbeschule.

Die Werkstattarbeit unterteilte sich fortan in die Bereiche Lehrbetrieb, Auftragsarbeit und Eigenproduktion. Durch die regelmäßigen Messebeteiligungen und den Aufbau eines Vertriebsnetzes wurden der Absatz der Werkstattprodukte gesichert und der Bekanntheitsgrad der Schule gesteigert. Der Umzug der Werkstätten in die Gebäude der Burg Giebichenstein 1921/22 brachte die Abtrennung von der ehemaligen Handwerkerschule und die Umbenennung in »Werkstät-

L'Ecole des Arts décoratifs de Burg Giebichenstein à Halle sur la Saale, dont le directeur était Paul Thiersch, se trouvait en situation de quasi-concurrence avec le Bauhaus. Thiersch qui avait pris la direction de l'école en 1915 avait transformé par paliers cet établissement d'enseignement artisanal plutôt insignifiant en une école des arts décoratifs moderne : l'ouverture de classes d'architecture et d'aménagement intérieur, de classes d'apprentissage pour femmes, de sculpture, de peinture et d'arts graphiques ainsi que la création de deux ateliers – l'un d'émail et l'autre de métal fin – permirent à Thiersch d'atteindre son but, c'est-à-dire faire donner à son établissement en 1918 le titre d'Ecole des arts décoratifs. Au cours de la période 1919/20 s'ouvrirent d'autres ateliers : travail sur bois, reliure, impression sur étoffe et papiers peints, textiles et céramique. En restructurant les ateliers d'apprentissage en ateliers de production dès l'été 1920, Thiersch devançait les changements au Bauhaus de Weimar et abandonnait ainsi le concept traditionnel d'école des arts décoratifs.

Les activités d'atelier se divisaient en enseignement professionnel, exécution des commandes et production personnelle. La participation régulière à des salons et l'organisation d'un réseau commercial assurèrent la vente des produits fabriqués dans les ateliers ainsi que la renommée de l'école. L'emménagement dans les bâtiments du Burg Giebichenstein en 1921/22 entraîna la scission définitive avec l'ancienne école d'apprentissage artisanal et le changement de nom en «Werkstätten der Stadt Halle, Staatlich-städtische Kunst-

**Hans Przyrembel &
Marianne Brandt,
1929/30**

Bowl
Brass
Designed by Marianne
Brandt
Metal workshop of
Hans Przyrembel,
Leipzig
Height: 9.1 cm

Schale
Messing
Entwurf Marianne
Brandt
Metallwerkstatt Hans
Przyrembel, Leipzig
Höhe: 9,1 cm

Coupe en laiton
Création Marianne
Brandt
Atelier de métal Hans
Przyrembel, Leipzig
Hauteur: 9,1 cm

87

Burg Giebichenstein State and Municipal School of Applied Arts). A workshop for book printing was added in 1922, a workshop for advertising – including a photography class – in 1927 and a porcelain workshop in 1930.

Like the work of the Bauhaus in Weimar during the same period, the style of the products made at Burg Giebichenstein in the early 20s was influenced by the spirit of Expressionism. The adoption of sculptural elements from the sphere of ›free‹ art gave new forms to traditional household goods. It was not until the mid-20s that the workshops in Halle took on a more soberly objective style of design, as evidenced particularly in the objects created by the metal and ceramics workshops. In contrast to the Bauhaus, however, the work at the Burg Giebichenstein school retained a stronger bias towards craftsmanship. Whereas the Bauhaus workshops in Weimar were transformed into design laboratories for industrial products from 1922/23 onwards, the pace of change at Burg Giebichenstein in Halle was somewhat less radical. In comparison to the relatively dogmatic and distinctly intellectual attitude which was becoming increasingly entrenched at the Bauhaus in Dessau, the school of Burg Giebichenstein continued to uphold a more traditional concept of craftsmanship and workshop production which gave the individual greater artistic freedom.

ten der Stadt Halle, Staatlich-städtische Kunstgewerbeschule Burg Giebichenstein«. Zu den bereits vorhandenen Werkstätten kamen 1922 die Werkstatt für Buchdruck, 1927 die Werkstatt für Werbearbeit – der eine Fotoklasse angegliedert wurde – und schließlich 1930 die Porzellanwerkstatt.

Der Stil der »Burgprodukte« wurde – ähnlich wie die zeitgleichen Arbeiten des Weimarer Bauhauses – in den frühen 20er Jahren von einem expressionistischen Geist geprägt. Ehemals traditionell gestaltete Gebrauchsgeräte erhielten durch die Einbringung plastischer Formen, die der freien Kunst entnommen waren, neue Ausprägungen. Erst Mitte der 20er Jahre setzte sich auch in den Werkstätten der Stadt Halle eine sachlichere Formgebung durch, was sich besonders in den Objekten der Metall- und Keramikwerkstatt dokumentiert. Die Hallesche Kunstgewerbeschule blieb jedoch im Gegensatz zum Bauhaus immer stärker kunstgewerblich ausgerichtet. Der in Weimar ab 1922/23 vollzogene Wandel der Werkstätten zu Entwurfslaboratorien für industrielle Produkte fand in Halle in dieser konsequenten Form nicht statt. Gegenüber der eher doktrinären und stark intellektuellen Grundhaltung, die sich am Dessauer Bauhaus mehr und mehr durchsetzte, zeichnete sich Burg Giebichenstein durch eine traditionsverbundene Auffassung von Handwerk und Werkstattarbeit aus, die der künstlerischen Freiheit des einzelnen noch größere Entfaltungsmöglichkeiten ließ.

gewerbeschule Burg Giebichenstein», Ateliers de la ville de Halle, école des arts décoratifs étatique et communale de Burg Giebichenstein». Aux ateliers existants s'ajoutèrent en 1922 l'atelier d'imprimerie du livre en 1927 celui de la publicité – avec une section photographie – et en 1930, l'atelier de porcelaine.

Le style des «produits Burg» étaient imprégnés au début des années vingt – à l'instar de la production du Bauhaus de Weimar – d'un esprit expressionniste. Les formes traditionnelles données autrefois aux objets utilitaires prirent une nouvelle apparence grâce aux éléments empruntés aux arts plastiques. Des formes plus objectives s'imposèrent aussi au milieu des années vingt dans les Ateliers de la ville de Halle, comme le montrent les objets en métal et en céramique. Le travail de l'école ne dépassa pas le domaine des arts décoratifs - au contraire du Bauhaus. La transformation des ateliers de Weimar en laboratoires pour la conception de produits industriels dès 1922/23 ne s'effectua pas de façon aussi radicale à Halle. A l'opposé de l'attitude très intellectuelle et doctrinaire qui prévalait de plus en plus au Bauhaus de Dessau, l'école de Burg Giebichenstein accordait encore une place importante à l'artisanat et au travail en atelier, laissant ainsi à la liberté artistique de ses élèves une plus grande latitude.

In 1925, Marcel Breuer designed the first tubular steel furniture at the Bauhaus in Dessau. One of his earliest models was the tubular steel »club chair«, the later B3 which came to be known as the »Wassily« chair. Unlike the prototype, which was welded together, the model which went into production in 1926 at the Standard-Möbel Lengyel & Co. furniture factory in Berlin had bolted connections for ease of transportation. From 1929 onwards, the Thonet furniture factory took over the production and marketing of Marcel Breuer's tubular steel furniture.

1925 entwickelte Marcel Breuer am Bauhaus Dessau die ersten Möbel aus gebogenem Stahlrohr. Zu den frühesten Modellen gehörte ein »Stahlklubsessel«, der spätere B 3, besser bekannt unter der Bezeichnung »Wassily«-Stuhl. Im Gegensatz zum Prototyp, der im Umfeld des Dessauer Bauhauses zusammengeschweißt wurde, war schon das ab 1926 von der Firma Standard-Möbel Lengyel & Co. in Berlin produzierte Serienmodell verschraubt und damit leichter zu transportieren. Ab 1929 übernahm dann die Firma Thonet AG die Produktion und Vermarktung der Stahlrohrmöbel Marcel Breuers.

En 1925, Marcel Breuer crée au Bauhaus de Dessau les premiers meubles en tube d'acier courbé. Parmi les tout premiers modèles se trouvait le «fauteuil club en acier», le futur B 3, plus connu sous le nom de fauteuil Wassily. A l'inverse du prototype soudé au Bauhaus de Dessau, le modèle de série fabriqué à partir de 1926 par la firme Standard-Möbel Lengyel & Co. est vissé et plus facile ainsi à transporter. A partir de 1929, c'est la maison Thonet SA qui assurera la fabrication et la diffusion des meubles en tubes d'acier de Marcel Breuer.

Marcel Breuer,
1925/26

Club chair B 3
Tubular steel, welded,
original fabric
Bauhaus Dessau
Height: 75 cm

Clubsessel B 3
Stahlrohr, verschweißt,
originale Stoffbespan-
nung
Bauhaus Dessau
Höhe: 75 cm

Fauteuil club B 3
Tubes en acier soudé,
tissu original
Bauhaus Dessau
Hauteur: 75 cm

**Marcel Breuer,
c. 1930**

Seating
Chrome-plated tubu-
lar steel, bolted con-
nections, fabric
Thonet AG, France
Height: 76 cm
(Club chair)

Sitzgruppe
Stahlrohr, verchromt,
verschraubt, Stoffbe-
spannung
Thonet AG, Frankreich
Höhe: 76 cm
(Clubsessel)

**Ensemble de fau-
teuils**
Tubes d'acier chromé,
vissés et garniture tissu
Thonet AG, France
Hauteur: 76 cm
(fauteuil club)

Marcel Breuer, 1926

Club chair B 3
Nickelled tubular steel,
bolted connections,
steel thread
Standard-Möbel
Lengyel & Co., Berlin
Height: 76 cm

Clubsessel B 3
Stahlrohr, vernickelt,
verschraubt,
Eisengarnbespannung
Standard-Möbel
Lengyel & Co., Berlin
Höhe: 76 cm

Fauteuil club B 3
Tubes d'acier nickelés,
vissés, tissu en fil glacé
de coton
Standard-Möbel
Lengyel & Co., Berlin
Hauteur: 76 cm

Following his initial experimentation in the use of bent tubular steel as a new material for furniture, Marcel Breuer went on to design a whole series of standardised tubular steel furnishings. Breuer's basic structural principle was based on the pursuit of maximum functionality and minimum weight at the most economical production cost. The furniture factory of Standard-Möbel Lengyel & Co., which initially produced all his tubular steel furniture (and in which Breuer temporarily held a financial interest), was taken over by Thonet in 1929.

Marcel Breuer, 1926/27

Chair B 5 and armchair B 11
Nickelled tubular steel, bolted connections, steel thread
Standard-Möbel Lengyel & Co., Berlin
Height: 87 cm

Stuhl B 5 und Armlehnstuhl B 11
Stahlrohr, vernickelt, verschraubt, Eisengarnbezug
Standard-Möbel Lengyel & Co., Berlin
Höhe: 87 cm

Chaise B 5 et fauteuil à accoudoirs B 11
en tubes d'acier nickelés, vissés et tissu en fil de coton glacé
Standard-Möbel Lengyel & Co., Berlin
Hauteur: 87 cm

Marcel Breuer, 1928/29

Sitzmaschine B 25
Chrome-plated tubular steel, bolted connections, wood painted black, woven cane
Thonet AG, Germany
Height: 108 cm

Sitzmaschine B 25
Stahlrohr, verchromt, verschraubt, Holz, schwarz lackiert, Rohrgeflecht
Thonet AG, Deutschland
Höhe: 108 cm

Sitzmaschine B 25
en tubes d'acier chromé, bois laqué noir et cannage
Thonet AG, Allemagne
Hauteur: 108 cm

Ausgehend von seinen ersten Erfahrungen mit der Verwendung von gebogenem Stahlrohr als neuen Möbelwerkstoff, entwarf Marcel Breuer eine ganze Serie von Stahlrohr-Typenmöbeln. Durchgehendes Konstruktionsprinzip Breuers war dabei die Erreichung optimaler Funktionalität bei minimalem Gewicht und geringstem Produktionspreis. Die Firma Standard-Möbel Lengyel & Co., die zunächst alle seine Stahlrohrmöbel produzierte und an der Breuer auch kurzzeitig finanziell beteiligt war, wurde aufgrund geschäftlicher Mißerfolge 1929 von der Möbelfirma Thonet AG übernommen.

Marcel Breuer créa une série entière de meubles types en tubes d'acier à partir de ses premières expériences sur le tube d'acier employé comme matériau de base dans les meubles. Le principe de construction de Breuer était d'obtenir une fonction pratique maximum pour un poids minimum et un prix de production le plus bas possible. La firme Standard-Möbel Lengyel & Co. produit au début tous les meubles en tubes d'acier de Breuer – pendant un temps celui-ci a d'ailleurs une participation financière dans l'entreprise – mais à la suite de difficultés commerciales, elle est reprise en 1929 par la fabrique de meubles Thonet AG.

**Marcel Breuer,
c. 1930**

Desk B 91
*Chrome-plated tubular steel, wood painted black
Thonet AG, Germany
Width: 125 cm*

Schreibtisch B 91
*Stahlrohr, verchromt,
Holz, schwarz lackiert
Thonet AG,
Deutschland
Breite: 125 cm*

Bureau B 91
*en tube d'acier chromé et bois laqué noir
Thonet AG, Allemagne
Largeur: 125 cm*

**Marcel Breuer,
1925/26**

**Nest of tables
B 9 – B 9c**
*Chrome-plated tubular steel, wood painted black
Thonet AG, Germany
Height: 60 cm*

**Satz Teetische
B 9 – B 9c**
*Stahlrohr, verchromt,
Holz, schwarz lackiert
Thonet AG,
Deutschland
Höhe: 60 cm*

**Série de tables à thé
B 9 – B 9c**
*en tube d'acier chromé et bois laqué noir
Thonet SA, Allemagne
Hauteur: 60 cm*

**Marcel Breuer,
1925**

Chair B 6
*Chrome-plated
tubular steel,
wood painted black
Standard-Möbel
Lengyel & Co., Berlin
Height: 88 cm*

Stuhl B 6
*Stahlrohr, verchromt,
Holz, schwarz lackiert
Standard-Möbel
Lengyel & Co., Berlin
Höhe: 88 cm*

Chaise B 6
*en tube d'acier chromé et bois laqué noir
Standard-Möbel
Lengyel & Co., Berlin
Hauteur: 88 cm*

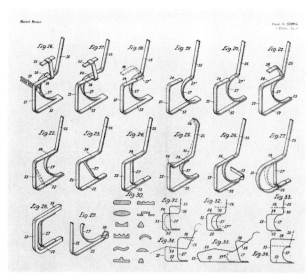

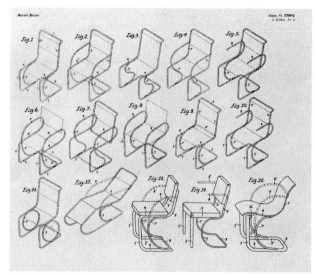

Marcel Breuer,
1933

Patent drawings for
steel and aluminium
chair frames

Patentzeichnungen für
federnde Stuhlgestelle
aus Stahl und Alumini-
um

Dessins de brevet pour
cadres en acier et en
aluminium de sièges à
ressorts

Marcel Breuer,
1933/34

Chair
Aluminium,
moulded plywood
Embru-Werke AG,
Rüti/Zurich
Height: 74 cm

Stuhl
Aluminium,
Sperrholz, geformt
Embru-Werke AG,
Rüti/Zürich
Höhe: 74 cm

Chaise
en aluminium et
contreplaqué cintré
Embru-Werke AG,
Rüti/Zürich
Hauteur: 74 cm

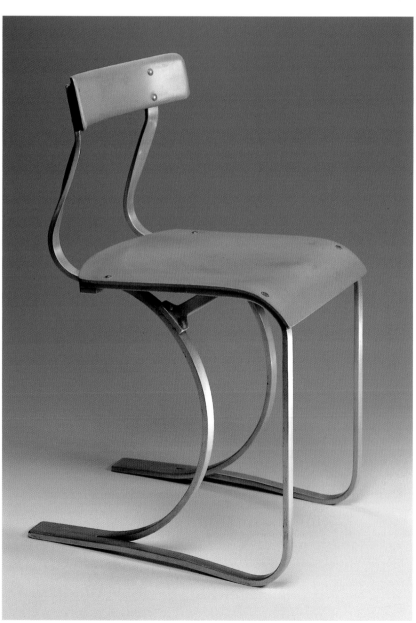

By 1932, Marcel Breuer had patented his designs for flat steel and tubular aluminium chair frames. In 1933, a competition launched by the Paris-based company Alliance Aluminium Cie. prompted Breuer to design a number of different chair and armchair types in tubular aluminium which were then produced by Embru-Werke AG and marketed by the »Wohnbedarf« company in Zurich. Later, Breuer's aluminium furniture was also produced under licence by the Arnold company in Schorndorf and the Stylclair company in Lyon.

Bereits 1932 sicherte sich Marcel Breuer in Deutschland die Patente für federnde Stuhlgestelle aus Flachstahl und Aluminium. Im Zusammenhang mit einem Wettbewerb der Pariser Firma Alliance Aluminium Cie. entwarf Breuer 1933 verschiedene Stuhl- und Sesseltypen aus federndem Aluminium, die nach erfolgreicher Prämierung von den Embru-Werken AG hergestellt und von der Firma Wohnbedarf in Zürich vertrieben wurden. Die Aluminiummöbel Breuers wurden später auch von den Firmen Arnold in Schorndorf und Stylclair in Lyon in Lizenz produziert.

Dès 1932, Marcel Breuer s'assure pour l'Allemagne les brevets de cadres métalliques pour sièges à ressorts.
A l'occasion d'un concours lancé par la firme parisienne Alliance Aluminium Cie. Breuer créa en 1933 divers fauteuils et chaises en aluminium à ressorts qui seront primés puis fabriqués par la société Embru et diffusés par la firme Wohnbedarf de Zurich. Ces meubles seront ensuite copiés sous licence par les sociétés Arnold de Schorndorf et Stylclair de Lyon.

Marcel Breuer, 1933/34

Armchair
Stainless steel, moulded plywood
Embru-Werke AG, Rüti/Zurich
Height: 73 cm

Armlehnstuhl
Edelstahl, Sperrholz, geformt
Embru-Werke AG, Rüti/Zürich
Höhe: 73 cm

Fauteuil à accoudoirs
en acier spécial et contreplaqué cintré
Embru-Werke AG, Rüti/Zurich
Hauteur: 73 cm

**Ludwig Mies van
der Rohe, 1927**

Group of seats
Nickelled tubular steel,
leather
Berliner Metallgewer-
be Joseph Müller,
Berlin
Height: 77 cm
(armchair)

Sitzgruppe
Stahlrohr, vernickelt,
Lederbespannung
Berliner Metallgewer-
be Joseph Müller,
Berlin
Höhe: 77 cm
(Armlehnstuhl)

**Ensemble de fau-
teuils**
Tube d'acier nickelé et
garniture en cuir
Berliner Metallgewer-
be Joseph Müller,
Berlin
Hauteur: 77 cm
(fauteuil à accoudoirs)

**Ludwig Mies van
der Rohe, 1927**

Armchair MR 20
Nickelled tubular steel,
leather
Berliner Metallgewer-
be Joseph Müller,
Berlin
Height: 77 cm

Armlehnstuhl MR 20
Stahlrohr, vernickelt,
Lederbespannung
Berliner Metallgewer-
be Joseph Müller,
Berlin
Höhe: 77 cm

**Fauteuil tubulaire à
accoudoirs MR 20**
Acier nickelé
garniture cuir
Berliner Metallgewer-
be Joseph Müller,
Berlin
Hauteur: 77 cm

In 1925, Ludwig Mies van der Rohe was put in charge of the Werkbund exhibition »Die Wohnung« (The Home), for which he developed the so-called Weißenhof chair – a tubular steel cantilever chair without back legs, produced by the Berlin-based company Joseph Müller from 1927 onwards. His design was inspired by Mart Stam's design for a chair without back legs which did not function on the cantilever principle, and which had also been designed for the same exhibition.

1925 wurde Ludwig Mies van der Rohe mit der Leitung der Werkbundausstellung »Die Wohnung«, die als Teil der Weißenhofausstellung für das Jahr 1927 geplant war, beauftragt. Mies van der Rohe entwickelte aus diesem Anlaß das erste zugleich hinterbeinlose und freischwingende Stuhlmodell aus Stahlrohr. Der sogenannte Weißenhof-Stuhl wurde ab 1927 von der Firma Berliner Metallgewerbe Joseph Müller hergestellt. Sein Entwurf wurde angeregt von dem ersten hinterbeinlosen, aber noch kantigen und nicht freischwingenden Stuhltyp Mart Stams, den dieser ebenfalls im Zusammenhang mit der Weißenhofausstellung entworfen hatte.

En 1925, Ludwig Mies van der Rohe fut chargé de la direction de l'exposition du Werkbund «Die Wohnung» (La Maison) prévue comme anticipant l'exposition Weißenhof de 1927. Il crée à cette occasion le premier modèle de chaise en tubes d'acier à piètement suspendu et sans pieds postérieurs, la célèbre «Weißenhof». Cette chaise sera produite à partir de 1927 par la firme Berliner Metallgewerbe Joseph Müller. Pour cette création, Mies van der Rohe s'est inspiré d'un modèle de Mart Stam, la première chaise sans pieds arrière mais aux formes encore anguleuses et non supendue, que ce dernier avait conçue lui aussi pour l'exposition Weißenhof.

95

Ludwig Mies van der Rohe, 1927

Armchair MR 20
Nickelled tubular steel, woven cane
Berliner Metallgewerbe Joseph Müller, Berlin
Height: 80 cm

Armlehnstuhl MR 20
Stahlrohr, vernickelt, Rohrgeflecht
Berliner Metallgewerbe Joseph Müller, Berlin
Höhe: 80 cm

Fauteuil à accoudoirs MR 20
Tube d'acier nickelé et cannage
Berliner Metallgewerbe Joseph Müller, Berlin
Hauteur: 80 cm

Ludwig Mies van der Rohe, 1927

Seating	**Sitzgruppe**	**Ensemble de fauteuils**
Nickelled tubular steel, woven cane	Stahlrohr, vernickelt, Rohrgeflecht	Tube d'acier nickelé et cannage
Berliner Metallgewerbe Joseph Müller, Berlin	Berliner Metallgewerbe Joseph Müller, Berlin	Berliner Metallgewerbe Joseph Müller, Berlin
Height: 80 cm (armchair)	Höhe: 80 cm (Armlehnstuhl)	Hauteur: 80 cm (fauteuil à accoudoirs)

In 1923, László Moholy-Nagy took over as artistic director of the metal workshop at the Bauhaus in Weimar. He was assisted by the silversmith Christian Dell. Under Moholy-Nagy, it developed from a traditional silversmith workshop into an experimental design workshop for industrial metalwork, as typified by Wilhelm Wagenfeld's table lamp based on a prototype by Carl J. Juckers – produced from 1923 onwards at the Bauhaus metal workshop under the designation MT 8.

1923 übernahm László Moholy-Nagy als Formmeister die künstlerische Leitung der Metallwerkstatt am Staatlichen Bauhaus Weimar. Ihm zur Seite stand als Werkmeister der Silberschmied Christian Dell. Typisch für den Wandel der Werkstatt unter Moholy-Nagy von einer traditionellen Silberschmiede zu einer experimentellen Entwurfswerkstatt für industrielles Metalldesign ist die von Wilhelm Wagenfeld entwickelte Tischlampe: Ausgehend von einem Grundmodell Carl J. Juckers wurde sie ab 1923 in der Metallwerkstatt des Bauhauses unter der Typbezeichnung MT 8 in Serie produziert.

En 1923, László Moholy-Nagy prend la direction artistique de l'atelier de métal comme maître de la forme au Bauhaus de Weimar. Le maître d'atelier était l'orfèvre Christian Dell. Sous la direction de Moholy-Nagy, l'évolution de l'atelier d'orfèvrerie traditionnelle en un atelier expérimental de design industriel est achevée et illustrée par la lampe de table de Wilhelm Wagenfeld: créée à partir d'un modèle de base de Carl J. Juckers, elle fut fabriquée en série à l'atelier de métal du Bauhaus sous l'appellation MT 8.

Christian Dell, 1922

Decanter
Electroplated nickel silver, ebony
Bauhaus Weimar, metal workshop
Height: 22,5 cm

Weinkanne
Alpacca, versilbert, Ebenholz
Bauhaus Weimar, Metallwerkstatt
Höhe: 22,5 cm

Cruche à vin
Argentan argenté et bois d'ébène
Bauhaus Weimar, atelier de métal
Hauteur: 22,5 cm

Walter Gropius, 1923

Office of Walter Gropius, Bauhaus Weimar

Direktionszimmer von Walter Gropius, Bauhaus Weimar

Bureau de direction de Walter Gropius, Bauhaus Weimar

Wilhelm Wagenfeld, 1924

Table lamp MT 8
Nickelled brass, cast iron, opalescent glass
Bauhaus Weimar, metal workshop
Height: 36.5 cm

Tischlampe MT 8
Messing, vernickelt, Gußeisen, Opalglas
Bauhaus Weimar, Metallwerkstatt
Höhe: 36,5 cm

Lampe de table MT 8
Laiton nickelé, fonte et verre opalisé
Bauhaus Weimar, atelier de métal
Hauteur: 36,5 cm

98

Marianne Brandt's metal designs were to become synonymous with the »Bauhaus style«. In her very first year at the Bauhaus, under the influence of Moholy-Nagy, she designed an ashtray based on simple stereometric forms. In 1926, Josef Albers designed a functional tea glass in a combination of heat-resistant laboratory glass, steel and porcelain. The tea glass illustrated here (Herbert Bayer collection) also has the Meißen china saucer used only in the early phase of production.

Die Metallarbeiten Marianne Brandts wurden zu Synonymen des »Bauhausstils«. Noch in ihrem ersten Lehrjahr entwarf sie, stark von Moholy-Nagy beeinflußt, einen Aschenbecher, den sie aus einfachen stereometrischen Grundformen konstruierte. Josef Albers entwickelte 1926 am Bauhaus Dessau aus der Kombination eines hitzebeständigen Laborglases mit V2 A-Stahl und Porzellan ein funktionales Teeglas. Das hier abgebildete Teeglas aus dem Nachlaß von Herbert Bayer ist noch mit dem Unterteller aus Meißner Porzellan ausgestattet, der nur in der Frühphase der Produktion verwendet wurde.

Les réalisations de Marianne Brandt deviendront synonymes de «Style Bauhaus». Elle crée dès sa première année d'apprentissage, fortement influencée par Moholy-Nagy, un cendrier dont la construction résulte de formes fondamentales simples et stéréométriques. En 1926, au Bauhaus de Dessau, Josef Albers conçoit un verre à thé fonctionnel fait en verre de laboratoire résistant à la chaleur, en acier V2 A et en porcelaine. Le verre à thé exposé ici provenant de la succession de Herbert Bayer est encore muni d'une soucoupe en porcelaine de Meißen qui ne sera employée qu'au début de la production.

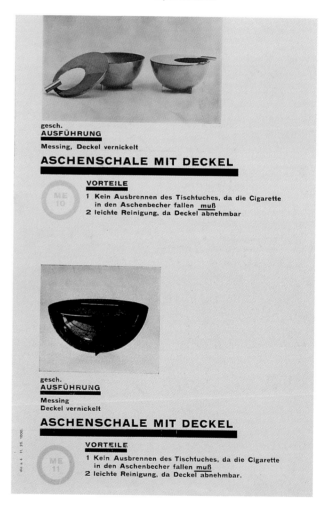

Marianne Brandt, 1924

Ashtray
Brass, nickel-plated lid
Bauhaus Weimar,
metal workshop
Height: 6.1 cm

Aschenbecher
Messing,
Deckel vernickelt
Bauhaus Weimar,
Metallwerkstatt
Höhe: 6,1 cm

Cendrier
en laiton,
couvercle nickelé
Bauhaus Weimar,
atelier de métal
Hauteur: 6,1 cm

Herbert Bayer, 1925

Brochure advertising
Bauhaus products
Bauhaus Dessau, print-
workshop

Werbeprospekt
für Bauhausprodukte
Bauhaus Dessau,
Werkstatt für Druck
und Reklame

Prospectus publicitaire
pour les réalisations
du Bauhaus
Bauhaus Dessau,
atelier d'imprimerie
et de réclame

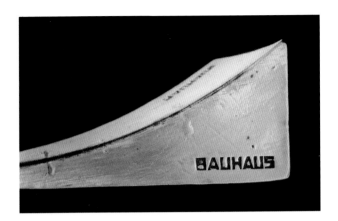

**Erich Consemüller,
1926/27**

*Photo of tea glasses
designed by
Josef Albers
Bauhaus Dessau*

*Fotografie von Teeglä-
sern nach Entwurf von
Josef Albers
Bauhaus Dessau*

*Photographie de ver-
res à thé créés
par Josef Albers
Bauhaus Dessau*

Josef Albers, 1926

Tea glass
*Glass, V2 A-steel, ebo-
ny, porcelain
Bauhaus Dessau,
Jenaer Glaswerke
Schott & Gen.
Krupp AG,
Meißen porcelain
factory
Height: 5 cm*

Teeglas
*Laborglas, V2 A-Stahl,
Ebenholz, Porzellan
Bauhaus Dessau,
Jenaer Glaswerke
Schott & Gen.,
Krupp AG,
Porzellanmanufaktur
Meißen
Höhe: 5 cm*

Verre à thé
*Verre de laboratoire ,
acier V2 A, bois d'ébè-
ne et porcelaine
Bauhaus Dessau,
Jenaer Glaswerke
Schott & Gen.,
Krupp AG,
Manufacture de
porcelaine Meißen
Hauteur: 5 cm*

Hans Przyrembel, a trained locksmith, studied at the Bauhaus in Weimar and Dessau from 1924 onwards. After completing the basic course, he began a silversmith apprenticeship in the metal workshop, where his previous knowledge of metalworking soon assured him an important role. In 1928, he left the Bauhaus to take over the metal workshop of Wolfgang Tümpel in Halle, before moving to Leipzig in 1929. Karl Raichle, who had spent only one semester at the Bauhaus in Dessau, founded a pewterworks in 1928/29 in Urach (later moving to Meersburg on Lake Constance) where he continued to pursue the design principles of the Bauhaus.

**Hans Przyrembel,
c. 1926**

Tea caddy
Nickelled brass
Bauhaus Dessau,
metal workshop
Height: 20.5 cm

Teedose
Messing, vernickelt
Bauhaus Dessau,
Metallwerkstatt
Höhe: 20,5 cm

Boîte à thé
en laiton nickelé
Bauhaus Dessau,
atelier de métal
Hauteur: 20,5 cm

**Hans Przyrembel,
1929/30**

Necklace
Gold, facet-cut
turmalines
Metal workshop Hans
Przyrembel, Leipzig
Length: 39.5 cm

Collier
Gold, facettierte
Turmaline
Metallwerkstatt Hans
Przyrembel, Leipzig
Länge: 39,5 cm

Collier
en or et tourmaline
facettée
Atelier de métal Hans
Przyrembel, Leipzig
Longueur: 39,5 cm

Der gelernte Schlosser Hans Przyrembel studierte ab 1924 am Bauhaus in Weimar und Dessau. Nach Absolvierung des Vorkurses begann er eine Lehre als Silberschmied in der Metallwerkstatt, in der er wegen seiner Vorkenntnisse schon bald eine wichtige Position einnahm. 1928 verließ er das Bauhaus und übernahm zunächst die Metallwerkstatt von Wolfgang Tümpel in Halle, bevor er sich 1929 in Leipzig niederließ. Karl Raichle, der nur ein Semester am Bauhaus in Dessau verbrachte, gründete 1928/29 in Urach (später in Meersburg am Bodensee) eine Zinnschmiede, in der er die Gestaltungsprinzipien des Bauhauses verarbeitete.

Hans Przyrembel, serrurier de formation, étudie à partir de 1924 au Bauhaus de Weimar et de Dessau. Après le cours préliminaire, il commence un apprentissage d'orfèvre à l'atelier de métal où il joue bientôt un rôle important grâce à ses connaissances préalables. Il quitte l'école en 1928 et reprend la direction de l'atelier de métal de Wolfgang Tümpel à Halle avant de s'installer à son compte en 1929 à Leipzig. Karl Raichle qui ne passe qu'un semestre au Bauhaus de Dessau fonde en 1928/29 une orfèvrerie d'objets d'étain à Urach (plus tard à Meersbourg sur le lac de Constance) où il met en pratique les principes du Bauhaus.

Karl Raichle,
c. 1928/29

Teapot
Pewter, ebony
Pewtersmiths K. & E.
Raichle, Urach
Height: 16 cm

Teekanne
Zinn, Ebenholz
Zinnschmiede K. & E.
Raichle, Urach
Höhe: 16 cm

Théière
en étain et bois
d'ébène
K. & E. Raichle Etainier, Urach
Hauteur: 16 cm

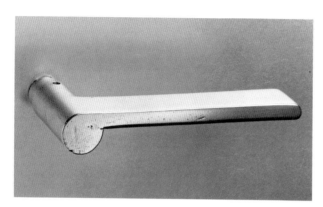

Casting stamp of
bronzecasters S. A.
Loevy, Berlin

Gußstempel der Bron-
zegießerei &
Baubeschlägefabrik
S. A. Loevy, Berlin

Cachet en fonte de la
Fonderie S. A. Loevy
de Berlin

**Wilhelm Wagenfeld,
1928**

Door handle
Nickelled brass
Bronzecasters
S. A. Loevy, Berlin
Length: 11.5 cm

Türdrücker
Messing, vernickelt
Bronzegießerei &
Baubeschlägefabrik
S. A. Loevy, Berlin
Länge: 11,5 cm

Loquet
en laiton nickelé
Fonderie
S. A. Loevy, Berlin
Longueur: 11,5 cm

**Wilhelm Wagenfeld,
1927/29**

Tea caddy M 15
Brass
Bauhochschule
Weimar,
metal workshop
Height: 13.5 cm

Teebüchse M 15
Messing, innen
versilbert
Bauhochschule
Weimar,
Metallwerkstatt
Höhe: 13,5 cm

Boîte à thé M 15
en laiton
Bauhochschule
Weimar,
atelier de métal
Hauteur: 13,5 cm

Following the dissolution of the Bauhaus in Weimar, Wilhelm Wagenfeld became assistant to Richard Winkelmayer at the metal workshop of the Staatliche Bauhochschule in Weimar. In 1928, he then took charge of the workshop. Though geometrically less severe, his metalware designs of this period are still very much in the tradition of the Weimar Bauhaus.

Nach der Auflösung des Weimarer Bauhauses arbeitete Wilhelm Wagenfeld zunächst als Assistent von Richard Winkelmayer in der Metallwerkstatt der Staatlichen Bauhochschule Weimar. 1928 übernahm er dann die Leitung der Werkstatt. Seine Metallwarenentwürfe aus dieser Zeit stehen zwar noch ganz in der Tradition des Weimarer Bauhauses, lösen sich aber in ihrer Gestaltung doch von der strengen geometrischen Formensprache.

Après la dissolution du Bauhaus à Weimar, Wilhelm Wagenfeld travaille d'a bord comme assistant de Richard Winkelmayer à l'atelier de métal de la Staatliche Bauhochschule de Weimar (Ecole technique supérieure de Construction), puis, en 1928, il reprend la direction de l'atelier. Ses créations de l'époque sont encore dans la grande tradition du Bauhaus de Weimar mais elles se libèrent de son vocabulaire des formes géométrique et sévère.

Wilhelm Wagenfeld, 1929/30

Tea warmer
Nickelled brass, opalescent glass
Metalware manufacturers
Walter & Wagner, Schleiz
Height: 10.5 cm

Teewärmer
Messing vernickelt, Opalglas
Metallwarenfabrik
Walter & Wagner, Schleiz
Höhe: 10,5 cm

Chauffe-thé
en laiton nickelé et verre opalisé
Usine d'articles métalliques
Walter & Wagner, Schleiz
Hauteur: 10,5 cm

Marianne Brandt probably created the teamaker illustrated here (Albert Krause collection) while she was still at the Bauhaus in Dessau. According to the previous owner, this was a gift from Brandt to Krause while they were both at the institute for industrial design in Berlin. After she left the Bauhaus, Marianne Brandt worked as a designer for the Ruppelwerk in Gotha between 1930 and 1932/33. On the basis of the available processing techniques there, she developed a uniform product design asserting the design concepts of the Bauhaus within an industrial enterprise.

Vermutlich noch am Bauhaus Dessau fertigte Marianne Brandt die abgebildete Teemaschine aus dem Nachlaß von Albert Krause. Nach Angaben des Vorbesitzers handelt es sich um ein Geschenk Brandts an Krause, das sie ihm während ihrer gemeinsamen Zeit am Institut für industrielle Gestaltung in Berlin vermachte. Nach ihrem Weggang vom Bauhaus arbeitete Marianne Brandt zwischen 1930 und 1932/33 für die Ruppelwerk GmbH in Gotha als Entwerferin im Bereich Kunstgewerbe. Hier entwickelte sie, ausgehend von den vorgefundenen Verarbeitungstechniken, ein einheitliches Produktdesign, das die Gestaltungskonzepte des Bauhauses in einem Industrieunternehmen durchsetzte.

C'est probablement encore au Bauhaus que Marianne Brandt réalise la machine à thé présentée ici, provenant de la succession d'Albert Krause. Selon les indications fournies par le précédent propriétaire, il s'agit d'un cadeau que M. Brandt a offert à Krause du temps de leurs activités communes à l'Institut de Création industrielle de Berlin. Après sa formation au Bauhaus, Marianne Brandt travaille entre 1930 et 1932/33 comme conceptrice pour l'usine d'articles métalliques Ruppelwerk de Gotha . Elle y développe à partir des techniques de transformation déjà établies un design de produit unitaire, introduisant les concepts du Bauhaus dans une entreprise industrielle.

Marianne Brandt, 1928/30

Teamaker
Brass, ebony
Probably Bauhaus Dessau,
metal workshop
Height: 20.5 cm

Teemaschine
Messing, Ebenholz
Vermutlich Bauhaus Dessau,
Metallwerkstatt
Höhe: 20,5 cm

Machine à thé
Laiton et bois d'ébène
Probablement Bauhaus Dessau,
atelier de métal
Hauteur: 20,5 cm

**Marianne Brandt,
1930/32**

Bookends
Sheet steel, poly-
chrome lacquer
Ruppelwerk GmbH,
Gotha
Height: 12 cm

Paar Buchstützen
Stahlblech, polychro-
me Lackierung
Ruppelwerk GmbH,
Gotha
Höhe: 12 cm

Deux appui-livres
en tôle d'acier et vernis
polychrome
Ruppelwerk GmbH,
Gotha
Hauteur: 12 cm

105

**Marianne Brandt,
1930/32**

Napkin ring
Sheet steel, yellow
lacquer
Metalware manufac-
turers Ruppelwerk
GmbH, Gotha
Height: 13.5 cm

Serviettenhalter
Stahlblech, gelbe
Lackierung
Metallwarenfabrik
Ruppelwerk GmbH,
Gotha
Höhe: 13,5 cm

Porte-serviettes
Tôle d'acier, laqué jau-
ne
Usine d'articles metalli-
ques Ruppelwerk
GmbH, Gotha
Hauteur: 13,5 cm

**Marianne Brandt,
1930/32**

Ink well
Sheet steel, chromed,
painted, pressed glass
Metalware manufac-
turers Ruppelwerk
GmbH, Gotha
Height: 8 cm

Tintenfaß
Stahlblech, verchromt,
schwarz lackiert,
Preßglas
Metallwarenfabrik
Ruppelwerk GmbH,
Gotha
Höhe: 8 cm

**Encrier en tôle d'a-
cier**
chromé, laqué noir et
verre pressé
Usine d'articles métalli-
ques Ruppelwerk
GmbH, Gotha
Hauteur: 8 cm

In 1926, Christian Dell, former master of the Bauhaus metal workshop in Weimar, took over the newly established metalwork class at Frankfurt Art School. In addition to teaching and designing silverware, he began to design lighting and lamps. One of Dell's earliest industrially produced lamp designs is the »Rondella-Polo«. The fully nickel-plated version illustrated here is extremely rare. At the same time as Dell, Hans Warnecke ran another metalwork class at Frankfurt Art School, oriented more strongly towards the applied arts.

1926 übernahm Christian Dell, der ehemalige Werkmeister der Metallwerkstatt am Weimarer Bauhaus, die Leitung der neugegründeten Metallklasse an der Frankfurter Kunstschule. Neben seiner pädagogischen Arbeit und der Ausführung von Silbergeräten begann er hier seine Karriere als Entwerfer für Beleuchtungskörper. Zu den frühesten industriell gefertigten Lampenentwürfen Dells gehört das Modell »Rondella-Polo«, das in der hier vorliegenden völlig vernickelten Version von großer Seltenheit ist. Hans Warnecke leitete parallel zu Dell eine zweite Metallklasse an der Frankfurter Kunstschule, die jedoch stärker kunstgewerblich ausgerichtet war.

En 1926, Christian Dell, ancien maître d'atelier au Bauhaus de Weimar, prend la direction de la nouvelle classe de métal à la Frankfurter Kunstschule (école d'art de Francfort). Outre son travail d'enseignant et la réalisation d'ustensiles en argent, il y commence sa carrière de concepteur d'objets d'éclairage. Parmi ses premières lampes fabriquées industriellement figure le modèle «Rondella-Polo», présenté ici en version nickelée d'une grande rareté. Hans Warnecke dirigeait une autre classe de travail sur métal de la Frankfurter Kunstschule mais entièrement tournée vers les arts décoratifs.

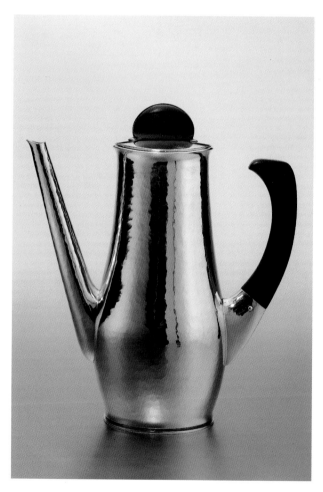

**Hans Warnecke,
c. 1930**

Teapot	**Teekanne**	**Théière**
Silver, ebony	Silber, Ebenholz	en argent et
Frankfurter Kunst-	Frankfurter Kunst-	bois d'ébène
schule, metal work-	schule, Metallwerkstatt	Frankfurter Kunst-
shop	Höhe: 15,5 cm	schule, atelier de métal
Height: 15.5 cm		Hauteur: 15,5 cm

**Christian Dell,
1927/29**

Coffee pot	**Kaffeekanne**	**Cafetière**
Silver, ebony	Silber, Ebenholz	en argent et bois
Frankfurter Kunst-	Frankfurter Kunst-	d'ébène
schule,	schule,	Frankfurter Kunst-
metal workshop	Metallwerkstatt	schule,
Height: 21 cm	Höhe: 21 cm	atelier de métal
		Hauteur: 21 cm

DAS FRANKFURTER REGISTER 1

"RONDELLA" TISCH- UND STÄNDER- (ATELIER) LAMPE

ENTWURF UND KONSTRUKTION: Chr. Dell, Lehrer an der Kunstschule Frankfurt am Main. HERSTELLUNG: Richard Franke, Weißfrauenstraße 14-16, Frankfurt am Main

DIE STÄNDER-(ATELIER)LAMPE
Fuß polierte Ebenholzplatte mit starkem vernickeltem Metallring. Standrohr und Lampenarm vernickelt und poliert
HÖHE 1,78 cm   PREIS: 75 M.
Einfache Ausführung mit Metallfuß und Aluminium-Reflektor in Vorbereitung

DIE TISCHLAMPE
Bellere Ausführung: Der Reflektor und Fuß aus Kupfer
Einfache Ausführung: Reflektor Aluminium, Fuß schwarze Eisenplatte · Bei beiden Standrohr und Lampenarm Messing, vernickelt, poliert
HÖHE bei hochgestelltem Lampenarm 54 cm
PREIS: Bellere Ausführ. 33 M. Einfache Ausführ. 25 M.

*Das Frankfurter
Register 1, 1928*

Brochure advertising
lamps designed by
Christian Dell

*Werbeprospekt für
Lampen nach Entwurf
von Christian Dell*

Prospectus publicitaire
pour des lampes
créées par Christian
Dell

**Christian Dell,
1928/29**

**»Rondella-Polo«
table lamp**
Brass and copper, nickel-plated, cast iron
Lamp manufacturers
Rondella,
Oberursel/Frankfurt/M.
Height: 33.5 cm

**Tischlampe
»Rondella-Polo«**
Messing und Kupfer,
vernickelt, Gußeisen
Beleuchtungskörperfabrik Rondella, Oberursel/Frankfurt a.M.
Höhe: 33,5 cm

**Lampe de table
«Rondella-Polo»**
en laiton, cuivre
nickelé et fonte
Usine de luminaires
Rondella,
Oberursel/Francfort
Hauteur: 33,5 cm

In 1920, at Dornburg, some 30 kilometres from Weimar, the Weimar Bauhaus established a ceramics workshop under the artistic direction of the sculptor Gerhard Marcks and the local potter Max Krehan. With the development of new ceramic designs by Otto Lindig and Theodor Bogler around 1922/23, which could be mass produced by means of a casting process, the previously artisanal ceramic workshop took on the character of a productive workshop in which industrial production processes could be simulated using new forms.

Die Keramikwerkstatt des Weimarer Bauhauses wurde 1920 im etwa 30 Kilometer von Weimar entfernten Dornburg unter der künstlerischen Leitung des Bildhauers Gerhard Marcks und des einheimischen Töpfers Max Krehan eingerichtet. Durch die Entwicklung neuer keramischer Gefäß-Typen von Otto Lindig und Theodor Bogler ab 1922/23, die im Gießverfahren seriell vervielfältigt werden konnten, erhielt auch die zu Anfang eher kunsthandwerklich ausgerichtete Keramikwerkstatt den Charakter einer Produktivwerkstatt, in der industrielle Produktionsverfahren unter Verwendung neuer Formen simuliert werden konnten.

En 1920, l'atelier de céramique du Bauhaus de Weimar est installé à Dornburg à 30 km de Weimar et dirigé par le sculpteur Gerhard Marcks et le potier local Max Krehan. A partir de 1922/23, grâce à l'élaboration par Otto Lindig et Theodor Bogler de modèles standard inédits pouvant être reproduits en série par coulage, cet atelier aménagé au départ de façon artisanale prend rapidement le caractère d'un atelier de production où peuvent être simulés des procédés de production industriels avec utilisation de nouvelles formes .

Otto Lindig, 1923

Cocoa pot	**Kakaokanne**	**Chocolatière**
Stoneware, grey glaze	Steinzeug, hellgraue	Grès et vernis bleu clair
Bauhaus Weimar,	Überlaufglasur	Bauhaus Weimar,
ceramics workshop,	Bauhaus Weimar,	atelier céramique,
Dornburg	Keramikwerkstatt,	Dornburg
Height: 23.5 cm	Dornburg	Hauteur: 23,5 cm
	Höhe: 23,5 cm	

Otto Lindig, 1931

Dish with lid	**Deckeldose**	**Boîte à couvercle**
Stoneware,	Steinzeug, weiß-graue	Grès, vernis blanc-gris
white-grey glaze	Überlaufglasur	Atelier céramique
Ceramics workshop	Keramische Werkstatt	Otto Linding, Dornburg
Otto Lindig, Dornburg	Otto Lindig, Dornburg	Hauteur: 22,5 cm
Height: 22.5 cm	Höhe: 22,5 cm	

Otto Lindig, 1923

Cocoa pot
Stoneware,
white-grey glaze
Bauhaus Weimar,
ceramics workshop,
Dornburg
Height: 14.7 cm

Kakaokanne
Steinzeug, weiß-graue
Überlaufglasur
Bauhaus Weimar,
Keramikwerkstatt,
Dornburg
Höhe: 14,7 cm

Chocolatière
grès, vernis blanc-gris
Bauhaus Weimar,
atelier de céramique,
Dornburg
Hauteur: 14,7 cm

Theodor Bogler, 1923

Teapot
Stoneware, grey glaze
Bauhaus Weimar,
ceramics workshop,
Dornburg
Height: 10.5 cm

**Kombinationstee-
kanne**
Steinzeug, hellgraue
Überlaufglasur
Bauhaus Weimar,
Keramikwerkstatt,
Dornburg
Höhe: 10,5 cm

Théière combinée
Grès et vernis bleu clair
Bauhaus Weimar,
atelier de céramique,
Dornburg
Hauteur: 10,5 cm

The cooperation between the Schott & Gen. glassworks in Jena and artists from the Bauhaus in Weimar dates back to 1925, the year in which Gerhard Marcks developed his prototype of the »Sintrax« coffee maker. In 1931, Wilhelm Wagenfeld, working freelance for Schott & Gen., re-designed a major collection of household glassware. It was on the basis of this experience that he was appointed artistic director of the Vereinigte Lausitzer Glaswerke AG (VLG) in Weißwasser in 1935. With his work for the VLG glassworks, Wagenfeld made the transition from an artisanal designer to an industrial designer.

Die Zusammenarbeit der Jenaer Glaswerke Schott & Gen. mit Künstlern des Weimarer Bauhauses geht auf das Jahr 1925 zurück, in dem Gerhard Marcks den Prototyp der »Sintrax«-Kaffeemaschine entwickelte. Ab 1931 übernahm dann Wilhelm Wagenfeld als freier künstlerischer Mitarbeiter von Schott & Gen. die Neugestaltung einer großen Kollektion von Haushaltsgläsern. Basierend auf diesen Erfahrungen, wurde er 1935 zum künstlerischen Leiter der Vereinigten Lausitzer Glaswerke AG (VLG) in Weißwasser berufen. Mit seiner Arbeit für die VLG vollzog Wagenfeld am konsequentesten den Wandel von einem Entwerfer für Kunstgewerbe zu einem Industriedesigner.

La collaboration entre les Jenaer Glaswerke Schott & Gen. (verrerie de Jena) et les artistes du Bauhaus de Weimar remonte à l'année 1925 au cours de laquelle Gerhard Marcks conçoit le prototype de la machine à café Sintrax. A partir de 1931, Wilhelm Wagenfeld étudie en tant que collaborateur extérieur de Schott & Gen. un nouveau programme de création consistant en une grande collection de verres ménagers. Fort de ces expériences acquises, il est nommé en 1935 à la direction artistique d'une verrerie de Weißwasser, les Vereinigten Lausitzer Glaswerke AG (VLG). Wagenfeld est l'artiste qui avec son travail aux VLG réussit le mieux le passage de créateur spécialisé dans les arts appliqués à celui de designer industriel.

**Gerhard Marcks,
c. 1925**

»Sintrax« coffee maker	**»Sintrax«- Kaffeemaschine**	**Machine à café «Sintrax»**
Heat-resistant glass, black-stained wood, chrome Glassworks Schott & Gen., Jena Height: 30.7 cm	Feuerfestes Glas, Holz, schwarz gebeizt, Metall, verchromt Jenaer Glaswerke Schott & Gen., Jena Höhe: 30,7 cm	en verre à feu, bois teinté noir et métal chromé Schott & Gen., Jena Hauteur: 30,7 cm

**Wilhelm Wagenfeld,
1931**

»Sintrax« coffee maker	**»Sintrax«- Kaffeemaschine**	**Machine à café «Sintrax»**
Heat-resistant glass, plastic, wood, aluminium Glassworks Schott & Gen., Jena Height: 37 cm	Feuerfestes Glas, Kunststoff, Holz, Aluminium Jenaer Glaswerke Schott & Gen., Jena Höhe: 37 cm	en verre à feu, plastique, bois et aluminium Verrerie Schott & Gen., Jena Hauteur: 37 cm

Wilhelm Wagenfeld,
c. 1930

Tea set
Heat-resistant glass
Glassworks
Schott & Gen., Jena
Height: 11 cm
(teapot)

Teeservice
Feuerfestes Glas
Jenaer Glaswerke
Schott & Gen., Jena
Höhe: 11 cm
(Teekanne)

Service à thé
en verre à feu
Verrerie
Schott & Gen., Jena
Hauteur: 11 cm
(théière)

111

Wilhelm Wagenfeld,
1938

»Kubus«
storage glasses
Moulded glass
Vereinigte Lausitzer
Glaswerke AG,
Weißwasser
Height: 21.5 cm

»Kubus«-
Vorratsgeschirr
Preßglas
Vereinigte Lausitzer
Glaswerke AG,
Weißwasser
Höhe: 21,5 cm

Vaisselle de réserve
«Kubus»
en verre pressé
Vereinigte Lausitzer
Glaswerke AG,
Weißwasser
Hauteur: 21,5 cm

In his first year at the Bauhaus carpentry workshop, Erich Dieckmann designed his own furniture models for the »Versuchshaus am Horn«. In 1926, he took over the artistic direction of the carpentry and interior-design department of the Staatliche Bauhochschule Weimar, where he designed his standard furniture based on simple cubic forms. In 1931, after his dismissal from the staff of the Bauhochschule Weimar on political grounds, Dieckmann was offered a teaching post as furniture designer at the Kunstgewerbeschule Burg Giebichenstein in Halle.

Schon während seines ersten Lehrjahres in der Bauhaus-Tischlerwerkstatt entwarf Erich Dieckmann eigene Möbelmodelle, die im »Versuchshaus am Horn« Verwendung fanden. 1926 übernahm er die künstlerische Leitung der Abteilung Tischlerei und Innenausbau an der Staatlichen Bauhochschule Weimar. Hier entwickelte er seine sogenannten Typenmöbel, die er aus einfachen, kubischen Formen konstruierte. Nach seiner politisch bedingten Entlassung als Lehrkraft der Bauhochschule Weimar erhielt Dieckmann 1931 die Möglichkeit, an der Kunstgewerbeschule Burg Giebichenstein in Halle seine Tätigkeit als Pädagoge und Möbelentwerfer fortzusetzen.

Dès sa première année d'apprentissage à l'atelier de menuiserie, Erich Dieckmann conçoit ses propres modèles de meubles qui trouvent leur emploi au «Versuchshaus am Horn». En 1926, il prend la direction artistique de l'atelier de menuiserie et de décoration intérieure à la Staatliche Bauhochschule Weimar (école technique supérieure de construction de Weimar). C'est là qu'il élabore ses types de meubles construits à partir de formes cubiques et simples. Après son licenciement pour des raisons politiques, il est invité en 1931 à continuer ses activités de pédagogue et de créateur de meubles à la Kunstgewerbeschule Burg Giebichenstein.

Erich Dieckmann, 1930/31

Armchair
Ash, beech,
woven cane
Kunstgewerbeschule
Burg Giebichenstein,
Halle, carpentry workshop
Height: 72 cm

Armlehnstuhl
Esche, Buche,
Rohrgeflecht
Kunstgewerbeschule
Burg Giebichenstein,
Halle, Tischlerwerkstatt
Höhe: 72 cm

Fauteuil à accoudoirs
en frêne, hêtre et cannage
Kunstgewerbeschule
Burg Giebichenstein,
Halle, atelier de menuiserie
Hauteur : 72 cm

**Erich Dieckmann,
1930/31**

Chair profiles, various
prototypes

Stuhlprofile, Entwick-
lungsreihe von ver-
schiedenen Stuhltypen

Profils de chaise, pha-
ses d'étude de diffé-
rents types de chaises

**Erich Dieckmann,
1926/27**

Armchair	**Sessel**	**Fauteuil**
Stained beech, blue fabric	Buche, dunkel gebeizt, blauer Stoffbezug	en hêtre foncé et garniture bleue
Bauhochschule Weimar, furniture workshop	Bauhochschule Weimar, Möbelwerkstatt	Bauhochschule Weimar, atelier de menuiserie
Height: 58 cm	Höhe: 58 cm	Hauteur: 58 cm

**Erich Dieckmann,
c. 1926**

Chair	**Stuhl**	**Chaise**
Oak, woven cane	Eiche, Rohrgeflecht	en chêne et cannage
Staatliche Bauhochschule Weimar, furniture workshop	Staatliche Bauhochschule Weimar, Möbelwerkstatt	Staatliche Bauhochschule Weimar, atelier de meubles
Height: 79 cm	Höhe: 79 cm	Hauteur: 79 cm

In 1923, the Berlin sculptor Karl Müller became the new artistic director of the metal workshop at the Kunstgewerbeschule Burg Giebichenstein in Halle. Under Müller's direction, the workshop became a leading centre of German metal design. Parallel to the developments at the Bauhaus, the metal workshop at Burg Giebichenstein also made the transition from an artisanal metalsmith workshop to an experimental design workshop, albeit less radically than at the Bauhaus. The focal point of interest at Burg Giebichenstein remained one of artisanal craftsmanship, however providing more scope for individuality than the Bauhaus.

1923 wurde der Berliner Ziseleur und Metallbildhauer Karl Müller als neuer künstlerischer Leiter der Metallwerkstatt an die Kunstgewerbeschule Burg Giebichenstein in Halle berufen. Unter der Leitung Müllers entwickelte sich die Werkstatt zu einem führenden Zentrum der deutschen Metallgestaltung. Analog zu den Entwicklungen am Bauhaus vollzog sich auch in der Metallwerkstatt der Burg Giebichenstein, wenn auch in abgeschwächter Form, der Wandel von einer kunsthandwerklichen Metallschmiede zu einer experimentellen Entwurfswerkstatt. Im Mittelpunkt der Interessen stand hier jedoch immer die handwerkliche Ausbildung, die, weniger doktrinär als am Bauhaus, der künstlerischen Individualität größere Spielräume ließ.

En 1923, le ciseleur et sculpteur sur métaux Karl Müller est nommé directeur artistique de l'atelier de métal de la Kunstgewerbeschule Burg Giebichenstein à Halle. Sous sa direction , l'atelier devient un centre important de l'art du métal en Allemagne. Cet atelier de travail artisanal des métaux se transforme, à l'instar de ce qui se passe au Bauhaus, en un atelier de création expérimental. Mais à la différence du Bauhaus, la formation artisanale reste au centre de l'enseignement dispensé et par son caractère moins doctrinaire laisse une plus grande liberté à l'individualité artistique.

Karl Müller, c. 1929

Mocca set	**Mokkaservice**	**Service à moka**
Silver, ivory	Silber, Elfenbein	en argent et ivoire
Kunstgewerbeschule	Kunstgewerbeschule	Kunstgewerbeschule
Burg Giebichenstein,	Burg Giebichenstein,	Burg Giebichenstein,
Halle, metal workshop	Halle, Metallwerkstatt	Halle, atelier de métal
Height: 12.8 cm	Höhe: 12,8 cm	Hauteur: 12,8 cm
(Mocca pot)	(Mokkakanne)	(cafetière à moka)

Karl Müller,
c. 1929/30

Mocca pot	**Mokkakanne**	**Cafetière à moka**
Brass	Messing	en laiton
Kunstgewerbeschule	Kunstgewerbeschule	Kunstgewerbeschule
Burg Giebichenstein,	Burg Giebichenstein,	Burg Giebichenstein,
Halle, metal workshop	Halle, Metallwerkstatt	Halle, atelier de métal
Height: 18 cm	Höhe: 18 cm	Hauteur: 18 cm

Metal workshop die of
the Kunstgewerbe-
schule Burg Giebichen-
stein Halle

Prägestempel der Me-
tallwerkstatt der
Kunstgewerbeschule
Burg Giebichenstein,
Halle

Coin de l'atelier de mé-
tal de la Kunstgewer-
beschule Burg Giebi-
chenstein à Halle

115

Karl Müller,
c. 1930

Tea caddy
Brass
Kunstgewerbeschule
Burg Giebichenstein,
Halle, metal workshop
Height: 13.5 cm

Teedose
Messing
Kunstgewerbeschule
Burg Giebichenstein,
Halle, Metallwerkstatt
Höhe: 13,5 cm

Boîte à thé
en laiton
Kunstgewerbeschule
Burg Giebichenstein,
Halle, atelier de métal
Hauteur: 13,5 cm

After training at the Handwerkerschule (Crafts School) in Halle and studying at the Bauhaus in Weimar, Lili Schultz became director of the enamel workshop at the Kunstgewerbeschule Burg Giebichenstein in Halle in 1925. Under her direction, the hitherto strongly decorative and expressionistic style of the enamel workshop evolved into a more sober and functional form of expression. An example of this development is the tea caddy illustrated, several versions of which were produced by the enamel workshop in the late 20s on the basis of her design.

Nach einer Ausbildung an der Handwerkerschule in Halle und einem Studienaufenthalt am Bauhaus Weimar übernahm Lili Schultz 1925 die Leitung der Emailwerkstatt an der Kunstgewerbeschule Burg Giebichenstein in Halle. Unter ihrer Führung wandelte sich der vorher stark von dekorativen und expressionistischen Elementen geprägte Stil der Emailwerkstatt zu einer mehr sachlichen und funktionsorientierten Ausdrucksweise. Stellvertretend für diese Entwicklung steht die abgebildete Teebüchse, die nach ihrem Entwurf gegen Ende der 20er Jahre von der Emailwerkstatt in mehreren Variationen ausgeführt wurde.

Lili Schultz prend en 1925 la direction de l'atelier d'émail de la Kunstgewerbeschule Burg Giebichenstein après avoir été formée à la Handwerkschule de Halle et fait un séjour au Bauhaus de Weimar. Sous sa direction, le style de l'atelier jusque-là fortement imprégné d'éléments décoratifs et expressionnistes évolue peu à peu en une forme d'expression plus sobre et fonctionnelle. La boîte à thé reproduite ici est une illustration de cette évolution; créée à la fin des années vingt, cette boîte sera fabriquée en plusieurs versions par l'atelier d'émail.

Karl Müller,
c. 1927/30

Cake stand
Silver, glass
Kunstgewerbeschule
Burg Giebichenstein,
Halle, metal workshop
Diameter: 32.2 cm

Tortenplatte
Silber, Glas
Kunstgewerbeschule
Burg Giebichenstein,
Halle, Metallwerkstatt
Durchmesser: 32,2 cm

Plat à gâteau
Argent et verre
Kunstgewerbeschule
Burg Giebichenstein,
Halle, atelier de métal
Diamètre: 32,2 cm

Hayno Focken,
c. 1935

Fruit bowl
Brass
Metal workshop
Hayno Focken, Lahr
Width: 40 cm

Obstschale
Messing
Metallwerkstatt
Hayno Focken, Lahr
Breite: 40 cm

Coupe à fruits
en laiton
Atelier de métal de
Hayno Focken, Lahr
Largeur: 40 cm

Lili Schultz, c. 1928

Tea caddy
Tombac, polychrome
champlevé enamel
Kunstgewerbeschule
Burg Giebichenstein,
Halle
Height: 10.4 cm

Teebüchse
Tombak, polychromer
Grubenschmelz
Kunstgewerbeschule
Burg Giebichenstein,
Halle
Höhe: 10,4 cm

Boîte à thé
en tombac et
émail polychrome
Kunstgewerbeschule
Burg Giebichenstein,
Halle
Hauteur: 10,4 cm

Karl Müller, c. 1932

Spoon, fork
Silver
Kunstgewerbeschule
Burg Giebichenstein,
Halle, metal workshop
Length: 22.1 cm
(spoon)

Löffel, Gabel
Silber
Kunstgewerbeschule
Burg Giebichenstein,
Halle, Metallwerkstatt
Länge: 22,1 cm
(Löffel)

Cuillère et fourchette
en argent
Kunstgewerbeschule
Burg Giebichenstein,
Halle, atelier de métal
Longueur: 22,1 cm
(cuillère)

The metalwork of goldsmith and silver-smith Wolfgang Tümpel clearly indicates the influences of the two leading pre-war art schools. In 1922, Tümpel began an apprenticeship as a silversmith at the Bauhaus in Weimar, which he completed in Karl Müller's metal workshop at the Kunstgewerbeschule Burg Giebichenstein in Halle. In addition to silversmith work, he·also designed lamps, some of which were produced in small quantities in the metal workshop. The teamaker based on stereometric forms was produced in his first own »Werkstatt für Gefäße – Schmuck – Beleuchtung« (workshop for dishes, jewellery, lamps) which he founded in Halle in 1927.

In den Metallarbeiten des Gold- und Sil-berschmieds Wolfgang Tümpel werden die Einflüsse der beiden bedeutendsten Kunstschulen der Vorkriegszeit sichtbar. 1922 begann Tümpel eine Lehre als Sil-berschmied am Weimarer Bauhaus, die er 1925 in der Metallwerkstatt Karl Müllers an der Kunstgewerbeschule Burg Giebichenstein in Halle abschloß. Neben der reinen Silberschmiedearbeit beschäf-tigte er sich hier auch mit dem Entwurf von Beleuchtungskörpern, von denen eini-ge in der Metallwerkstatt in Kleinserien produziert wurden. Die aus stereometri-schen Formen zusammengesetzte Teema-schine entstand in seiner ersten eigenen »Werkstatt für Gefäße – Schmuck – Be-leuchtung«, die er 1927 in Halle gründete.

Les travaux en or et en argent de l'or-fèvre Wolfgang Tümpel sont très nette-ment influencés par les deux grandes éco-les d'art d'avant-guerre. En 1922, Tüm-pel commence un apprentissage d'or-fèvre au Bauhaus de Weimar qu'il achève-ra en 1925 à l'atelier de métal de la Kunstgewerbeschule Burg Giebichenstein de Halle, sous la direction de Karl Müller. Outre son travail d'orfèvre, il se met à créer des appareils d'éclairage dont cer-tains sont produits en petite série à l'ate-lier. La machine à thé aux formes stéréo-métriques est née dans son premier ate-lier «Werkstatt für Gefäße- Schmuck- Be-leuchtung» (atelier d'assiettes, de joaille-rie et de luminaires) ouvert en 1927 à Halle.

Wolfgang Tümpel, 1927

Teamaker
Nickelled brass, wood
Metal workshop
Wolfgang Tümpel,
Halle
Height: 28.3 cm

Teemaschine
Messing, vernickelt,
Holz
Metallwerkstatt
Wolfgang Tümpel,
Halle
Höhe: 28,3 cm

Machine à thé
en laiton nickelé
et bois
Atelier de métal
Wolfgang Tümpel,
Halle
Hauteur : 28,3 cm

Stand selling products from the metal workshop of the Burg Giebichenstein School of Applied Art, Halle (c. 1927)

Verkaufsstand mit Erzeugnissen der Metallwerkstatt der Kunstgewerbeschule Burg Giebichenstein, Halle (ca. 1927)

Stand de vente des réalisations de l'atelier de métal de l'école Burg Giebichenstein, Halle vers 1927

Wolfgang Tümpel, c. 1928

Prototype teamaker

Erstausformung der Teemaschine

Première ébauche de la machine à thé

119

Wolfgang Tümpel, 1926/27

Table lamp
Nickelled brass, opalescent glass
Kunstgewerbeschule Burg Giebichenstein, Halle, metal workshop
Height: 30 cm

Tischlampe
Messing, vernickelt, Opalglas
Kunstgewerbeschule Burg Giebichenstein, Halle, Metallwerkstatt
Höhe: 30 cm

Lampe de table
en laiton nickelé et verre opalisé
Kunstgewerbeschule Burg Giebichenstein, Halle, atelier de métal
Hauteur: 30 cm

1919/20, a ceramics workshop was established at the Handwerkerschule (Crafts School) in Halle, the forerunner of the Kunstgewerbeschule Burg Giebichenstein, under the artistic direction of sculptor Gustav Weidanz. After a successful pottery apprenticeship at the Bauhaus in Weimar, Marguerite Friedlaender became director of the workshop in 1925 and brought it international renown. Her husband, Franz Rudolf Wildenhain, continued her work at the new workshop, where he became director in 1930, being replaced in 1934 by Hubert Griemert.

1919/20 wurde an der Handwerkerschule der Stadt Halle, der Vorgängerinstitution der späteren Kunstgewerbeschule Burg Giebichenstein, unter der künstlerischen Leitung des Bildhauers Gustav Weidanz eine Keramikwerkstatt eingerichtet. Nach einer erfolgreich abgeschlossenen Töpferlehre am Bauhaus Weimar übernahm Marguerite Friedlaender 1925 die Leitung der Werkstatt und brachte diese zu internationaler Bedeutung. Franz Rudolf Wildenhain, Ehemann von Marguerite Friedlaender, führte dann ab 1930 ihre Arbeit als neuer Leiter der Werkstatt fort, bevor 1934 schließlich Hubert Griemert die Leitung übernahm.

En 1919/20, la Handwerkerschule (école d'artisanat) de Halle, prédécesseur de la Kunstgewerbeschule Burg Giebichenstein, ouvre un atelier de céramique sous la direction du sculpteur Gustav Weidanz. Après un apprentissage achevé avec succès au Bauhaus de Weimar, Marguerite Friedlaender prend la direction du nouvel atelier en 1925 qui grâce à elle acquerra bientôt une renommée internationale. Franz Rudolf Wildenhain, mari de Marguerite Friedlaender, continue le travail de sa femme à la direction de l'atelier à partir de 1930 avant que Hubert Griemert n'en prenne la direction en 1934.

Gustav Weidanz, 1922

Teapot	**Teekanne**	**Théière**
Stoneware,	Steinzeug,	en grès et vernis
dark blue glaze	dunkelblaue Glasur	bleu foncé
Kunstgewerbeschule	Kunstgewerbeschule	Kunstgewerbeschule
Burg Giebichenstein,	Burg Giebichenstein,	Burg Giebichenstein,
Halle,	Halle,	Halle,
ceramics workshop	Keramikwerkstatt	atelier de céramique
Height: 13 cm	Höhe: 13 cm	Hauteur: 13 cm

**Franz Rudolf
Wildenhain, c. 1930**

Plant pot	**Übertopf**	**Cache-pot**
Stoneware, brown underglaze painting Kunstgewerbeschule Burg Giebichenstein, Halle, ceramics workshop Height: 17 cm	Steinzeug, braune Unterglasurbemalung Kunstgewerbeschule Burg Giebichenstein, Halle, Keramikwerkstatt Höhe: 17 cm	en grès et peinture noire sous vernis Kunstgewerbeschule Burg Giebichenstein, Halle, atelier de céramique Hauteur: 17 cm

**Marguerite
Friedlaender, 1926/27**

Dish with lid	**Deckeldose**	**Boîte à couvercle**
Stoneware, black matt glaze Kunstgewerbeschule Burg Giebichenstein, Halle, ceramics workshop Height: 21.5 cm	Steinzeug, schwarze Mattglasur Kunstgewerbeschule Burg Giebichenstein, Halle, Keramikwerkstatt Höhe: 21,5 cm	en grès et vernis mat noir Kunstgewerbeschule Burg Giebichenstein, Halle, atelier de céramique Hauteur: 21,5 cm

**Hubert Griemert,
c. 1935**

Dish with lid	**Deckeldose**	**Boîte à couvercle**
Stoneware, grey glaze Kunstgewerbeschule Burg Giebichenstein, Halle, ceramics workshop Height: 18.5 cm	Steinzeug, graue Über-laufglasur Kunstgewerbeschule Burg Giebichenstein, Halle, Keramikwerkstatt Höhe: 18,5 cm	en grès et vernis gris Kunstgewerbeschule Burg Giebichenstein, Halle, atelier de céramique Hauteur: 18,5 cm

The cooperation with the KPM state porcelain factory in Berlin which began in 1929 led to the establishment of a separate porcelain workshop at the Kunstgewerbeschule Burg Giebichenstein in Halle under the artistic direction of Marguerite Friedlaender. In 1930, she developed the »Hallesche Form« tea and coffee set for KPM, which became a major commercial success, particularly with the »gold rings« (1931) decor by Trude Petri. In contrast, Gerhard Marcks, »Tiergarten« tea set designed in 1932/37 for KPM was not produced.

Aus der 1929 vereinbarten Zusammenarbeit mit der Staatlichen Porzellanmanufaktur Berlin (KPM) resultierte die Einrichtung einer separaten Porzellanwerkstatt an der Kunstgewerbeschule Burg Giebichenstein in Halle unter der künstlerischen Leitung von Marguerite Friedlaender. 1930 entwickelte sie hier für die KPM das Tee- und Kaffeeservice »Hallesche Form«, das vor allem mit dem Werksdekor »Goldringe« (1931) von Trude Petri zu einem großen Verkaufserfolg wurde. Das 1932/37 von Gerhard Marcks für die KPM entworfene Teeservice »Tiergarten« ging dagegen nicht in Serie.

Suite à la décision de collaborer avec la manufacture nationale de porcelaine de Berlin (Staatliche Porzellanmanufaktur Berlin = KPM), un atelier de porcelaine est créé à la Kunstgewerbeschule Burg Giebichenstein de Halle sous la direction de Marguerite Friedlaender. En 1930 elle crée pour le KPM le service à café et à thé «Hallesche Form», un vrai succès commercial, en partie aussi le mérite de Trude Petri avec son décor «Anneaux d'or» (1931). En revanche le service à thé «Tiergarten» de Gerhard Marcks créé en 1932/37 pour le KPM ne sera pas fabriqué en série.

122

Marguerite Friedlaender, 1930/31

»Hallesche Form« tea set
Porcelain, »gold ring« decor
KPM state porcelain factory, Berlin, and Kunstgewerbeschule Burg Giebichenstein, Halle, porcelain and metal workshop
Height: 12 cm (teapot)

Teeservice »Hallesche Form«
Porzellan, Dekor »Goldringe«
Staatliche Porzellanmanufaktur Berlin (KPM) und Kunstgewerbeschule Burg Giebichenstein, Halle, Porzellan- und Metallwerkstatt
Höhe: 12 cm (Teekanne)

Service à thé «Hallesche Form»
en porcelaine et décor «anneaux d'or»
Manufacture nationale de porcelaine de Berlin (KPM) et Kunstgewerbeschule Burg Giebichenstein, Halle, atelier de céramique et de métal
Hauteur: 12 cm (théière)

**Marguerite
Friedlaender, 1930**

**Teapot
»Hallesche Form«**
Celadon-porcelain
KPM state porcelain
factory, Berlin
Height: 12 cm

**Teekanne
»Hallesche Form«**
Seladonporzellan
Staatliche Porzellanma-
nufaktur Berlin (KPM)
Höhe: 12 cm

**Théière
«Hallesche Form»**
En porcelaine céladon
Manufacture nationa-
le de porcelaine de
Berlin (KPM)
Hauteur: 12 cm

**Gerhard Marcks,
1932**

**Teapot
»Tiergarten«**
Porcelain, copper
Kunstgewerbeschule
Burg Giebichenstein,
Halle, porcelain and
metal workshop
Height: 12.3 cm

**Teekanne
»Tiergarten«**
Porzellan, Kupfer
Kunstgewerbeschule
Burg Giebichenstein,
Halle, Porzellan- und
Metallwerkstatt
Höhe: 12,3 cm

**Théière
«Tiergarten»**
en porcelaine et cuivre
Kunstgewerbeschule
Burg Giebichenstein,
Halle, atelier de céra-
mique et de métal
Hauteur: 12,3 cm

**Marguerite
Friedlaender, 1930**

**Tea-extract pot
»Hallesche Form«**
Porcelain, brown un-
derglaze painting,
partly gilded
KPM state porcelain
factory, Berlin
Height: 9 cm

**Tee-Extraktkanne
«Hallesche Form»**
Porzellan, braune Un-
terglasurmalerei, teil-
weise vergoldet
Staatliche Porzellanma-
nufaktur Berlin (KPM)
Höhe: 9 cm

**Petit pot pour ex-
trait de thé »Halle-
sche Form«**
en porcelaine et pein-
ture brune sous vernis,
en partie doré
Manufacture nationa-
le de porcelaine de
Berlin (KPM)
Hauteur: 9 cm

International Style

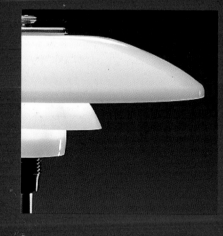

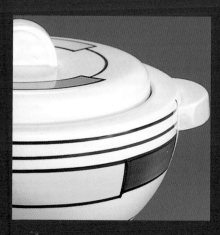

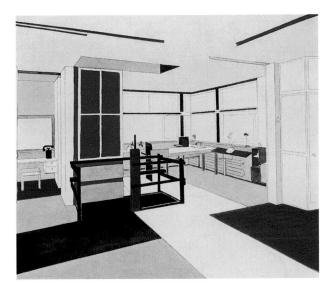

Gerrit Thomas Rietveld, 1924

Isometric drawing of the interior of the Rietveld-Schroeder House in Utrecht

Isometrische Darstellung der Einrichtung des »Rietveld-Schröder«-Hauses, Utrecht

Isométrie de la maison «Rietveld-Schröder» à Utrecht

International Style

In the period between the two great wars, the industrialised world was swept by radical political, social, technical and economic change. Increasing mechanisation, and the rationalisation of life it involved, led to structural changes which transformed the very face of the modern world. New systems of transportation, marketing and communications brought a hitherto unparalleled international dimension to industry, technology and trade. These profound changes also affected the design of interior fittings and everyday appliances. The new role of the designer evolved from the world of the craftsman, seeking new forms based on functional concepts of production technology. Although the craftsman continued to exist alongside the industrial designer, he too began to seek increasingly functional design forms, many of which also influenced industrial design. The regionally diverse design experiments which emerged in the wake of the reform movement around the turn of the century concentrated in the late 20s and early 30s to become an international style based on the use of elementary structural principles.

Der Internationale Stil

Der Zeitraum zwischen den beiden Weltkriegen wurde geprägt durch den radikalen politischen, sozialen, technischen und ökonomischen Wandel innerhalb der industrialisierten Gesellschaft. Die zunehmende Technisierung und die damit verbundene Rationalisierung des Lebens veränderte das Erscheinungsbild und die Strukturen der modernen Welt. Durch die Entwicklung neuer Verkehrs-, Vertriebs- und Kommunikationssysteme kam es zu einer internationalen Vernetzung von Industrie, Technik und Handel. Diese massiven Veränderungen wirkten sich auch auf die Gestaltung von Inneneinrichtungen und Gebrauchsgeräten aus. Aus dem Beruf des Entwerfers für Kunstgewerbe entwickelte sich das Arbeitsfeld des Designers, der, ausgehend von funktionalen und produktionstechnischen Erwägungen, neue Formen für den alltäglichen Gebrauch entwarf. Neben dem Industriedesigner existierte aber weiterhin der Beruf des Kunsthandwerkers, der in seinen Arbeiten nun vermehrt nach sachlichen, funktionsorientierten Gestaltungsmöglichkeiten suchte, die wiederum in vielen Fällen auf die industrielle Formfindung vorbildlich wirkten. Die vor dem Ersten Weltkrieg – ausgehend von der Reformbewegung um die Jahrhundertwende – regional noch recht unterschiedlichen Gestaltungsexperimente verdichteten sich in den späten 20er und frühen 30er Jahren zu einem internationalen Stil, dessen Grundlage die gemeinsame Verwendung elementarer Konstruktionsprinzipien bildete.

Le Style international

La période de l'entre-deux-guerres fut marquée par des transformations profondes sur le plan politique, social, technologique et économique dans les sociétés industrialisées. Le rôle croissant de la technique et son corollaire, la rationalisation de la vie, changea l'image et les structures du monde moderne. Le développement de nouveaux systèmes de transport, de commercialisation et de communication entraîna la création d'un réseau international de l'industrie, de la technologie et du commerce. Ces bouleversements ne restèrent pas sans conséquence sur la conception de l'aménagement d'intérieur et des objets à usage courant. C'est à partir du métier de concepteur travaillant dans les arts décoratifs que s'était développé le champ d'activité du designer : celui-ci créait de nouvelles formes pour l'usage de la vie courante en tenant compte de considérations fonctionnelles et de questions techniques concernant la production. Le métier d'artisan d'art continuait d'exister : ce dernier recherchait de plus en plus des formes fonctionnelles et sobres qui, à leur tour, influençaient souvent la création dans l'industrie. Les expérimentations dans ce domaine, qui, avant la première guerre mondiale – avec l'apparition du mouvement de réforme vers 1900 – étaient restées disparates, commencèrent à converger dans les années vingt et trente pour former un style international, basé essentiellement sur l'emploi commun de principes de construction élémentaires.

*Eva Stricker-Zeisel,
1928/29*

Teaset
*Earthenware,
polychrome painted
Majolika-Fabrik
Schramberg
Height: 13.5 cm
(teapot)*

Teeservice
*Steingut, polychrome
Bemalung
Majolika-Fabrik
Schramberg
Höhe: 13,5 cm
(Teekanne)*

Service à thé
*en grès, peinture
polychrome
Majolika-Fabrik
Schramberg
Hauteur: 13,5 cm*

The term International Style was coined by Henry-Russell Hitchcock and Philip Johnson in their 1932 publication »The International Style: Architecture since 1922«. As the title suggests, the architecture of the modern avantgarde between the two wars became the umbrella form of a new style combining the principles of Dutch De Stijl, Russian Constructivism and German Bauhaus on the basis of analytical principles and rational considerations.

The Dutch De Stijl movement, which took its name from Theo van Doesburg's art periodical »De Stijl« (1917-1931), became the leading proponent of Constructivist principles in art, architecture and design. Its leading representatives included painter and architect van Doesburg, painter Piet Mondrian, furniture designer and architect Gerrit Thomas Rietveld and architect and designer Jacobus Johannes Pieter Oud. The De Stijl artists succeeded in extending their art, based on elementary structures and absolute abstraction, to include the fields of architecture and applied art. In the field of design, Rietveld's furniture, from 1917 onwards, particularly his famous »Red/Blue« chair (1917/23), came to epitomise a collective design approach in quest of uniform basic forms.

Der Begriff des »Internationalen Stils« wurde 1932 durch das von Henry-Russell Hitchcock und Philip Johnson veröffentlichte Buch »The International Style: Architecture since 1922« eingeführt. Die Architektur der modernen Avantgarde zwischen den beiden Weltkriegen wurde, wie bereits der Titel des Buches ausdrückt, zur übergeordneten Orientierungsform eines neuen Stils, der die von De Stijl in Holland, dem russischen Konstruktivismus und dem Bauhaus in Deutschland geschaffenen Grundlagen einer auf analytischen Prinzipien und rationalen Überlegungen basierenden Kunst in sich vereinte.

Die holländische De Stijl-Bewegung, deren Name aus der zwischen 1917 und 1931 von Theo van Doesburg herausgegebenen Kunstzeitschrift »De Stijl« hervorgegangen war, wurde zum Vorreiter der konstruktivistischen Prinzipien in Kunst, Architektur und Design. Zu ihren wichtigsten Vertretern zählten neben dem Maler und Architekten van Doesburg der Maler Piet Mondrian, der Möbeldesigner und Architekt Gerrit Thomas Rietveld und der Architekt und Designer Jacobus Johannes Pieter Oud. Den Künstlern des De Stijl gelang es, ihre auf der Konstruktion nach Elementargesetzen und absoluter Abstraktion beruhende Kunst auch auf die Gebiete der Architektur und der angewandten Kunst auszudehnen. Im Bereich Design waren die ab 1917 von Rietveld entworfenen Möbel, allen voran der berühmte »Rot-Blau«-Stuhl (1917/23), die wesentlichen Träger einer kollektiven, nach einheitlichen Grundformen suchenden Gestaltungsweise.

La notion de «Style international» fut introduite en 1932 par le livre de Henry-Russell Hitchcock et de Philip Johnson «The International Style : Architecture since 1922». L'architecture avant-gardiste de l'entre-deux-guerres devint, ainsi que le titre du livre le suggère, la forme supérieure et directive d'un nouveau style, synthèse de divers éléments d'un art se basant sur des principes analytiques et des considérations rationnelles. Tous ces éléments avaient été élaborés par le mouvement De Stijl en Hollande, le constructivisme russe et le Bauhaus allemand.

Le mouvement De Stijl qui tire son nom de la revue «De Stijl», publiée par Theo van Doesburg entre 1917 et 1931, devint le précurseur des principes constructivistes dans l'art, l'architecture et le design. Ses représentants les plus importants étaient, outre le peintre et architecte van Doesburg, le peintre Piet Mondrian, l'architecte et concepteur de meubles Gerrit Thomas Rietveld et l'architecte et designer Jacobus Johannes Pieter Oud. Les artistes du mouvement De Stijl réussirent à étendre leur art, construit selon des lois élémentaires et une abstraction absolue, au domaine de l'architecture et des arts appliqués. En ce qui concerne la stylique, les meubles de Rietveld construits à partir de 1917 – surtout la fameuse chaise «Rouge-Bleu» de 1917/1923 – étaient les réalisations les plus représentatives d'un mode de création collectif, à la recherche de formes fondamentales uniques.

Karl Raichle, c. 1930

Candle holder
Pewter
Pewterware
manufacturers
K. & E. Raichle, Urach
Height: 23.5 cm

Kerzenleuchter
Zinn
Zinnschmiede
K. & E. Raichle, Urach
Höhe: 23,5 cm

Bougeoir
en étain
Orfèvre
K. & E. Raichle, Urach
Hauteur: 23,5 cm

Russian Constructivism began with the Suprematism propagated by Kasimir Malevich from 1913 onwards. Initially restricted to painting, it sought the abstraction of all artistic concepts by means of a few elementary forms and colours (especially black, red and white). In the course of the Revolution with its utopian concepts of collectivism, the Russian avantgarde was quick to place its art at the service of the new society. The abstraction of design elements previously limited to the fine arts was now applied to all fields of daily life, including the architecture and applied arts of Eastern Europe.

Alongside the International Style, a new direction was taking hold, particularly in France and America, which was to take its name from the great 1925 exhibition in Paris, the »Exposition Internationale des Arts Décoratifs et Industries Modernes«. A typical feature of Art Deco was its combination of stereometric cubist forms with geometric decors. In its purest form, Art Deco was a luxury art, using such sumptuously expensive materials as tropical woods, bronze and ivory and, being produced artisanally, was affordable only to a small circle of wealthy buyers. Moreover, Art Deco was a purely decorative art which, in spite of its use of contemporary forms and decors suggesting modernity, did not actually contribute towards a progressive development of design.

Der russische Konstruktivismus hatte seinen Ausgangspunkt im von Kazimir Malevich ab 1913 propagierten Suprematismus. Zunächst auf die Malerei beschränkt stellte er alle Gedanken der Kunst durch wenige elementare Formen und Farben (vor allem Schwarz, Rot und Weiß) stark abstrahiert dar. Im Zuge der Revolution und der in diesem Zusammenhang aufgekommenen sozialistischen Utopien des Zusammenlebens setzte sich auch die russische Avantgarde-Kunst für den Dienst in der neuen Gesellschaft ein. Die zunächst auf die bildende Kunst beschränkte Abstraktion der Gestaltungselemente wurde nun auch auf die Bereiche des alltäglichen Lebens, der Architektur und der angewandten Kunst Osteuropas übertragen.

Parallel zum Internationalen Stil existierte das Art Déco, das in Frankreich und Amerika seine stärkste Ausprägung erfuhr und mit der Ausstellung »Exposition Internationale des Arts Décoratifs et Industries Modernes« 1925 in Paris, seinen Höhepunkt erreichte. Typisch für das Art Déco war die Verbindung stereometrischer Formen des Kubismus mit geometrischen Dekoren. Art Déco in seiner reinsten Ausführung war eine Luxuskunst, die durch die Verwendung kostspieliger Materialien wie z.B. Tropenhölzern, Bronze oder Elfenbein sowie die rein kunsthandwerkliche Ausführung nur für einen kleinen Kreis von potenten Käufern erschwinglich war. Zudem war das Art Déco eine reine Dekorationskunst, die zwar durch die Verwendung zeitgemäßer Formen und Dekore den Anspruch auf Modernität erhob, aber nicht zu einer Weiterentwicklung des Designs führte.

L'origine du constructivisme russe se trouvait dans le suprématisme propagé par Kazimir Malevitch à partir de 1913. Il le limita d'abord à la peinture où il présenta toutes les préoccupations de l'art juste par quelques formes élémentaires et des couleurs primaires (surtout le noir, le rouge et le blanc) très abstraites. Dans la foulée de la révolution d'octobre et des utopies socialistes, l'art d'avant-garde russe se mit lui aussi au service de la nouvelle société. L'abstraction des formes d'abord limitée aux arts plastiques passa ensuite dans le domaine de la vie courante, de l'architecture et des arts appliqués de l'Europe de l'Est.

En même temps que le Style international, l'Art déco se répandait aussi en France et aux Etats-Unis où il laissa son empreinte et atteignit son apogée avec l'Exposition internationale des Arts décoratifs et industries modernes de Paris en 1925. Ce style se distinguait par l'association des formes stéréométriques du cubisme et des décors géométriques. Dans sa forme la plus pure, l'Art déco était un art de luxe réalisé dans des matériaux coûteux comme les bois tropicaux, le bronze et l'ivoire et d'une qualité artisanale parfaite, accessible seulement à un petit cercle d'élus fortunés. De plus l'Art déco était un art de décoration pur qui s'il prétendit à la modernité ne joua pas pour autant de rôle dans l'évolution du design.

In 1917/18, the Dutch cabinetmaker and architect Gerrit Thomas Rietveld developed the prototype of the »Red/Blue« chair which was to establish his reputation as a De Stijl artist. Rietveld applied the same design principle to his »Militar« chair in 1923. The typical De Stijl colours highlight the sculptural effects of Rietveld's furniture, while emphasising their structural design.

1917/18 entwickelte der holländische Möbeltischler und Architekt Gerrit Thomas Rietveld aus einfachen Vierkanthölzern und rechtwinkligen Holzplatten den Prototyp seines sogenannten »Rot-Blau«-Stuhls, der seinen Ruf als De Stijl-Künstler begründete. Das gleiche Gestaltungsprinzip verwendete Rietveld auch bei dem »Militar«-Stuhl aus dem Jahr 1923. Die polychrome Lackierung in den typischen De Stijl-Farben unterstützt die plastische Wirkung der Möbel Rietvelds und betont gleichzeitig ihren konstruktiven Aufbau.

En 1917/18, l'architecte menuisier hollandais Gerrit Thomas Rietveld élabore le prototype de sa fameuse chaise «Rouge-bleu» à partir de simples morceaux quadrangulaires et de plaques en bois carrées. Ce modèle lui vaudra sa réputation d'artiste De Stijl. Rietveld reprend le même principe de construction pour sa chaise «Militar» datant de 1923. La laque polychrome dans les tons typiques du De Stijl accentue l'effet plastique des meubles de Rietveld et souligne en même temps leur structure constructive.

**Gerrit Thomas
Rietveld, 1917/23**

»Red/Blue« chair
Beech, painted
Cabinetmaker G. A.
van de Groenekan,
Utrecht
Height: 88 cm

»Rot-Blau«-Stuhl
Buche, polychrom
lackiert
Möbeltischler G.A.
van de Groenekan,
Utrecht
Höhe: 88 cm

**Chaise
«Rouge-bleu»**
Hêtre et laque
polychrome
Menuisier G. A. van
de Groenekan, Utrecht
Hauteur: 88 cm

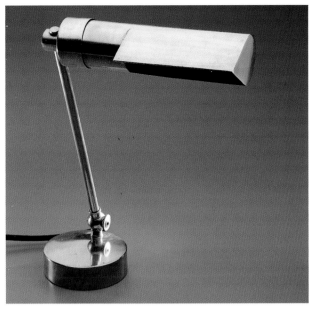

Jacobus Johannes
Pieter Oud, 1928

»Giso 405«
table lamp
Nickelled copper
Metalware manufac-
turers Gispen, Rotter-
dam & Amsterdam
Height: 30 cm

Tischlampe
»Giso 405«
Kupfer, vernickelt
Metallwarenfabrik
Gispen, Rotterdam &
Amsterdam
Höhe: 30 cm

Lampe de table
«Giso 405»
Cuivre nickelé
Usine d'articles métalli-
ques Gispen, Rotter-
dam & Amsterdam
Hauteur: 30 cm

Gerrit Thomas
Rietveld, 1923

»Militar« chair
Oak, bolted connec-
tions, black/white
lacquer
Cabinetmakers G.A.
van de Groenekan,
Utrecht
Height: 90 cm

»Militar«-Stuhl
Eiche, verschraubt,
schwarz-weiße
Lackierung
Möbeltischler G.A.
van de Groenekan,
Utrecht
Höhe: 90 cm

Chaise «Militar»
en chêne vissé,
laqué noir et blanc
Menuisier G. A. van
de Groenekan, Utrecht
Hauteur: 90 cm

Dining room with furniture designed by Alvar Aalto, 1937/38, displayed by Bowman Bros., London

Speisezimmer mit Möbeln nach Entwurf von Alvar Aalto, 1937/38 ausgestellt im Möbelhaus Bowman Bros., London

Salle à manger garnie de meubles créés par Alvar Aalto, exposés en 1937/38 dans le magasin d'ameublement Bowman Bros. à Londres.

In 1929, the Finnish architect Alvar Aalto began designing furniture in moulded plywood. His experiments with laminated beechwood – which he soon began using for the framework structure of his furniture – allowed him to translate the modern design principles of tubular steel furniture to the natural material, wood. His armchair model no. 41, which became famous under the name »Paimio«, was designed by Aalto in 1931/32. As the Paimio Sanatorium, built to his design, had already been completed in 1929, this armchair was clearly not included in the initial furnishings of the house.

Alvar Aalto, 1931/32

»Paimio« armchair, model no. 41
Plywood, birch, solid, layered and moulded
Oy Huonekalu-ja Rakennustyötehdas AB, Turku, Finland
Height: 67 cm

Sessel »Paimio«, Modell-Nr. 41
Sperrholz, Birke, massiv, geschichtet und geformt
Oy Huonekalu-ja Rakennustyötehdas AB, Turku, Finnland
Höhe: 67 cm

Fauteuil «Paimio», modèle 41
en contreplaqué, bouleau massif, lamellé et cintré
Oy Huonekalu-ja Rakennnustyötehdas AB, Turku, Finlande
Hauteur: 67 cm

Ab 1929 beschäftigte sich der finnische Architekt Alvar Aalto mit dem Entwurf von Möbeln aus geformtem Sperrholz. Seine Experimente mit schichtverleimtem Birkenholz – das er schon bald für die Rahmenkonstruktionen seiner Möbel benutzte – ermöglichten ihm, die modernen Gestaltungsprinzipien von Stahlrohrmöbeln auf den natürlichen Werkstoff Holz zu übertragen. Den Sessel mit der Modellnummer 41, der unter der Bezeichnung »Paimio«-Sessel Berühmtheit erlangte, entwarf Aalto erst 1931/32. Da das nach seinen Plänen erbaute Sanatorium Paimio aber bereits 1929 fertiggestellt war, kann dieser Sesseltyp nicht zu der Grundausstattung des Hauses gehört haben.

L'architecte finlandais Alvar Aalto commence à créer des meubles en contreplaqué cintré en 1929. Ses expérimentations sur du bouleau lamellé et collé dont il va bientôt se servir pour faire les cadres de ses meubles lui permettent de transposer les principes modernes de conception de meubles en tubes d'acier sur le bois, matériau naturel. Le modèle Nr. 41, fauteuil devenu célèbre sous le nom de «Paimio», n'a été créé qu'en 1931/32. Etant donné que le sanatorium Paimio construit d'après ses plans est déjà prêt en 1929, il est impossible que ce fauteuil ait fait partie de l'ameublement de base de l'établissement.

Poul Henningsen, c. 1927

PH table lamp
Nickelled brass, bakelite, opalescent glass, matt glass
Louis Poulsen, Copenhagen
Height: 45 cm

PH-Tischleuchte
Messing, vernickelt, Bakelit, Opal- und Mattglas
Louis Poulsen, Kopenhagen
Höhe: 45 cm

Lampe de table PH
en laiton nickelé, bakélite, verre mat opalisé.
Louis Poulsen, Copenhague
Hauteur: 45 cm

Alvar Aalto, 1935/36

Tea trolley
Plywood, birch, solid, laminated and moulded
Oy Huonekalu-ja Rakennustyötehdas AB, Turku, Finland
Width: 90 cm

Teewagen
Sperrholz, Birke, massiv, geschichtet und geformt
Oy Huonekalu-ja Rakennustyötehdas AB, Turku, Finnland
Breite: 90 cm

Table à thé
en contreplaqué, bouleau massif, lamellé et cintré
Oy Huonekalu-ja Rakennustyötehdas AB, Turku, Finlande
Largeur: 90 cm

The furniture by Serge Chermayeff and Eckart Muthesius shows typical examples of International Style. Chermayeff, who was born in Russia, established a reputation towards the end of the 20s as an interior designer for leading London furnishing stores. His work combined the influences of French Art Deco with the Constructivist elements of functionalist modernism. Muthesius realised a similar concept in 1930 with his furniture designs for the palace of the Indian Maharaja of Indore, built to his plans.

Die Möbel von Serge Chermayeff und Eckart Muthesius sind typische Vertreter des Internationalen Stils. Chermayeff, gebürtiger Russe, machte sich gegen Ende der 20er Jahre einen Namen als Entwerfer von Inneneinrichtungen für führende Londoner Einrichtungshäuser. Seine Arbeiten verbanden Einflüsse des französischen Art Déco mit konstruktivistischen Elementen der funktionalen Moderne. Ein ähnliches Konzept verwirklichte Muthesius 1930 in den Möbelentwürfen für den nach seinen Plänen erbauten Palast des indischen Maharadschas von Indore.

Les meubles de Serge Chermayeff et d'Eckart Muthesius sont des exemples typiques du Style international. Russe de naissance, Chermayeff se fait un nom en tant que créateur d'intérieurs pour de grands magasins d'ameublement londoniens à la fin des années vingt. Ses réalisations associent l'influence de l'Art Déco français avec des éléments constructivistes du style moderne fonctionnel. En 1930, Muthesius utilise un concept similaire pour créer les meubles du palais du maharajah d'Indore construit d'après ses plans.

Serge Chermayeff,
1929/30

Sideboard	**Anrichte**	**Bahut**
Mahogany, padouk, sanarah	Mahagoni, Padouk, Sanarah	Mahagoni, padouk et sanarah
Waring & Gillow Ltd., London	Warring & Gillow Ltd., London	Warring & Gillow Ltd., Londres
Width: 138 cm	Breite: 138 cm	Largeur: 138 cm

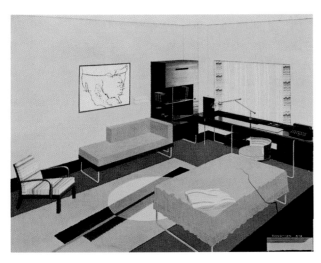

**Serge Chermayeff,
1928/29**

Design for a study

*Entwurf für ein
Arbeitszimmer*

Ebauche d'un
bureau de travail

**Eckart Muthesius,
1930/33**

**Bureau for the palace of the Maharaja
of Indore**
Black painted maple,
ivory, glass
Height: 120 cm

**Sekretär für den
Palast des Maharadschas von Indore**
Ahorn, schwarz lakkiert, Elfenbein, Glas
Höhe: 120 cm

**Secrétaire pour le
palais du maharajah
d'Indore**
Erable laqué noir,
ivoire et verre
Hauteur: 120 cm

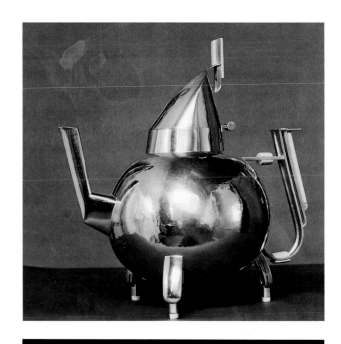

**Theodor Wende,
1927**

Teapot
*Silver, ivory
Badische Kunstgewer-
beschule Pforzheim,
silversmith workshop
Height: 27 cm*

Teekanne
*Silber, Elfenbein
Badische Kunstgewer-
beschule Pforzheim,
Silberschmiede-
werkstatt
Höhe: 27 cm*

Théière
*en argent et ivoire
Badische Kunstgewer-
beschule Pforzheim,
atelier d'orfèvrerie
Hauteur: 27 cm*

134

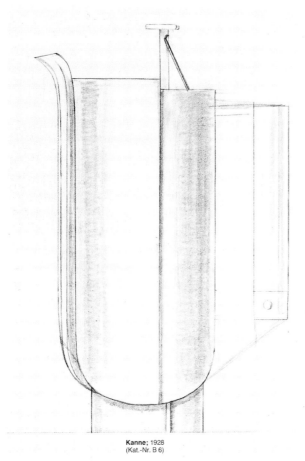

Kanne; 1928
(Kat.-Nr. B 6)

**Theodor Wende,
1928**

Design for the coffee-
pot

Entwurfszeichnung für
die Kaffeekanne

Dessin d'étude de la
cafetière

**Theodor Wende,
1928**

Coffeepot
*Silver, ivory
Badische Kunstgewer-
beschule Pforzheim,
silversmith workshop
Height: c. 25 cm*

Kaffeekanne
*Silber, Elfenbein
Badische Kunstgewer-
beschule Pforzheim,
Silberschmiede-
werkstatt
Höhe: ca. 25 cm*

Cafetière
*en argent et ivoire
Badische Kunstgewer-
beschule Pforzheim,
atelier d'orfèvrerie
Hauteur: 25 cm*

In 1921, Theodor Wende took over the goldsmith and silversmith master class at the Badische Kunstgewerbeschule (School of Applied Arts) in Pforzheim. His designs for objects and jewellery combined the functional design principles expounded by the Bauhaus in the 20s with his own distinctively imaginative formal language in a blend of contemporary architectonic and sculptural elements.

1921 übernahm Theodor Wende die Leitung der Meisterklasse für Gold- und Silberschmiedekunst an der Badischen Kunstgewerbeschule in Pforzheim. Seine Entwürfe für Geräte und Schmuck verbanden die vom Bauhaus propagierten sachlichen Gestaltungstendenzen der 20er Jahre mit einer für ihn typischen, phantasievollen Formensprache, die zeitgenössische architektonische und plastische Elemente in sich vereinte.

En 1921 Theodor Wende prend la direction de la classe de maître artisan à l'atelier d'orfèvrerie de la Badische Kunstgewerbeschule (Ecole des Arts décoratifs) de Pforzheim. Ses créations d'ustensiles et de bijoux associent les principes de création propagés par le Bauhaus dans les années vingt avec un vocabulaire des formes bien à lui, plein d'imagination et alliant des éléments architectoniques et plastiques de cette époque.

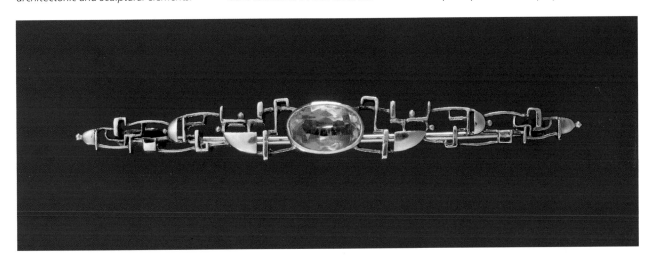

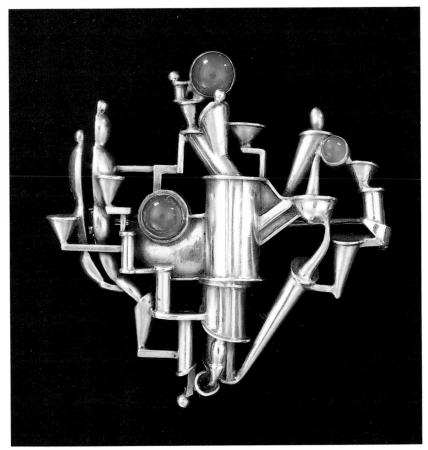

Theodor Wende, 1921

Brooch
Silver, chrysoprase cabochons
Badische Kunstgewerbeschule Pforzheim, silversmith workshop
Height: 5 cm

Brosche
Silber, Chrysopras-Cabochons
Badische Kunstgewerbeschule Pforzheim, Silberschmiedewerkstatt
Höhe: 5 cm

Broche
en argent et cabochons de chrysoprase
Badische Kunstgewerbeschule Pforzheim, atelier d'orfèvrerie
Hauteur: 5 cm

Theodor Wende, 1924/25

Brooch
Gold, facet-cut aquamarine
Badische Kunstgewerbeschule Pforzheim, silversmith workshop
Length: 5.8 cm

Brosche
Gold, facettierter Aquamarin
Badische Kunstgewerbeschule Pforzheim, Silberschmiedewerkstatt
Länge: 5,8 cm

Broche
en or et aigue-marine taillée en facettes
Badische Kunstgewerbeschule Pforzheim, atelier d'orfèvrerie
Longueur: 5,8 cm

From 1916 to 1936, the goldsmith and silversmith Emmy Roth ran a metal art workshop in the Charlottenburg district of Berlin. Her metalwork designs of the late 20s and early 30s are highly distinctive, combining high standards of craftsmanship with modern design. Another typical feature of her work is the reference to contemporary architectural designs, as is evident in a comparison of one of her works with Erich Mendelsohn's »Einstein Tower« (1920/21). As a Jew, Emmy Roth was forced to leave Nazi Germany in 1936, emigrating first to Palestine and later to the USA.

Von ca. 1916 bis 1936 betrieb die Gold- und Silberschmiedin Emmy Roth in Berlin-Charlottenburg eine Werkstatt für Metallkunst. Ihre Metallarbeiten aus den späten 20er und frühen 30er Jahren zeichnen sich durch eine eigenständige Gestaltung aus, die handwerkliche Perfektion mit moderner Formgebung verband. Typisch auch für ihre Entwürfe ist die Einbeziehung zeitgenössischer architektonischer Vorbilder, wie der Vergleich einer ihrer Arbeiten mit dem »Einsteinturm« von Erich Mendelsohn (1920/21) zeigt. Aufgrund der Anfeindung, die sie im nationalsozialistischen Deutschland wegen ihrer jüdischen Religon erlebte, emigrierte Emmy Roth 1936 zunächst nach Palästina und später in die USA.

De 1916 à 1936 environ, l'orfèvre Emmy Roth dirige un atelier d'objets d'art en métal à Berlin-Charlottenbourg. Ses réalisations de la fin des années vingt et du début des années trente se caractérisent par leur style très original unissant la perfection artisanale et un dessin très moderne. Typique aussi de ses créations, l'inclusion de modèles architectoniques contemporains, comme le montre clairement une comparaison faite entre l'une de ses créations et la «Tour d'Einstein» d'Erich Mendelsohn (1920/21). En raison de l'hostilité croissante de l'Allemagne national-socialiste envers les Juifs, Emmy Roth émigre en 1936 en Palestine puis plus tard aux Etats-Unis.

**Erich Mendelsohn,
1919/20**

Einstein Tower,
Potsdam

Einsteinturm,
Potsdam

La tour d'Einstein,
Potsdam

Emmy Roth, c. 1929

Sugar sprinkler
Silver
Silversmith workshop
Emmy Roth, Berlin
Height: 14 cm

Puderzuckerstreuer
Silber
Silberschmiede-
werkstatt
Emmy Roth, Berlin
Höhe: 14 cm

Sucrier à saupoudrer
en argent
atelier d'orfèvrerie
Emmy Roth, Berlin
Hauteur: 14 cm

Emmy Roth, 1930/31

Mocca set	**Mokkaservice**	**Service à moka**
Silver, horn	Silber, Horn	en argent et en corne
Silversmith workshop	Silberschmiede-	Atelier d'orfèvrerie
Emmy Roth, Berlin	werkstatt	Emmy Roth, Berlin
Height: 21 cm	Emmy Roth, Berlin	Hauteur: 21 cm
(Mocca pot)	Höhe: 21 cm	(cafetière à moka)
	(Mokkakanne)	

Before the Second World War, the silver-ware manufacturers Bruckmann & Söhne and the Württembergische Metallwarenfabrik (WMF) ranked amongst the world's leading producers of industrially manufactured silverware. Both companies strove to include the functionalistic formal trends of the 20s in their production of everyday appliances. Goldsmith and silversmith Paula Straus was employed as a designer for Bruckmann & Söhne from 1925. Later, like the architect Fritz August Breuhaus de Groot, she also designed silverware for the Württembergische Metallwarenfabrik.

Die Silberwarenfabrik Bruckmann & Söhne und die Württembergische Metallwarenfabrik (WMF) gehörten vor dem Zweiten Weltkrieg zu den weltweit größten Produzenten von industriell hergestellten Silberwaren. Beide Unternehmen bemühten sich, in ihrer Produktion von Gebrauchsgeräten die sachlichen Formtendenzen der 20er Jahre aufzunehmen. Die Gold- und Silberschmiedin Paula Straus war ab 1925 im Entwurfsatelier von Bruckmann & Söhne tätig. Später entwarf sie, wie auch der Architekt Fritz August Breuhaus de Groot, Silberwaren für die Württembergische Metallwarenfabrik.

La «Silberwarenfabrik Bruckmann & Söhne» (fabrique d'argenterie Bruckmann et Fils) et la Württembergische Metallwarenfabrik (fabrique d'articles métalliques du Wurtemberg) font partie avant la 2ème guerre mondiale des plus grands fabricants d'objets en argent produits industriellement. Les deux firmes s'efforcent d'intégrer dans leurs articles les formes sobres des années vingt. L'orfèvre Paula Straus travaille dans l'atelier de créations de Bruckmann & Söhne à partir de 1925. Plus tard elle créera des objets en argent pour la Württembergische Metallwarenfabrik, comme d'ailleurs l'architecte Fritz August Breuhaus de Groot.

Fritz August Breuhaus de Groot, c. 1930

Cream jug and sugar bowl on tray	**Sahnegießer und Zuckerschale auf Tablett**	**Pot à crème et sucrier sur plateau**
Silver, ebony	Silber, Ebenholz	Argent et bois d'ébène
Württembergische Metallwarenfabrik (WMF), Geislingen	Württembergische Metallwarenfabrik (WMF), Geislingen	Württembergische Metallwarenfabrik (WMF), Geislingen
Width: 24.2 cm (tray)	Breite: 24,2 cm (Tablett)	Largeur: 24, 2 cm (plateau)

Kaffee- und Teeservice, Silber gedrückt mit Ebenholzhandhaben, Kaffeekanne 126,— RM.
Teekanne 129,— RM., Rahmkanne 52,— RM., Zuckerschale mit Deckel 75,— RM., Teedose 75,— RM.,
Tablett oval 180,— RM.

Paula Straus, 1926

*Tea and coffee set
Silverware manufac-
turers Bruckmann &
Söhne, Heilbronn*

*Kaffee- und Teeservice
Silberwarenfabrik
Bruckmann & Söhne,
Heilbronn*

*Service à café et à thé
Manufacture d'objets
en argent
Bruckmann & Söhne,
Heilbronn*

139

Paula Straus, c. 1926

Tea set	**Teeservice**	**Service à thé**
Silver, ebony	Silber, Ebenholz	en argent et bois d'-
Silverware manufac-	Silberwarenfabrik	ébène
turers Bruckmann &	Bruckmann & Söhne,	Manufacture d'objets
Söhne, Heilbronn	Heilbronn	en argent
Height: 13 cm	Höhe: 13 cm	Bruckmann & Söhne,
(Teapot)	(Teekanne)	Heilbronn
		Hauteur: 13 cm
		(théière)

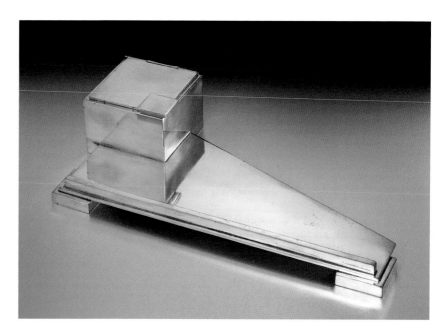

Karl Heubler, c. 1927

Writing set
Brass, glass
Reimann-Schule,
Berlin,
metal workshop
Width: 23.5 cm

Schreibzeug
Messing, Glaseinsatz
Reimann-Schule,
Berlin,
Metallwerkstatt
Breite: 23,5 cm

Ecritoire
en laiton et verre
Reimann-Schule,
Berlin,
atelier de métal
Largeur: 23,5 cm

140

**Reimann-Schule,
c. 1930/31**

Candle holder
Copper
Chase Brass & Copper
Company,
Waterbury/Con.
Height: 15.2 cm

Kerzenleuchter
Kupfer
Chase Brass & Copper
Company,
Waterbury/Con.
Höhe: 15,2 cm

Bougeoir
en cuivre
Chase Brass & Copper
Company,
Waterbury/Con.
Hauteur: 15,2 cm

In 1902, Albert Reimann established a private school for small sculpture in Berlin, which was officially awarded the status of a school of arts and crafts in 1913. The Reimann school developed in the course of the 20s and 30s into one of the most progressive institutes of modern design in Germany. From 1905 onwards, Karl Heubler was in charge of the school's metal workshop, which he brought to international renown. As the result of a touring exhibition of the American Federation of Arts which was shown in several American towns in 1930/31, the school was able to enter into cooperation with the American Chase Company.

1902 gründete Albert Reimann in Berlin eine private Schule für Kleinplastik, die 1913 den offiziellen Status einer Kunst- und Kunstgewerbeschule erhielt. Die sogenannte Reimann-Schule entwickelte sich während der 20er und 30er Jahre zu einem der fortschrittlichsten Lehrinstitute für moderne Formgebung in Deutschland. Ab 1905 leitete Karl Heubler die Metallwerkstatt der Schule und führte sie zu internationaler Bedeutung. Die Zusammenarbeit mit der amerikanischen Chase Company resultierte aus der erfolgreichen Beteiligung der Reimann-Schule an einer Wanderausstellung der American Federation of Arts, die 1930/31 in mehreren amerikanischen Städten zu sehen war.

En 1902, Albert Reimann ouvre à Berlin une école privée d'art plastique qui se verra attribuer officiellement en 1913 le statut d'école d'art et d'arts décoratifs. L'école Reimann devient dans les années vingt et trente l'un des établissements d'enseignement des arts plastiques modernes les plus progressistes d'Allemagne. A partir de 1905, Karl Heubler dirige l'atelier de métal de l'école et fait de celle-ci un établissement d'envergure internationale. La collaboration avec la Chase Company américaine est la conséquence directe de la participation réussie de l'école Reimann à une exposition itinérante de l'American Federation of Arts que de nombreuses villes américaines accueillent entre 1930 et 1931.

**Henry Dreyfuss,
1935**

**Thermos flask
with tray**
Aluminium, steel,
glass, rubber
American Thermos
Bottle Company,
Norwich/Con.
Height: 19.8 cm

**Thermoskanne
mit Tablett**
Aluminium, Stahl,
Glas, Gummi
American Thermos
Bottle Company,
Norwich/Con.
Höhe: 19,8 cm

**Thermos
avec plateau**
Aluminium, acier,
verre et caoutchouc
American Thermos
Bottle Company,
Norwich/Con.
Hauteur: 19,8 cm

**The Kalo Shops,
c. 1918**

Egg warmers
Silver, ebony
The Kalo Shops,
Chicago & New York
Height: 17 cm

Eierwärmer
Silber, Ebenholz
The Kalo Shops,
Chicago & New York
Höhe: 17 cm

Chauffe-œufs
en argent et
bois d'ébène
The Kalo Shops,
Chicago & New York
Hauteur: 17 cm

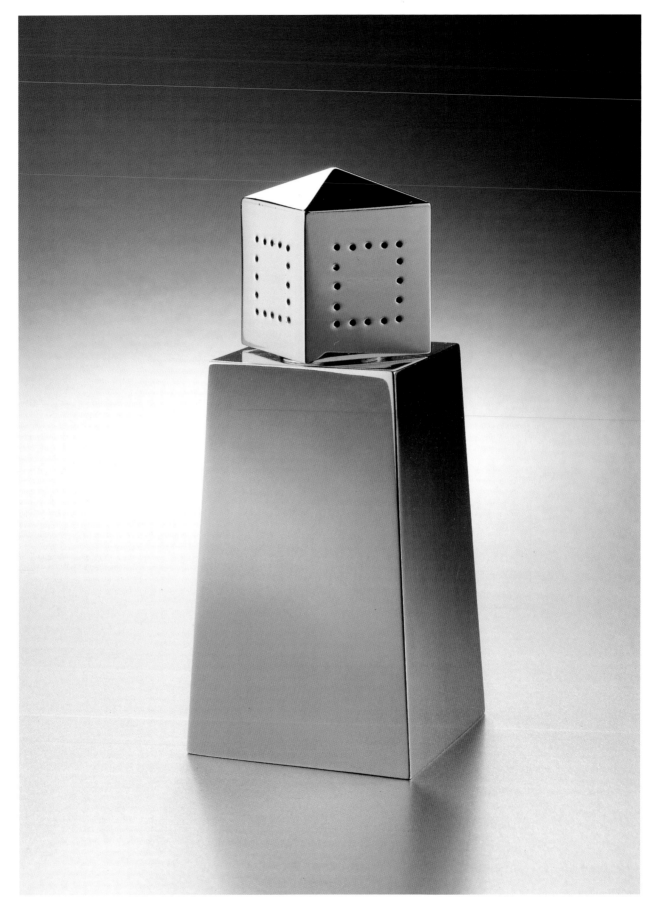

Valéry Bizouard, 1938

Sugar sprinkler	**Puderzuckerstreuer**	**Sucrier à saupoudrer**
Silver	Silber	en argent
Silverware manufac-	Silberwarenfabrik	Orfèvrerie Tétard
turers Tétard Frères,	Tétard Frères, Paris	Frères, Paris
Paris	Höhe: 13,5 cm	Hauteur: 13,5 cm
Height: 13.5 cm		

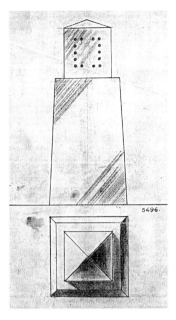

Valéry Bizouard, 1938

Design for the sugar sprinkler

Entwurfszeichnung, Puderzuckerstreuer

Etude de sucrier à saupoudrer

Italy, c. 1930

Coffee maker, jug and sugar bowl
Brass, plastic
Height: 32 cm
(coffee maker)

Mokkamaschine, Kanne und Zuckerdose
Messing, Kunststoff
Höhe: 32 cm
(Mokkamaschine)

Machine à moka, cafetière et sucrier
Laiton et plastique
Hauteur: 32 cm
(machine à moka)

Kay Fisker, 1929

Tea set
Silver, ivory
Silverware manufactu-
res Anton Michelsen,
Copenhagen
Height: 14 cm
(teapot)

Teeservice
Silber, Elfenbein
Silberschmiede
Anton Michelsen,
Kopenhagen
Höhe: 14 cm
(Teekanne)

Service à thé
en argent et en ivoire
Orfèvre
Anton Michelsen,
Copenhague
Hauteur: 14 cm
(théière)

Kay Fisker, 1926

Decanter
Silver
Silverware manufactu-
res Anton Michelsen,
Copenhagen
Height: 24.5 cm

Weinkanne
Silber
Silberschmiede
Anton Michelsen,
Kopenhagen
Höhe: 24,5 cm

Cruche à vin
en argent
Orfèvrerie
Anton Michelsen,
Copenhague
Hauteur: 24,5 cm

Right from the beginning of the 20th century, Scandinavian silverware was of outstanding craftsmanship and functional design. The silverware manufacturers Georg Jensen, Anton Michelsen and Frantz Hingelberg, all based in Copenhagen, were leading figures in their field. From about 1925, the Michelsen company produced designs by the Danish architect Kay Fisker. Fisker's modernistic forms broke new ground for the further development of Scandinavian silversmith art.

Bereits seit Anfang des 20. Jahrhunderts zeichneten sich die skandinavischen Silberwaren durch ihre handwerkliche Perfektion und materialgerechte Gestaltung aus. Eine führende Stellung auf dem Gebiet der dänischen Silberschmiedekunst nahmen die Silberschmieden Georg Jensen, Anton Michelsen und Frantz Hingelberg ein, die alle in Kopenhagen ansässig waren. Ab ca. 1925 produzierte die Firma Michelsen Silbergeräte nach Entwürfen des dänischen Architekten Kay Fisker. Die modernistischen Formen Fiskers waren für die weitere Entwicklung der skandinavischen Silberschmiedekunst richtungweisend.

Dès le début du XXème siècle, les objets en argent fabriqués en Scandinavie se distinguent par leur perfection artisanale et leur forme adaptée au matériau. Les orfèvreries Georg Jensen, Anton Michelsen et Frantz Hingelberg, tous de Copenhague, occupent le premier rang dans l'art de l'orfèvrerie dans leur pays. A partir de 1925 environ, la firme Michelsen réalise des ustensiles en argent d'après des créations de l'architecte danois Kay Fisker. Les formes modernistes élaborées par Kay Fisker joueront un rôle directeur dans l'évolution de l'orfèvrerie en Scandinavie.

Gustav Pedersen, 1935

Tea set
Silver, ebony
Silverware manufactures Georg Jensen, Copenhagen
Height: 22.5 cm
(teapot)

Teeservice
Silber, Ebenholz
Silberschmiede Georg Jensen, Kopenhagen
Höhe: 22,5 cm
(Teekanne)

Service à thé
en argent et bois d'ébène
Orfèvrerie Georg Jensen, Copenhague
Hauteur: 22,5 cm

Svend Weihrauch, c. 1931

Teapot
Silver, bakelite
Silverware manufacturers Frantz Hingelberg, Aarhus
Height: 12.5 cm

Teekanne
Silber, Bakelit
Silberwarenfabrik Frantz Hingelberg, Aarhus
Höhe: 12,5 cm

Service à thé
en argent et bakélite
Manufacture d'objets en argent Frantz Hingelberg, Aarhus
Hauteur: 12,5 cm

After the 1917 October Revolution, Russian ceramics were also used as vehicles of Communist propaganda. The Constructivist plate decor by Sergei V. Chekhonin, for example, bears the symbol of hammer and sickle. From 1923, the state porcelain factory in Petrograd also produced ceramics in the Supremacist style, strongly influenced by the work of Kasimir S. Malevich. The writing set designed by Nikolai M. Suetin applies Malevich's art theories to an everyday household item.

Nach der Oktoberrevolution 1917 wurde auch die russische Porzellankunst in den Dienst der kommunistischen Propaganda gestellt. So zeigt der konstruktivistisch gestaltete Tellerdekor von Sergei V. Chekhonin das Symbol von Hammer und Sichel. Ab 1923 entstanden in der Staatlichen Porzellanmanufaktur in Petrograd auch Porzellane im suprematistischen Stil, die stark von den Arbeiten Kazimir S. Malevichs beeinflußt waren. Das Schreibzeug, nach einem Entwurf von Nikolai M. Suetin, integriert die Kunstlehre Malevichs in einen Gegenstand des alltäglichen Lebens.

Sergei Vasilievich Chekhonin, 1919

Propaganda plate
Porcelain,
polychrome painting
State porcelain
factory, Petrograd
Diameter: 14.4 cm

Propagandateller
Porzellan, polychrome
Überglasurbemalung
Staatliche Porzellanmanufaktur, Petrograd
Durchmesser: 14,4 cm

Assiette de propagande
en porcelaine et
peinture polychrome
sur vernis
Manufacture nationale de porcelaine,
Pétrograd
Diamètre: 14,4 cm

Après la révolution d'octobre 1917, l'art de la porcelaine est mis lui aussi en Russie au service de la propagande communiste. Ainsi le décor constructiviste de l'assiette de Sergei V. Chekhonin présente-t-il la faucille et le marteau. A partir de 1923 des porcelaines, très influencées par les travaux de Kazimir S. Malévich, sont réalisées dans le style suprématiste par la manufacture nationale de porcelaine de Pétrograd. L'écritoire, d'après une création de Nikolaï M. Suétin, intègre les principes artistiques de Malévich dans un objet de la vie courante.

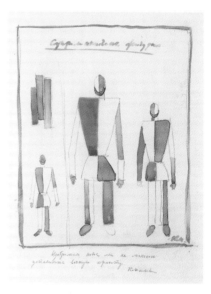

Nikolai Mikhailovich Suetin, 1923

Writing set
Porcelain, polychrome painting
State porcelain factory, Petrograd
Height: 13 cm

Schreibzeug
Porzellan, polychrome Überglasurbemalung
Staatliche Porzellanmanufaktur, Petrograd
Höhe: 13 cm

Ecritoire
en porcelaine et peinture polychrome sur vernis
Manufacture nationale de porcelaine, Pétrograd
Hauteur:13 cm

Kazimir Severinovich Malevich, 1923

Suprematist clothing design
Pencil and watercolour on paper
34 cm x 25.5 cm

Entwurf für suprematistische Kleidung
Bleistift und Aquarell auf Papier
34 cm x 25,5 cm

Modèle de vêtement suprématiste
Crayon et aquarelle sur papier
34 cm x 25,5 cm

The cylindrical glass vase with facetted and cut propaganda motifs in the style of the Czech avantgarde, by Zdenek Juna, a student at the Prague School of Applied Arts, was probably produced to celebrate the foundation of the Communist Party of Czechoslovakia (1921). The design of the two silver pots from the silver workshop of Frantisek Bibus & Sohn in Moravská Trebová indicates that the trend towards functional design of everyday appliances was already widespread in Czechoslovakia in the early 30s.

Vermutlich anläßlich des Gründungsjahres der Kommunistischen Partei der Tschechoslowakei (1921) fertigte Zdenek Juna, ein Schüler der Kunstgewerbeschule Prag, die zylindrische Glasvase mit geschliffenen und geschnittenen Propagandamotiven im Stile der tschechischen Avantgarde. Die Formgebung der beiden Silberkannen aus der Silberschmiedewerkstatt von Frantisek Bibus & Sohn in Moravská Trebová belegt, daß auch in der tschechischen Kunstgewerbeproduktion der frühen 30er Jahre die Tendenz zur funktionalen Gestaltung von Gebrauchsgeräten weit verbreitet war.

A l'occasion certainement de l'année de fondation du parti communiste tchèque (1921), Zdenek Juna, élève à l'Ecole des Arts décoratifs de Prague, réalise un vase en verre cylindrique, orné de motifs de propagande taillés et gravés, très dans le style de l'avant-garde tchèque. Les formes des deux pots en argent provenant de l'atelier d'orfèvrerie de Frantisek Bibus & Fils de Moravská Trebová montrent que la tendance à créer des formes fonctionnelles est largement répandue dans les arts décoratifs tchèques au début des annéees trente.

148

Zdenek Juna, 1921

Vase
Glass, cut decor
School of Applied
Arts, class of
V. H. Brunner
Height: 28.5 cm

Vase
Glas, geschnittener
und geschliffener
Dekor
Kunstgewerbeschule
Prag, Fachklasse
V. H. Brunner
Höhe: 28,5 cm

Vase
en verre, décor gravé
et taillé
Ecole des Arts
décoratifs
de Prague, classe de
V. H. Brunner
Hauteur: 28,5 cm

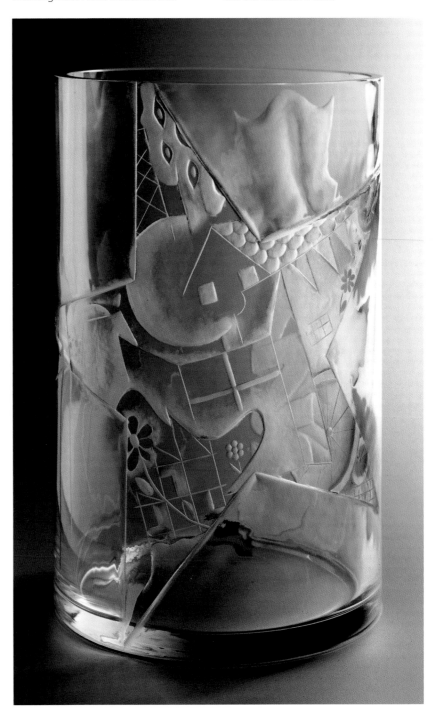

**Frantisek Bibus &
Sohn, c. 1930**

Teapot
*Silver, ebony
silverware manufactu-
res Frantisek Bibus &
Son, Moravská Trebová
Height: 14 cm*

Teekanne
*Silber, Ebenholz
Silberschmiede Franti-
sek Bibus & Sohn,
Moravská Trebová
Höhe: 14 cm*

Théière
*Argent et bois
d'ébène
Orfèvre Frantisek
Bibus & Fils,
Moravská Trebová
Hauteur: 14 cm*

**Frantisek Bibus &
Sohn, c. 1930**

Coffeepot
*Silver, ebony
Silverware manufactu-
res Frantisek Bibus &
Son, Moravská Trebová
Height: 27.5 cm*

Kaffeekanne
*Silber, Ebenholz
Silberschmiede Franti-
sek Bibus & Sohn,
Moravská Trebová
Höhe: 27,5 cm*

Cafetière
*en argent et bois
d'ébène
Orfèvre Frantisek
Bibus & Fils,
Moravská Trebová
Hauteur: 27,5 cm*

In 1923, Margarete Heymann-Marks founded the »Hael workshops for artistic ceramics« in Marwitz near Velten together with her first husband, Gustav Loebenstein. The forms and decors of her mass-produced tableware indicate the influence of constructivist modernism, as do Eva Stricker-Zeisel's designs for the Schramberger Majolikafabrik. Stricker-Zeisel emigrated in 1932, first to the Soviet Union, where she worked as a designer and artistic director in the porcelain industry of the Russian Republic, and later, in 1938, to the USA, where she continued her career as a porcelain and ceramics designer of international rank.

Margarete Heymann-Marks gründete 1923 in Marwitz bei Velten zusammen mit ihrem ersten Ehemann Gustav Loebenstein die »Hael-Werkstätten für künstlerische Keramik«. Die Formen und Dekore ihrer seriell produzierten Gebrauchsgeschirre stehen – wie auch die Entwürfe Eva Stricker-Zeisels für die Schramberger Majolikafabrik – unter dem Einfluß der konstruktivistischen Moderne. Stricker-Zeisel übersiedelte 1932 zunächst in die Sowjetunion und arbeitete dort als Entwerferin und künstlerische Direktorin für die Porzellanindustrie der Russischen Republik. 1938 emigrierte sie in die USA und setzte hier ihre Karriere als international tätige Porzellan- und Keramikdesignerin fort.

Margarete Heymann-Marks fonde en 1923 avec son mari Gustav Loebenstein à Marvitz près de Velten les «Hael-Werkstätten fur künstlerische Keramik» (Ateliers Hael de céramique d'art). Les formes et les décors de leurs vaisselles produites en série sont à l'instar des créations d'Eva Stricker-Zeisel pour la Schramberger Majolikafabrik influencées par les constructivistes. Eva Stricker-Zeisel émigre en 1932 en Union soviétique où elle travaille comme conceptrice et directrice artistique de l'industrie de la porcelaine de la République russe. Elle émigre ensuite en 1938 aux Etats-Unis et continue sa carrière internationale de créatrice dans la porcelaine et la céramique.

Margarete Heymann-Marks, c. 1930

Tea set
Stoneware, matt cream glaze with green/black painting Hael-Werkstätten, Marwitz Height: 15 cm (teapot)

Teeservice
Steingut, cremefarbene Mattglasur mit grün-schwarzer Bemalung Hael-Werkstätten, Marwitz Höhe: 15 cm (Teekanne)

Service à thé
Grès, vernis couleur crème et peinture vert-noir Hael-Werkstätten, Marwitz Hauteur : 15 cm (théière)

Advertisement for Hael ceramics, c. 1930

Werbung für Hael-Keramik, ca 1930

Publicité pour les céramiques Hael, vers 1930

Eva Stricker-Zeisel,
c. 1930

Tureen
Stoneware,
yellow glaze
Majolika-Fabrik
Schramberg
Height: 21 cm

Terrine
Steingut, gelbe Glasur
Majolika-Fabrik
Schramberg
Höhe: 21 cm

Terrine
Grès, vernis jaune,
Majolika-Fabrik
Schramberg
Hauteur: 21 cm

Josef Hillerbrand,
c. 1928

Tea set
Porcelain, yellow
underglaze painting
Nymphenburger porce-
lain factory
Height: 16 cm
(teapot)

Teeservice
Porzellan, gelbe
Unterglasurbemalung
Nymphenburger Por-
zellanmanufaktur
Höhe: 16 cm
(Teekanne)

Service à thé
en porcelaine et
peinture polychrome
sous vernis jaune
Manufacture de porce-
laine de Nymphenburg
Hauteur: 16 cm
(théière)

Wilhelm von Eiff,
c. 1930/31

Vase
Cut glass
Kunstgewerbeschule
Stuttgart, glass and
gem department
Height: 37.7 cm

Vase
Glas, geschnittener
Dekor
Kunstgewerbeschule
Stuttgart, Abteilung
für Glas- und Edel-
steinbearbeitung
Höhe: 37,7 cm

Vase
en verre, décor gravé
Kunstgewerbeschule
Stuttgart, section verre
et pierres précieuses
Hauteur: 37,7 cm

Nora Ortlieb,
c. 1929

Vase
Glass, cut decor
Kunstgewerbeschule
Stuttgart, glass and
gem department
Height: 27.5 cm

Vase
Glas, geschnittener
Dekor
Kunstgewerbeschule
Stuttgart, Abteilung
für Glas- und Edel-
steinbearbeitung
Höhe: 27,5 cm

Vase
en verre décor gravé
Kunstgewerbeschule
Stuttgart, section verre
et pierres précieuses
Hauteur : 27,5 cm

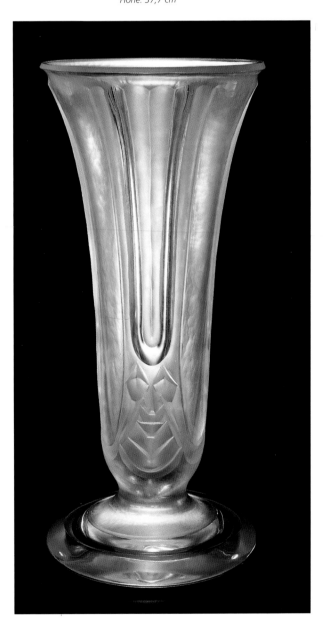

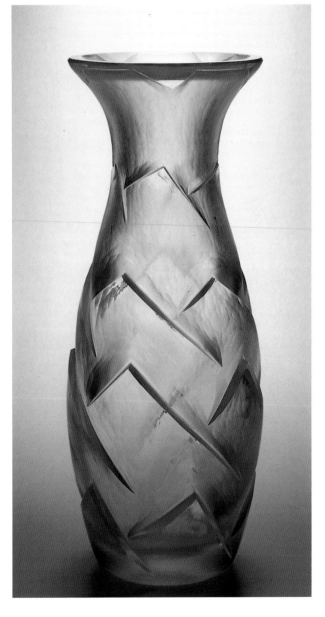

In 1921, a department of glass and gem processing was established at the Württembergische Kunstgewerbeschule (Württemberg School of Applied Arts) in Stuttgart under the artistic directorship of Wilhelm von Eiff. It was to be of decisive significance for the revival of the art of glassmaking in interwar Germany. In their work, von Eiff and his pupils combined traditional finishing processes with contemporary forms and new production processes. Similar design principles are also applied in the glass designs by Richard Süßmuth, which were mass-produced at his Penzig/Silesia workshop from 1924 onwards.

1921 wurde an der Württembergischen Kunstgewerbeschule in Stuttgart unter der künstlerischen Leitung Wilhelm von Eiffs eine Fachabteilung für Glas- und Edelsteinbearbeitung eingerichtet, die für die Erneuerung der Glaskunst in Deutschland zwischen den beiden Weltkriegen von entscheidender Bedeutung war. Von Eiff und seine Schüler verbanden in ihren Arbeiten traditionelle Veredlungstechniken für Glas mit zeitgemäßen Formen und neuen Herstellungsverfahren. Ähnliche Gestaltungsprinzipien liegen auch den Glasentwürfen Richard Süßmuths zugrunde, die ab 1924 in seiner Werkstatt in Penzig/Schlesien in Serie produziert wurden.

En 1921, une section verre et pierres précieuses est créée à la Württembergische Kunstgewerbeschule de Stuttgart sous la direction de Wilhelm von Eiff. Cette section joue un rôle capital dans le renouveau de l'art du verre en Allemagne entre les deux guerres. Von Eiff et ses Elèves associent dans leurs travaux les techniques traditionnelles d'affinage du verre avec des formes contemporaines et de nouveaux procédés de fabrication. Les mêmes principes sont à la base des créations en verre de Richard Süßmuth, produites en série à partir de 1924 dans son atelier de Penzig en Silésie.

**Richard Süßmuth,
c. 1928**

Vase
Glass, cut decor
Workshops
Richard Süßmuth,
Penzig/Silesia
Height: 23 cm

Vase
Glas, Keilschliffdekor
Werkstätten
Richard Süßmuth,
Penzig/Schlesien
Höhe: 23 cm

Vase
en verre décor taillé
en coin
Ateliers
Richard Süßmuth,
Penzig/Silésie
Hauteur: 23 cm

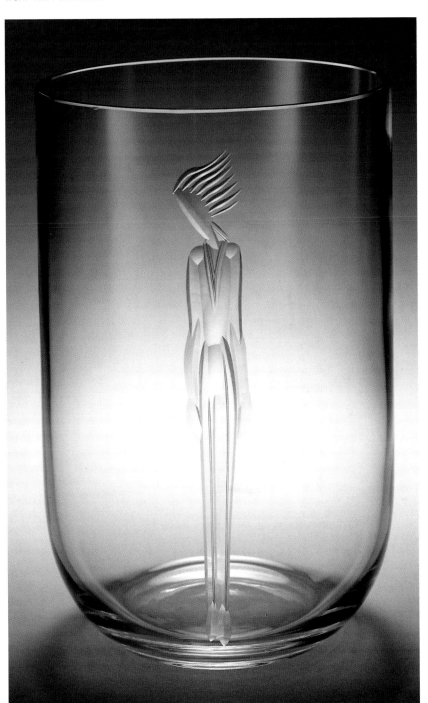

**Fachschule
Steinschönau, c. 1931**

Vase
Glass, polychrome
enamel and black
enamel decor
Fachschule Steinschö-
nau, departments
Dorn & Eiselt
Height: 19 cm

Vase
Glas, polychrome
Email- und
Schwarzlotbemalung
Fachschule Steinschö-
nau, Abteilungen
Dorn & Eiselt
Höhe: 19 cm

Vase
en verre, peinture
polychrome à l'émail
et au plomb noir fondu
Fachschule Steinschö-
nau, sections
Dorn & Eiselt
Hauteur: 19 cm

**Hendrik Petrus
Berlage, 1926**

Coffee set
Press glass,
coloured yellow
Glass works Leerdam
Height: 6.5 cm

Kaffeegedeck
Preßglas,
gelb eingefärbt
Glasfabrik Leerdam
Höhe: 6,5 cm

Service à café
en verre pressé et
teint en jaune
Verrerie Leerdam
Hauteur: 6,5 cm

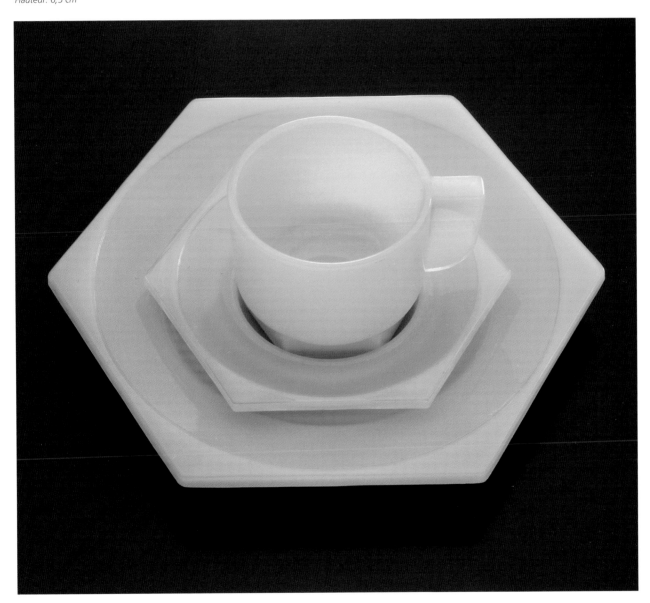

Biographies
Biographien
Biographies

Alvar Aalto
1898 - 1976

1916 - 1921 studied architecture at Helsinki Polytechnic ▦ 1921/22 exhibition designer in Sweden and Finland, working in various architecture offices ▦ 1923-1927 established his own architecture practice in Jyväskylä ▦ 1927-1933 transferred his practice to Turku, designed Paimio Sanatorium, set up an experimental workshop for plywood products together with Otto Korhonen and developed plywood furniture ▦ 1928 co-founded the »Congrès Internationaux d'Architec-

ture Moderne« (CIAM) ▦ from 1933 architecture practice in Helsinki, producing many architectural designs at home and abroad, designing furniture and other objects ▦ 1935 founded the »Artek« furniture factory with Mairea Gullichsen, developing and producing bonded and plywood furniture ▦ 1946-1948 visiting professor of architecture at Massachusetts Institute of Technology, Cambridge, USA ▦ from 1948 international work as town planner, architect and designer in Finland

1916-1921 Architekturstudium an der Technischen Universität Helsinki ▦ 1921/22 als Ausstellungsgestalter in Schweden und Finnland tätig, Mitarbeit in verschiedenen Architekturbüros ▦ 1923-1927 Aufbau eines eigenen Architekturbüros in Jyväskylä ▦ 1927-1933 Verlegung seines Büros nach Turku, Planung des Sanatoriums in Paimio, zusammen mit Otto Korhonen Aufbau einer Versuchswerkstatt für Sperrholzprodukte: Entwicklung von Schichtholzmöbeln ▦ 1928 Mitbegründer des »Congrès Internationaux d'Architecture Moderne« (CIAM) ▦ ab 1933 Aufbau eines Architekturbüros in Helsinki: zahlreiche Architekturentwürfe für das In- und Ausland, Entwurfstätigkeit für Möbel und Kunstgewerbe ▦ 1935 zusammen mit Mairea Gullichsen Gründung der Möbelfabrik »Artek«: Entwicklung und Produktion von Möbeln aus Schicht- und Sperrholz ▦ 1946-1948 Lehrauftrag für Architektur am Massachusetts Institute of Technology, Cambridge, USA ▦ ab 1948 international als Städteplaner, Architekt und Entwerfer in Finnland tätig

1916-1921 Etudes d'architecture à l'Université polytechnique d'Helsinki ▦ 1921/22 travaille comme concepteur d'expositions en Suède et en Finlande, collaboration à de nombreux cabinets d'architectes ▦ 923-1927 ouvre son propre cabinet d'architecte à Jyväskylä ▦ 1927-1933 transfert de son bureau à Turku, projet de sanatorium de Paimio, avec Otto Korhonen atelier expérimental de contreplaqué : élabora-

tion de meubles en bois lamellé ▦ 1928 co-fondateur des «Congrès Internationaux d'Architecture Modene» (CIAM) ▦ A partir de 1933 ouverture d'un cabinet d'architecte à Helsinki : nombreuses créations dans le pays et à l'étranger, activité créatrice dans le domaine du mobilier et des arts décoratifs ▦ 1935 fondation avec Mairea Gullichsen de la fabrique de meubles «Artek»: conception et fabrication de meubles en bois lamellé et contreplaqué ▦ 1948 chargé de cours d'architecture au Massachusetts Institute of Technology, Cambridge, USA ▦ A partir de 1948 travaille comme architecte urbaniste et concepteur en Finlande

Josef Albers 1888-1976

1905-1913 trained as a primary teacher and taught in Westphalia ▦ 1913-1915 studied at the Königliche Kunstschule (Royal Art School) Berlin ▦ 1916-1919 taught in Bottrop and studied at the Kunstgewerbeschule (School of Applied Art) in Essen under Jan Thorn-Prikker, creating his first glass window designs ▦ 1919-1920 studied at the Akademie der Bildenden Künste (Fine Arts Academy) in Munich ▦ 1920-1933 studied and taught at the Bauhaus in Weimar and Dessau, where, on completing the basic course in 1921, he helped to establish the glass-painting workshop as a journeyman, teaching basic courses and heading the glass workshops there from 1923, becoming a master in 1925 and giving classes on material theory and work theory, in 1928 becoming director of the carpentry workshop ▦ 1933 emigrated to the USA ▦ 1933-1949 taught at Black Mountain College/North Carolina ▦ 1950-1960 director of the department of design at Yale University, New Haven/Con. ▦ from 1960 visiting professor at various universities in America and Europe

1905-1913 Ausbildung zum Volksschullehrer, als Lehrer in Westfalen tätig ▦ 1913-1915 Studium an der Königlichen Kunstschule Berlin ▦ 1916-1919 als Lehrer in Bottrop tätig, Studium an der Kunstgewerbeschule Essen: Schüler von Jan Thorn-Prikker, erste Gestaltung von Glasfenstern ▦ 1919-1920 Studium an der Akademie der Bildenden Künste, München ▦ 1920-1933 Studium und Lehrauftrag am Bauhaus Weimar und Dessau: Vorkurs, ab 1921 als Geselle Aufbau der Werkstatt für Glasmalerei, ab 1923 teilweise Übernahme der Vorkurse und Leitung der Glaswerkstätte, 1925 Ernennung zum Bauhausmeister, Leitung der Klassen für Material- und Werklehre, ab 1928 Leitung aller Vorkurse und der Tischlerei ▦ 1933 Emigration in die USA ▦ 1933-1949 Lehrauftrag am Black Mountain College/North Carolina ▦ 1950-1960 Direktor des Department of Design an der Yale Universität, New Haven/Con. ▦ ab 1960 Gastprofessuren in Amerika und Europa

1905-1913 Formation d'instituteur, travaille comme professeur en West-

phalie ▦ 1913-1015 études à l'Académie royale des Beaux-Arts de Berlin ▦ 1916-1919 professeur à Bottrop, études à l'Ecole des Arts décoratifs d'Essen: élève de Jan Thorn-Prikker, première conception de fenêtres vitrées ▦ 1919-1920 études à l'Académie des Beaux-Arts de Munich ▦ 1920-1933 études et enseignement au Bauhaus de Weimar et de Dessau: cours préliminaire, à partir de 1921 nommé compagnon, crée l'atelier de peinture sur verre, en 1923 reprend en partie les cours préliminaires et direction de l'atelier du verre, 1925 nommé maître

du Bauhaus, donne les cours de théorie des matériaux et du travail, à partir de 1928 dirige tous les cours préliminaires et la menuiserie ▦ 1933 émigration aux USA ▦ 1933-1949 donne des cours au Black Mountain Collège/Caroline du Nord ▦ 1950-1960 directeur du département design à l'université de Yale, New Haven/Con. ▦ A partir de 1960 divers postes de professeur invité et chargé de cours en Amérique et en Europe

Herbert Bayer 1900-1985

1917-1918 military service ▦ 1919-1920 apprenticed to the architect Georg Schmidthammer in Linz, produced his first typographic works ▦ 1921 practical training in the studio of architect/designer Emanuel J. Margold, Darmstadt, designing packaging ▦ 1921-1923 studied at the Bauhaus in Weimar (basic course and wallpainting studies) ▦ 1923-1924 study trips to Italy and Berchtesgaden ▦ 1925-1928 taught at the Bauhaus in Dessau: journeyman's exam, appointment as teacher and junior master, head of the newly established printing workshop ▦ 1928-1938 set up his own studio for typography and visual communication in Berlin ▦ 1928/29 director of the »studio dorland« advertising agency, artistic adviser to Vogue magazine in Germany ▦ 1937 work in the exhibition of »Degenerate Art« ▦ 1938-1946 emigrated to the USA, worked as exhibition designer in New York, various teaching contracts ▦ 1946-1975 worked in Aspen/Col.: design advisor to the Aspen Institute and other institutions, private and public architecture contracts, continued involvement in the fields of advertising and typography ▦ 1975 lived in Montecito/Cal.

1917-1918 Kriegsdienst ▦ 1919-1920 Lehre im Architekturbüro von Georg Schmidthammer, Linz: erste typographische Arbeiten ▦ 1921 Praktikum im Atelier des Architekten und Entwerfers Emanuel J. Margold, Darmstadt: Entwürfe für Verpackungen ▦ 1921-1923 Studium am Bauhaus Weimar: Vorkurs, Lehre als Wandmaler ▒ 1923-1924 Studienaufenthalte in Italien und Berchtesgaden ▒ 1925-1928 Lehrauftrag am Bauhaus Dessau: Gesellenprüfung, Ernennung zum Lehrer und Jungmeister, Leitung der neu eingerichteten Werkstatt für Druck und Reklame ▒ 1928-1938 Aufbau eines eigenen Ateliers für Typographie und Werbegestaltung in Berlin ▒ 1928/29 Direktor der Werbeagentur »studio dorland«, künstlerischer Berater der Zeitschrift »Vogue« in Deutschland ▒ 1937 auf der Ausstellung »Entartete Kunst« vertreten

▒ 1938-1946 Emigration in die USA, in New York als Ausstellungsgestalter tätig, verschiedene Lehraufträge ▒ 1946-1975 in Aspen/Col. tätig: Gestaltungsberater des Kulturzentrums Aspen und anderer Institutionen, private und öffentliche Architekturaufträge, weiterhin im Bereich Werbung und Typographie tätig ▒ ab 1975 in Montecito/Cal. ansässig

1917-1918 Service militaire ▒ 1919-1920 apprentissage dans le cabinet d'architecte de Georg Schmidthammer, Linz: premiers travaux typographiques ▒ 1921 stage dans l'atelier de l'architecte concepteur Emanuel J. Margold à Darmstadt: créations d'emballages ▒ 1921-1923 études au Bauhaus de Weimar: cours préliminaire, apprentissage de peintre mural ▒ 1923-1924 séjour en Italie et à Berchtesgaden ▒ 1925-1928 chargé de cours au Bauhaus de Dessau : examen de compagnonnage, nomination d'enseignant et de jeune maître, direction du nouvel atelier d'imprimerie et de publicité ▒ 1928 -1938 création de son propre atelier typographique et publicitaire à Berlin ▒ 1928/29 directeur de l'agence de publicité «studio dorland», conseiller artistique de la revue Vogue en Allemagne ▒ 1937 représenté à l'exposition «l'art dégénéré» ▒ 1938- 1946 émigration aux USA, travaille à New York comme concepteur d'expositions, divers postes de chargé de cours ▒ 1946-1975 travaille à Aspen/Col.: conseiller artistique du centre culturel d'Aspen et d'autres institutions, commandes de constructions privées et publiques, continue à travailler dans la publicité et la typographie ▒ A partir de 1975 s'installe à Montecito/Cal.

Peter Behrens 1868-1940
1886-1889 studied at the art schools of Hamburg, Karlsruhe and Düsseldorf ▒ from 1890 worked as a painter and graphic artist in Munich ▒ 1893 founding member of the Munich Secession ▒ 1897 a cofounder of the »Vereinigte Werkstätten« (United Workshops) in Mu-

nich ▒ 1898 worked on »Pan« magazine ▒ 1899-1903 member of the Darmstadt artists' colony ▒ 1902/03 gave master classes at the Bavarian Museum of Arts and Crafts in Nuremberg ▒ 1903-1907 director of the Kunstgewerbeschule Düsseldorf ▒ 1907 founding member of the Deutscher Werkbund ▒ 1907 artistic adviser to AEG, Berlin, established a major architecture practice in Berlin, working with Walter Gropius, Ludwig Mies van der Rohe and Le Corbusier, prolific production of architectural and industrial designs in the years to follow ▒ 1909 de-

signed the AEG turbine hall ▒ 1922-1936 taught at the Akademie der Bildenden Künste (Academy of Fine Arts) in Vienna, giving master classes in architecture ▒ 1936 gave master classes in architecture at the Prussian Art Academy in Berlin

1886-1889 Studium an der Kunstgewerbeschule Hamburg, der Kunstschule Karlsruhe und der Düsseldorfer Akademie ▒ ab 1890 als Maler und Graphiker in München tätig ▒ 1893 Gründungsmitglied der Münchener Sezession ▒ 1897 Mitbegründer der »Vereinigten Werkstätten für Kunst im Handwerk«, München ▒ 1898 Mitarbeit an der Zeitschrift »Pan« ▒ 1899-1903 Mitglied der Darmstädter Künstlerkolonie ▒ 1902/03 Leitung der Meisterkurse am Bayerischen Gewerbemuseum, Nürnberg ▒ 1903-1907 Direktor der Kunstgewerbeschule Düsseldorf ▒ 1907 Gründungsmitglied des Deutschen Werkbundes ▒ ab 1907 künstlerischer Beirat der »Allgemeinen Elektricitätsgesellschaft« (AEG), Berlin, Aufbau eines großen Architekturbüros in Berlin: In dem Büro sind u.a. Walter Gropius, Ludwig Mies van der Rohe und Le Corbusier tätig, in den Folgejahren intensive Entwurfstätigkeit im Bereich Architektur und Industriedesign ▒ 1909 Entwurf der Turbinenhalle der AEG ▒ 1922-1936 Lehrauftrag an der Akademie der Bildenden Künste, Wien: Leitung der Meisterklasse für Architektur ▒ ab 1936 Lehrauftrag an der Preußischen Akademie der Künste Berlin: Leitung des Meisterateliers für Baukunst

1886-1889 Etudes à l'Ecole des Arts décoratifs de Hambourg, de l'Ecole des Beaux-Arts de Karlsruhe et de l'Académie de Düsseldorf ▒ à partir de 1890 peintre et graphiste à Munich ▒ 1893 membre fondateur de la Sécession munichoise ▒1897 cofondateur des Ateliers réunis de Munich ▒ 1898 collabore à la revue «Pan» ▒ 1899-1903 membre de la colonie d'artistes de Darmstadt ▒ 1902-1903 direction des cours de maîtres au Musée des Arts et Métiers bavarois à Nuremberg ▒ 1903-

1907 directeur de l'Ecole des Arts décoratifs de Düsseldorf ▒ 1907 membre fondateur du Deutscher Werkbund ▒ A partir de 1907 conseiller artistique de AEG, création d'un grand cabinet d'architecture à Berlin: travaille avec Walter Gropius, Ludwig Mies van der Rohe et le Corbusier, ensuite grande activité en architecture et en design industriel ▒ 1909 conception de l'usine de turbines de AEG ▒ 1922-1936 enseigne à l'Académie des Beaux-Arts de Vienne: direction de la classe d'architecture ▒ A partir de 1936 enseigne à l'Académie des Beaux-Arts de Berlin : dirige l'atelier d'architecture.

Max Benirschke 1880-1961
1895-1897 studied weaving in Mährisch-Schönberg ▒ 1997-1902 studied at the Kunstgewerbeschule (School of Applied Arts) in Vienna, attending classes by Alfred Roller and Josef Hoffmann, published his interior design ideas in the magazine »Das Interieur«, and studied at the Akademie der Bildenden Künste (Academy of Fine Arts) in Vienna ▒ 1902/03 freelance designer in Vienna ▒ 1903-1919 taught at the Kunstgewerbeschule (School of Applied Arts) in Dusseldorf, where he was assistant in Peter Behrens' architecture classes and in charge of a preparatory class, created numerous designs for architecture and industry, designed for the jewellery maker Theodor Fahrner of Pforzheim ▒ 1919-1936 taught at the Fachschule für Handwerk und Industrie (Trade School of Crafts and Industry) in Düsseldorf

1895-1897 Studium an der Fachschule für Weberei in Mährisch-Schönberg ▒ 1897-1902 Studium an der Kunstgewerbeschule Wien: Besuch der Klassen Alfred Roller und Josef Hoffmann, Veröffentlichung seiner Entwürfe für Inneneinrichtungen und Kunstgewerbe in der Zeitschrift »Das Interieur«, Studium an der Akademie der Bildenden Künste, Wien ▒ 1902/03 als selbständiger Entwerfer in Wien tätig ▒ 1903-1919 Lehrauftrag an der Kunstgewerbeschule Düsseldorf: Assistent der Architekturklasse von Peter Behrens, Leitung einer Vorbereitungsklasse, zahlreiche Entwürfe für Architektur und Kunstgewerbe, Entwurfstätigkeit für die Schmuckwarenfirma Theodor Fahrner, Pforzheim ▒ 1919-1936 Lehrauftrag an der Fachschule für Handwerk und Industrie in Düsseldorf

1895-1897 Etudes à l'Ecole technique de Tissanderie et de Tissage de Mährisch-Schönberg ▒ 1897-1902 études à l'Ecole des Arts décoratifs de Vienne dans la classe d'Alfred Roller et celle de Josef Hoffmann, publication de ses créations d'intérieurs et d'arts décoratifs dans la revue «Das Interieur», études à l'Académie des Beaux-Arts de Vienne ▒ 1902-1903 travaille à son compte comme concepteur à Vienne ▒ 1903-1919 chargé de cours à l'Ecole des Arts décoratifs de Düsseldorf: assistant de la classe d'architec-

ture Peter Behrens, direction d'une classe préparatoire, nombreuses créations en architecture et en arts décoratifs, travaille pour le fabricant de bijoux Theodor Fahrner à Pforzheim ▒ 1919-1936 enseigne à l'Ecole technique d'Artisanat et d'Industrie de Düsseldorf.

Hendrik Petrus Berlage 1856-1934
1875-1878 studied architecture at Zurich Polytechnic ▒ 1879-1881 study trips to Italy, Germany and Austria ▒ 1882-1889 employee and subsequently partner of the architect Theodorus Sanders in Amster-

dam ▒ 1889-1913 set up his own architecture practice in Amsterdam, designing office buildings for insurance companies, the Amsterdam stock exchange, urban development plans for various Dutch cities, and working in the field of interior design and applied arts ▒ 1900 cofounder of the applied-arts distributing company »'t Binnenhuis« ▒ 1911 visited America and was deeply influenced by the architecture of Louis Sullivan and Frank Lloyd Wright ▒ 1913 worked in The Hague, producing architectural designs for the Kröller-Müller family ▒ 1914-1919 headed the construction department of W.H. Müller & Co. ▒ 1919-1934 worked as a freelance architect in The Hague ▒ 1923 designed for the Leerdam glassware factory ▒ from 1924 taught architecture at the Delft Polytechnic

1875-1878 Architekturstudium am Polytechnikum Zürich ▒ 1879-1881 Reisen und Studien in Italien, Deutschland und Österreich ▒ 1882-1889 als Mitarbeiter und später als gleichberechtigter Partner im Architekturbüro von Theodorus Sanders in Amsterdam tätig ▒ 1889-1913 Aufbau eines eigenen Architekturbüros in Amsterdam: Entwurf und Ausführung von Bürobauten für Versicherungsgesellschaften, Planung der Amsterdamer Börse, Beschäftigung mit Stadterweiterungsplänen für verschiedene holländische Großstädte, Entwurfstätigkeit im Bereich Innenarchitektur und Kunstgewerbe ▒ 1900 Mitbegründer der kunstgewerblichen Vertriebsfirma »'t Binnenhuis« ▒ 1911 Amerikareise: starke Beeinflussung durch Bauten von Louis Sullivan und Frank Lloyd Wright ▒ ab 1913 in Den Haag tätig: Bautätigkeit für die Familie Kröller-Müller ▒ 1914-1919 Leitung der Bauabteilung der Firma W. H. Müller & Co. ▒ 1919 - 1934 als freier Architekt in Den Haag tätig ▒ ab 1923 Entwürfe für die Glaswarenfabrik Leerdam ▒ ab 1924 Lehrauftrag für Architektur an der Technischen Hochschule Delft

1875-1878 Etudes d'architecture à l'Ecole polytechnique de Zurich ▨ 1879-1881 voyages et études en Italie, Allemagne et Autriche ▨ 1882-1889 travaille comme collaborateur puis comme partenaire dans le cabinet d'architecture de Theodorus Sanders à Amsterdam ▨ 1889-1913 création de son propre bureau d'architecte à Amsterdam: plans et réalisations de bureaux pour des compagnies d'assurances, projet de la bourse d'Amsterdam, plans d'urbanisme pour diverses grandes villes hollandaises, activité dans le domaine de l'aménagement d'intérieurs et des arts décoratifs ▨ 1900 co-fondateur de la firme «'t' Binnenhuis» ▨ 1911 voyage en Amérique: fortement influencé par les constructions de Louis Sullivan et de Frank Lloyd Wright ▨ A partir de 1913 travaille à La Haye: construit pour la famille Kröller-Müller ▨ 1914-1919 dirige le service construction de la firme W.H. Müller & Co. ▨ 1919-1934 travaille comme architecte indépendant à La Haye ▨ A partir de 1923 créations pour la verrerie Leerdam ▨ A partir de 1924 chargé de cours d'architecture à l'Ecole technique supérieure de Delft.

Valéry Bizouard 1875-1945
Began designing gold- and silverware in Paris around 1898, entered various competitions and had his designs produced by the silversmiths A. Debain, Paris ▨ 1901 member of the »Société Nationale des Beaux Arts«, exhibited regularly ▨ 1919-1936 headed the design department of silversmiths Tétard Frères, Paris, and also designed for other French silverware manufacturers ▨ 1928-1936 his work was presented in exhibitions of the »Société des Artistes Décorateurs«

Ab ca. 1898 als Entwerfer für Gold- und Silberwaren in Paris tätig: Teilnahme an Metallkunstwettbewerben, Ausführung der Entwürfe durch die Silberschmiede A. Debain, Paris ▨ ab 1901 Mitglied der »Société Nationale des Beaux Arts«: regelmäßige Ausstellungsbeteiligung ▨ 1919-1936 Leiter des Entwurfsbüros der Silberschmiede Tétard Frères, Paris, Entwurfstätigkeit auch für andere französische Silberwarenhersteller ▨ 1928-1936 Ausstellungsbeteiligung innerhalb der »Société des Artistes Décorateurs«

A partir de 1898 travaille comme créateur d'objets en or et en argent à Paris: participation à des concours dans ce domaine, réalisation des créations par l'orfèvrerie A. Debain de Paris ▨ A partir de 1901 membre de la «Société nationale des Beaux-Arts»: participation régulière à des expositions ▨ 1919-1936 dirige le bureau de création des orfèvres Tétard Frères de Paris, travaille aussi pour d'autres fabricants français d'objets en métal précieux ▨ 1928-1936 participation à des expositions dans le cadre de la «Société des Artistes Décorateurs»

Franz Boeres 1872-1956
1886-1891 studied at the Kun-

stschule (Art School) in Hanau ▨ 1892-1900 modeller in the casting works of Paul Stotz, Stuttgart ▨ 1900 freelance artist and designer in Stuttgart, designing for the silverware manufacturers Bruckmann & Söhne in Heilbronn and the metalware manufacturers Seifert & Co. in Dresden, WMF in Geislingen and Erhard & Söhne in Schwäbisch Gmünd ▨ 1903-1919 designed for the jewellery maker Theodor Fahrner, Pforzheim ▨ 1910-1914 architect and designer for Robert Bosch in Stuttgart ▨ turned to painting around 1920

1886-1891 Studium an der Zeichenakademie Hanau ▨ 1892-1900 Modelleur in der Erzgießerei Paul Stotz, Stuttgart ▨ ab 1900 als selbständiger Künstler und Entwerfer in Stuttgart tätig: Entwürfe für die Silberwarenfabrik Bruckmann & Söhne, Heilbronn, die Metallwarenfabrik Seifert & Co., Dresden, die Württembergische Metallwarenfabrik, Geislingen, und die Metallwarenfabrik Erhard & Söhne, Schwäbisch Gmünd ▨ 1903-1919 Entwurfstätigkeit für die Schmuckwarenfirma Theodor Fahrner, Pforzheim ▨ 1910-1914 als Architekt und Entwerfer für den Industriellen Robert Bosch in Stuttgart tätig ▨ ab ca. 1920 Hinwendung zur Malerei

1886-1891 Etudes à l'académie de dessin de Hanau ▨ 1892-1900 modeleur à la fonderie Paul Stoltz de Stuttgart ▨ A partir de 1900 travaille comme artiste et créateur indépendant à Stuttgart: créations pour la fabrique d'objets en métal précieux Bruckmann & Söhne de Heilbronn, d'articles métalliques Seifert & Co. de Dresde, celle de Geislingen dans le Wurtemberg et la firme Erhard & Söhne de Schwäbisch Gmünd ▨ 1903-1919 travaille comme créateur pour le fabricant de bijoux Theodor Fahrner à Pforzheim ▨ 1910-1914 travaille comme architecte et concepteur pour l'industriel Robert Bosch à Stuttgart ▨ A partir de 1920 se consacre à la peinture

Theodor Bogler 1897-1968
1919/20 studied at the Bauhaus in Weimar ▨ 1920 studied architecture and art history at Munich University and Polytechnic ▨ 1920-1924 studied at the Bauhaus in Weimar, with an apprenticeship in the ceramics workshop in Dornburg, journeyman's exam, organisational and commercial responsibilities, designing prototypes for the Velten-Vordamm pottery factory ▨ 1925/26 head of the model and form workshop at the Velten-Vordamm pottery factory ▨ 1927-1933 entered the Benedictine Abbey of Maria Laach, studied theology and philosophy in Beuron and Maria Laach ▨ 1929 lived in Velten, his designs for the Velten pottery factory were adopted by the »Ars Liturgica« workshops at Maria Laach ▨ 1932 ordained as priest ▨ 1934-1938 designed for Hedwig Bollhagen's »HB-Werkstätten« in Marwitz near Velten ▨ 1936-1968 designed for the Majolica factory in Karlsruhe ▨ 1939-1948 Prior of the

Benedictine Abbey of Maria Laach ▨ from 1948 directed the »Ars Liturgica« art and publishing workshops in Maria Laach ▨ 1951 designed for various ceramics companies in Höhr-Grenzhausen

1919/20 Studium am Bauhaus Weimar ▨ 1920 Studium der Architektur und Kunstgeschichte an der Universität und Technischen Hochschule in München ▨ 1920-1924 Weiterführung des Studiums am Bauhaus Weimar: Lehre in der Keramikwerkstatt in Dornburg, Gesellenprüfung, Übernahme von organisatorischen und kaufmännischen Aufgaben, Entwurf von Prototypen für die Steingutfabrik Velten-Vordamm, Velten ▨ 1925/26 Leitung der Modell- und Formwerkstatt des Werks Velten der Steingutfabrike Velten-Vordamm ▨ 1927-1933 Eintritt in die Benediktinerabtei Maria Laach, Studium der Theologie und Philosophie in Beuron und Maria Laach ▨ 1929 Aufenthalt in Velten: Entwürfe Boglers für die Veltener Steingutfabrik werden von den Kunstwerkstätten »Ars Liturgica« in Maria Laach übernommen ▨ 1932 Priesterweihe ▨ 1934-1938 Entwurfstätigkeit für die »HB-Werkstätten« Hedwig Bollhagens, Marwitz bei Velten ▨ 1936-1968 Entwurfstätigkeit für die Majolika-Manufaktur Karlsruhe ▨ 1939-1948 Prior der Benediktinerabtei Maria Laach ▨ ab 1948 Leitung der Kunstwerkstätten und des Kunstverlages »Ars Liturgica« in Maria Laach ▨ ab 1951 Entwurfstätigkeit für verschiedene keramische Betriebe in Höhr-Grenzhausen

1919/20 Etudes au Bauhaus de Weimar ▨ 1920 études d'architecture et d'histoire de l'art à l'université et l'Ecole technique supérieure de Munich ▨ 1920-1924 continuation de ses études au Bauhaus de Weimar: apprentissage dans l'atelier de céramique à Dornburg, examen de compagnonnage, fonctions organisatrices et commerciales, conception de prototypes pour la poterie Velten-Vordamm à Velten ▨ 1925-26 dirige l'atelier de forme et de modèle de l'abbaye bénédictine de Maria Laach, études de théologie et de philosophie à Beuron et Maria Laach ▨ 1929 séjour à Velten; créations pour la poterie de Velten sont reprises par les ateliers «Ars Liturgica» de Maria Laach ▨ 1932 Prêtrise ▨ 1934-1938 activité pour les «HB Werkstätten» de Hedwig Bollhagen de Marwitz près de Velten ▨ 1936-1968 travaille pour la manufacture Majolika de Karlsruhe ▨ 1939-1948 prieur de l'abbaye bénédictine de Maria Laach ▨ A partir de 1948 dirige les ateliers et les éditions «Ars Liturgica» à Maria Laach ▨ A partir de 1951 travaille pour divers commerces de céramiques de Höhr-Grenzhausen

Marianne Brandt 1893-1983
1911-1917 studied at the Grand Ducal Saxon School of Fine Arts in Weimar ▨ 1917-1923 freelance artist in Weimar ▨ 1924-1929 studied and worked at the Bauhaus in Weimar, taking the basic course, the

metal workshop apprenticeship, the journeyman's exam, then becoming deputy director of the metal workshop, organising cooperative projects with the lighting industry and designing lamps for Körting & Matthiesen AG (KANDEM) of Leipzig, and Schwintzer & Gräff of Berlin ▨ 1929 worked in the architecture office of Walter Gropius, Berlin ▨ 1930-1932 drew up new concepts and designs for the applied arts division of the Ruppelwerk metalware factory in Gotha ▨ between 1933 and 1949 she withdrew from public life, working as a freelance artist in

Chemnitz ▨ 1949/50 taught in the woodwork, ceramics and metal department of the Hochschule für freie und angewandte Kunst (College of Fine and Applied Arts) in Dresden ▨ 1951-1954 worked at the Institut für Angewandte Kunst (Industrial Design School) in East Berlin ▨ in 1953/54 visited the People's Republic of China and organised the exhibition of German applied art on behalf of the German Democratic Republic ▨ she lived in Kirchberg/Saxony from 1976 onwards

1911-1917 Studium an der Großherzoglich Sächsischen Hochschule für Bildende Kunst Weimar ▨ 1917-1923 als freie Künstlerin in Weimar tätig ▨ 1924-1929 Studium und Arbeit am Bauhaus Weimar: Vorkurs, Lehre in der Metallwerkstatt, Gesellenprüfung, stellvertretende Leiterin der Metallwerkstatt, Organisation der Zusammenarbeit mit der Leuchtenindustrie: Lampenentwürfe für die Firmen Körting & Matthiesen AG (KANDEM), Leipzig, und Schwintzer & Gräff, Berlin ▨ 1929 Mitarbeit im Architekturbüro Walter Gropius, Berlin ▨ 1930-1932 für das Ruppelwerk in Gotha tätig: Neukonzeption und Entwurfsarbeit für den Bereich Kunstgewerbe ▨ 1933-1949 Rückzug in das Privatleben, als freie Künstlerin in Chemnitz tätig ▨ 1949/50 Lehrauftrag an der Hochschule für freie und angewandte Kunst Dresden: Abteilung für Holz, Keramik und Metall ▨ 1951-1954 Mitarbeit am Institut für angewandte Kunst, Berlin/Ost ▨ 1953/54 Aufenthalt in der Volksrepublik China: Betreuung der Ausstellung »Deutsche Angewandte Kunst« im Auftrag der Deutschen Demokratischen Republik ▨ ab 1976 in Kirchberg/Sachsen ansässig

1911-1917 Etudes à l'Académie royale des Beaux-Arts de Weimar ▨ 1917-1923 travaille comme artiste indépendante à Weimar ▨ 1924-1929 études et travail au Bauhaus de Weimar: cours préliminaires, apprentissage à l'atelier de métal, examen de compagnonnage, directrice adjointe de l'atelier de métal, organisation de la coopération avec l'industrie: créations de lampes pour les firmes Körting & Matthiesen AG (KANDEM) de Leipzig et Schwintzer & Gräff de Berlin ▓ 1929 collabore au bureau d'architecte de Walter Gropius à Berlin ▓ 1930-1932 travaille pour la Ruppelwerk de Gotha: nouvelle conception et travail de création dans le domaine «arts décoratifs» ▓ 1933-1949 peu d'activités en dehors de sa vie privée, travaille comme artiste indépendante à Chemnitz ▓ 1949-1950 chargée de cours à l'Ecole supérieure des Arts libres et appliqués de Dresde à la section bois, céramique et métal ▓ 1951 -1954 collaboration à l'Institut de l'Art appliqué de Berlin-Est ▓ 1953/54 séjour en Chine: chargée de l'exposition «L'art d'avant-garde allemand» par la République démocratique allemande ▓ Depuis 1976 vit à Kirchberg en Saxe

Marcel Breuer 1902-1981
1920 entered the Akademie für bildende Künste (Fine Arts Academy) in Vienna and trained in a Viennese architecture office ▓ 1920-1923 studied at the Bauhaus in Weimar, taking the basic course, the carpentry apprenticeship and journeyman's exam ▓ 1924 lived in Paris ▓ 1925-1928 headed the carpentry workshop at the Bauhaus in Dessau, where he created his first tubular steel furniture and standard house designs ▓ 1928 set up an architecture office in Berlin, primarily designing furniture and interior fittings ▓ 1933/34 visited Switzerland and Budapest, and worked with Farkas Molnár and Josef Fischer ▓ 1935-1937 emigrated to England, set up his own architecture office in London ▓ 1937-1941 moved to the USA, taught at the school of design at Harvard University, Cambridge, Mass. and set up an architecture office with Walter Gropius, which he ran alone from 1941-1946 ▓ 1946-1956 transferred his office to New York where his projects included plans for the Whitney Museum in New York and cooperation on the UNESCO building in Paris ▓ 1956 set up the »Marcel Breuer and Associates« architecture office in New York

1920 Studium an der Akademie für Bildende Künste, Wien, Praktikum in einem Wiener Architekturbüro ▓ 1920-1923 Studium am Bauhaus Weimar: Vorkurs, Lehre in der Tischlerei, Gesellenprüfung ▓ 1924 Parisaufenthalt ▓ 1925-1928 als Jungmeister Leitung der Möbelwerkstatt am Bauhaus Dessau: erste Entwürfe für Stahlrohrmöbel, Planung von Typen-Häusern ▓ ab 1928 Aufbau eines Architekturbüros in Berlin, vorwiegend Entwürfe für Möbel und Inneneinrichtungen ▓ 1933/34 Aufenthalt in der Schweiz und in Budapest, Zusammenarbeit mit Farkas Molnár und Josef Fischer ▓ 1935-1937 Emigration nach England, dort Aufbau eines eigenen Architekturbüros in London ▓ 1937-1941 Übersiedlung in die USA, Lehrtätigkeit an der School of Design an der Harvard University, Cambridge/Mass., Aufbau eines Architekturbüros zu-

sammen mit Walter Gropius ▓ 1941-1946 selbständige Weiterführung des Architekturbüros ▓ 1946-1956 Verlegung des Büros nach New York: Planung u.a. des Whitney Museums in New York und Mitarbeit am UNESCO-Gebäude in Paris ▓ ab 1956 Aufbau des Architekturbüros »Marcel Breuer and Associates«, New York

1920 Etudes à l'Académie des Beaux-Arts de Vienne, stage dans un cabinet d'architecte ▓ 1920-1923 études au Bauhaus de Weimar: cours

préliminaire, apprentissage de menuisier, examen de compagnonnage ▓ 1924 séjour à Paris ▓ 1925-1928 dirige en tant que jeune maître l'atelier de meubles au Bauhaus de Dessau: premières créations de meubles tubulaires, plans de types de maisons ▓ A partir de 1928 création de son propre bureau d'architecte à Berlin, surtout création de mobiliers ▓ 1933/34 séjour en Suisse et à Budapest, collaboration avec Farkas Molnár et Josef Fischer ▓ 1935-1937 émigre en Angleterre, création de son propre cabinet d'architecte à Londres ▓ 1937-1941 émigre aux USA, enseigne à la School of Design de Harvard à Cambridge/Mass., création d'un cabinet d'architectes avec Walter Gropius ▓ 1941-1946 dirige seul le cabinet ▓ 1946-1956 transfert du bureau à New-York: projet du musée Whitney de New York et collaboration à l'immeuble de l'UNESCO à Paris ▓ A partir de 1956 création du bureau d'architectes «Marcel Breuer and Associates» à New York

Fritz August Breuhaus de Groot 1883-1960
Attended the Barmen building school ▓ studied at the Düsseldorf Kunstgewerbeschule (School of Applied Arts) ▓ studied architecture at the polytechnics of Darmstadt and Düsseldorf ▓ around 1906 founded the Atelier F. A. Breuhaus & C. Mauve architecture practice in Düsseldorf, working as an architect, interior decorator and designer ▓ 1922/23 founded the Mikado-Werkstätte A.G. in Bonn ▓ during the 20s and 30s created interior designs for passenger ships, railway carriages and the Hindenburg Zeppelin ▓ 1928 taught in Munich ▓ 1930/31 lived in Berlin, teaching interior design and textile design at the »Contempora« private art studios there ▓ 1932 set up an architecture and design office with Heinrich Roßkotten in Berlin, designed and built several private and commercial houses and industrial units, worked intensively on designs for furniture, textiles, wallpapers, lamps etc.

Besuch der Baugewerkschule Barmen ▓ Studium an der Kunstgewerbeschule Düsseldorf ▓ Architekturstudium an den Technischen Hochschulen in Darmstadt und Düsseldorf ▓ ca. 1906 Gründung des Architekturbüros Atelier F. A. Breuhaus & C. Mauve in Düsseldorf: Entwürfe für Architektur, Inneneinrichtungen und Kunstgewerbe ▓ 1922/23 Gründung der Mikado-Werkstätte A.G., Bonn ▓ während der 20er und 30er Jahre Entwürfe für Inneneinrichtungen von Passagierschiffen, Eisenbahnwaggons und des Zeppelins »LZ 129 Hindenburg« ▓ ab 1928 Lehrauftrag in München ▓ ab 1930/31 in Berlin ansässig, Lehrauftrag an den privaten »Contempora Lehrateliers für neue Werkkunst«, Berlin: Klassen für Raumkunst und Textilentwurf ▓ ab 1932 Aufbau eines Architektur- und Entwurfsbüros in Partnerschaft mit Heinrich Roßkotten in Berlin: Planung und Ausführung zahlreicher Privat- und Geschäftshäuser sowie von Industrieanlagen, intensive Entwurfsarbeit für Möbel, Textilien, Tapeten, Lampen etc.

Fréquentation de l'école de construction de Barmen ▓ études à l'Ecole des Arts décoratifs de Düsseldorf ▓ études d'architecture à l'université de Darmstadt et de Düsseldorf ▓ vers 1906 fondation du cabinet d'architecture «Atelier F.A. Breuhaus & C. Mauve» à Düsseldorf: créations pour l'architecture, les arts décoratifs et l'aménagement d'intérieurs ▓ 1922/23 création de l'Ateliers Mikado AG à Bonn ▓ Années vingt et trente, créations d'intérieurs de maisons, de paquebots, de trains et du zeppelin «LZ 129 Hindenburg» ▓ A partir de 1928 chargé de cours à l'école privée «Contempora Lehrateliers für neue Werkkunst» de Berlin: classes de l'espace et du textile ▓ Dès 1932 création d'un cabinet d'architecture et de création sous forme de partenariat avec Heinrich Roßkotten à Berlin: plans et réalisation de nombreuses maisons et de magasins ainsi que d'installations industrielles, activité créatrice intensive de meubles, de textiles, de papiers muraux et de lampes etc.

Sergei Vasilievich Chekhonin 1878-1936
In 1896/97 studied at the Art Institute of St. Petersburg ▓ 1897-1900 studied painting at the »Princess Maria Tenishewa« private art school in St. Petersburg, where he attended master classes by Ilya Repin ▓ 1904-1906 worked at the »Abramtsewo« ceramics workshop in Moscow ▓ 1905/06 produced caricatures and comics for Russian revolutionary periodicals ▓ 1907 worked at the ceramics factory of Pyotr Vaulin in Kikerino near St. Petersburg ▓ 1910 member of the »World of Art« group, exhibited regularly until 1924 ▓ 1913-1918 official adviser to the Russian Ministry of Agriculture, adviser for applied arts and head of the school of enamelling in Rostov-Yaroslavky ▓ 1918-1927 artistic director of the Lomonosov porcelain factory in Petrograd/Len-

ingrad ▓ 1923/24 artistic director of the Volchov porcelain factory near Nowgorod ▓ 1928-1936 emigrated to France, where he became a freelance artist and designer in Paris, designing stage sets, jewellery and porcelain, and working for »Vogue« magazine

1896/97 Studium an der Zeichenschule der Gesellschaft zur Förderung der Künste, St. Petersburg ▓ 1897-1900 Studium der Malerei an der privaten Kunstschule »Prinzessin Maria Tenishewa«, St. Petersburg: Meisterschüler von Ilya Repin ▓ 1904-1906 in der Keramik-Werkstatt »Abramtsewo« in Moskau tätig ▓ 1905/06 Entwurf von Karikaturen und Bildgeschichten für russische Revolutionszeitungen ▓ 1907 in der Keramikfabrik von Pyotr Vaulin in Kikerino bei St. Petersburg tätig ▓ ab 1910 Mitglied der Künstlergruppe »Welt der Kunst«: bis 1924 regelmäßige Ausstellungsbeteiligungen ▓ 1913-1918 als offizieller Berater des russischen Landwirtschaftsministeriums tätig: Referent für Kunstgewerbe, Leitung der Kunstgewerbeschule für Emailtechnik in Rostov-Yaroslavky ▓ 1918-1927 künstlerische Leitung der Staatlichen Lomonosov-Porzellanmanufaktur, Petrograd/Leningrad ▓ 1923/24 künstlerischer Direktor der Volchov-Porzellanmanufaktur bei Nowgorod ▓ 1928-1936 Emigration nach Frankreich, als freischaffender Künstler und Entwerfer in Paris tätig: Bühnenentwürfe für Theater, Entwürfe für Schmuck und Porzellan, Mitarbeit am Magazin »Vogue«

1896/97 Etudes à l'école de dessin de la Société de promotion des arts de Saint-Pétersbourg ▓ 1897-1900 études de la peinture à l'école privée «Princesse Maria Tenishewa» de Saint-Pétersbourg: élève d'Ilya Repin ▓ 1904-1909 travaille à l'atelier de céramique «Abramtsewo» de Moscou ▓ 1905/06 caricatures et histoires en images pour des journaux révolutionnaires russes ▓ 1907 travaille dans l'atelier de céramique de Piotr Vaulin à Kikerino près de Saint-Pétersbourg ▓ A partir de 1910 membre du groupe d'artistes «Monde de l'art»: jusqu'en 1924 participation régulière à des expositions ▓ 1913-1918 conseiller officiel du ministère de l'agriculture: chargé des arts décoratifs, direction de l'école des techniques d'émail de Rostov-Yaroslavky ▓ 1918-1927 direction artistique de la manufacture nationale de porcelaine de Pétrograd ▓ 1923/24 directeur artistique de la manufacture de porcelaine Volchov près de Nowgorod ▓ 1928-1936 émigre en France et travaille comme artiste et concepteur indépendant à Paris: créations de décors pour le théâtre, créations de bijoux et de porcelaine, collaboration au magazine Vogue

Serge Chermayeff 1900
1918-1923 freelance journalist for Amalgamated Press in London ▓ 1922-1925 studied art and architecture in Germany, Austria, France and Holland ▓ 1924-1927 chief of

design for the decorating firm of E. Williams Ltd., London ▦ 1928-1931 director of the Modern Art Studio run by furniture manufacturers Waring & Gillow, London, designed interior fittings and accessories ▦ 1931-1939 worked as an independent architect and designer in London: 1933-1936 went into partnership with Erich Mendelsohn ▦ in 1939 emigrated to the USA ▦ 1940/41 settled in San Francisco ▦ 1942-1946 taught design at Brooklyn College, New York ▦ 1946-1951 director of the Institute of Design, Chicago ▦ 1952-1962 taught at the Massachusetts Institute of Technology, Harvard Graduate School of Design, Cambridge, USA ▦ 1962-1971 taught architecture at the Yale University School of Architecture in New Haven/Con. ▦ 1974 visiting professor at various universities ▦ in 1980 he was awarded an honorary doctorate by Ohio State University, Columbus

1910-1913 Besuch der Royal Drawing Society School, London ▦ 1918-1923 als freier Journalist für die »Amalgamated Press« in London tätig ▦ 1922-1925 Kunst- und Architekturstudium in Deutschland, Österreich, Frankreich und Holland ▦ 1924-1927 Leitung der Entwurfsabteilung des Einrichtungsgeschäftes E. Williams Ltd, London ▦ 1928-1931 Leitung des »Modern Art Studios« im Einrichtungshaus Warring & Gillow's, London: Entwürfe für Inneneinrichtungen und Zubehör ▦ 1931-1939 als selbständiger Architekt und Entwerfer in London tätig: 1933-1936 in Partnerschaft mit Erich Mendelsohn ▦ 1939 Emigration in die USA ▦ 1940/41 in San Francisco ansässig ▦ 1942-1946 Lehrauftrag für Design am Brooklyn College, New York ▦ 1946-1951 Direktor des Institut of Design, Chicago ▦ 1952-1962 Lehrauftrag am Massachusetts Institute of Technology, Harvard Graduate School of Design, Cambridge ▦ 1962-1971 Lehrauftrag für Architektur an der Yale University, School of Architecture, New Haven/Con. ▦ ab 1974 verschiedene Gastprofessuren ▦ 1980 Ehrendoktor der Ohio State University, Columbus

1910-1913 fréquente la Royal Drawing Society School de Londres ▦ 1918-1923 travaille comme journaliste indépendant au «Amalgamated Press» à Londres ▦ 1922-1925 études d'art et d'architecture en Allemagne, Autriche, France et Hollande ▦ 1924-1927 directeur du service de conception et de création du magasin d'ameublement E. Williams Ltd. de Londres ▦ 1928-1931 direction du «Modern Art Studio» dans le magasin d'ameublement Warring & Gillow's à Londres: créations d'intérieurs et d'accessoires ▦ 1931-1939 architecte et créateur indépendant à Londres: 1933-1936 en association avec Erich Mendelsohn ▦ 1939 émigre aux USA ▦ 1940/41 s'installe à San Francisco ▦ 1942-1946 chargé de cours de design au Brooklyn College de New York ▦ 1946-1951 directeur de l'Institut

of Design de Chicago ▦ 1952-1962 enseigne au Massachusetts Institute of Technology, Harvard Graduate School of Design, à Cambridge ▦ 1962-1971 enseigne l'architecture à Yale, School of Architecture, New Haven/Con. ▦ A partir de 1974 divers postes de professeurs invités ▦ 1980 Docteur honoris causa de la Ohio State University à Columbus

Christian Dell 1893-1974
1907-1911 apprentice silversmith at the silverware factory of Schleißner & Söhne in Hanau, Germany, and studied at the Zeichenakademie

(Drawing Academy) in Hanau ▦ 1911/12 journeyman silversmith in Dresden ▦ in 1912/13 enrolled at the Grand Ducal Saxon School of Applied Arts in Weimar ▦ 1914-1918 military service ▦ 1918-1920 worked for Hestermann & Ernst in Munich, initially as a journeyman, later as a master silversmith ▦ 1920 worked in the silversmith workshop of Emil Lettré, Berlin, later returning as a student to the Zeichenakademie in Hanau ▦ in 1921 set up a silversmith workshop in Hanau ▦ 1922-1925 master in the metal workshop at the Bauhaus in Weimar, working closely with László Moholy-Nagy ▦ 1926-1933 taught at Frankfurt Art School, where he directed the metal workshop and designed for the lighting industry ▦ in 1933 the Nazi regime removed him from the staff of Frankfurt Art School ▦ in 1939 set up a jewellery business in Wiesbaden

1907-1911 Lehre als Silberschmied in der Silberwarenfabrik Schleißner & Söhne, Hanau, Studium an der Zeichenakademie Hanau ▦ 1911/12 als Silberschmiedegeselle in Dresden tätig ▦ 1912/13 Studium an der Großherzoglich Sächsischen Kunstgewerbeschule Weimar ▦ 1914-1918 Kriegsdienst ▦ 1918-1920 bei der Firma Hestermann & Ernst in München, zunächst als Geselle, später als Silberschmiedemeister tätig ▦ 1920 Arbeit im Silberschmiedeatelier Emil Lettré, Berlin, danach als Meisterschüler erneutes Studium an der Zeichenakademie Hanau ▦ 1921 Gründung einer Silberschmiedewerkstatt in Hanau ▦ 1922-1925 Werkmeister in der Metallwerkstatt am Bauhaus Weimar, enge Zusammenarbeit mit László Moholy-Nagy ▦ 1926-1933 Lehrauftrag an der Kunstschule Frankfurt: Leitung der Metallwerkstatt, intensive Entwurfstätigkeit für die Leuchtenindustrie ▦ 1933 Entlassung als Lehrkraft der Frankfurter Kunstschule durch die Nationalsozialisten ▦ ab 1939 Aufbau eines Juweliergeschäftes in Wiesbaden

1907-1911 Apprentissage d'orfèvre à l'atelier de fabrication d'objets en argent Schleißner & Söhne à Hanau, études à l'académie de dessin de la même ville ▦ 1911/12 travaille comme compagnon orfèvre à Dresde ▦ 1912/13 études à l'Ecole des Arts décoratifs du Grand-Duché de Saxe à Weimar ▦ 1914-1918 service de guerre ▦ 1918-1920 travaille chez Hestermann & Ernst à Munich d'abord en tant que compagnon, ensuite comme maître artisan ▦ 1920 travaille dans l'atelier d'Emil Lettré à Berlin, puis à nouveau études à l'académie de dessin de Hanau ▦ 1921 création d'un atelier d'orfèvre à Hanau ▦ 1922-25 maître artisan à l'atelier de métal du Bauhaus de Weimar, collaboration étroite avec László Moholy-Nagy ▦ 1926-1933 enseigne à l'Ecole des Beaux-Arts de Francfort : direction de l'atelier de métal, activité fiévreuse de création pour l'industrie de l'éclairage ▦ 1933 licencié de son poste d'enseignant par les nationaux-socialistes ▦ A partir de 1939 création d'une bijouterie à Wiesbaden

Erich Dieckmann 1896-1944
1918-1920 studied architecture in Danzig ▦ 1921-1925 studied at the Bauhaus in Weimar (apprenticeship in the carpentry workshop and journeyman's exam) ▦ in 1925 stayed on at the carpentry workshop in Weimar after the Bauhaus moved to Dessau ▦ 1926-1930 directed the »furniture making and interior design« department at the Staatliche Bauhochschule in Weimar and designed furniture ▦ 1931-1933 taught at Burg Giebichenstein School of Applied Arts in Halle where he directed the carpentry workshop and designed tubular steel and cane furniture for industrial production ▦ in 1933 the Nazi regime removed him from the staff ▦ 1933-1936 unemployed, very little design work ▦ 1936-1939 member of the »Amt Schönheit der Arbeit« (Beauty of Labour Board) in Hanover ▦ 1939-1944 member of the »Deutsche Kunsthandwerk« (German Craftsmanship) board of the Chamber of Arts in Berlin

1918-1920 Architekturstudium an der Technischen Hochschule Danzig ▦ 1921-1925 Studium am Bauhaus Weimar: Vorkurs, Lehre in der Tischlerwerkstatt, Gesellenprüfung ▦ 1925 Weiterführung der Tischlerwerkstatt in Weimar nach Verlegung des Bauhauses nach Dessau ▦ 1926-1930 Leitung der Abteilung »Tischlerei und Innenarchitektur« an der Staatlichen Bauhochschule Weimar: intensive Entwurfstätigkeit für Möbel ▦ 1931-1933 Lehrauftrag an der Kunstgewerbeschule Burg Giebichenstein in Halle: Leitung der Tischlerwerkstatt, Entwürfe für serielle Stahlrohr- und Korbmöbel ▦ 1933 Entlassung als Lehrkraft durch die Nationalsozialisten ▦ 1933-1936 arbeitslos, kaum Entwurfstätigkeit ▦ 1936-1939 als Referent beim »Amt Schönheit der Arbeit« in Hannover tätig ▦ 1939-1944 als Referent für das »Deutsche Kunsthandwerk« bei der Reichskam-

mer der Bildenden Künste in Berlin tätig

1918-1920 Etudes d'architecture à l'Ecole technique supérieure de Danzig ▦ 1920-1925 études au Bauhaus de Weimar: cours préliminaire, apprentissage à la menuiserie, examen de compagnonnage ▦ 1925 reprend la direction de l'atelier de menuiserie après le transfert du Bauhaus à Dessau ▦ 1926-1930 direction de la section «menuiserie et aménagement d'intérieur» à l'Ecole technique supérieure de Construction de Weimar: création intensive

de meubles ▦ 1931-1933 chargé de cours à l'Ecole des Arts décoratifs de Burg Giebichenstein à Halle : direction de l'atelier de menuiserie, créations de meubles en série en tubes d'acier et en rotin ▦ 1933 licenciement de son poste d'enseignant par les nationaux-socialistes ▦ 1933-1936 sans travail, presque pas d'activité créatrice ▦ 1936-1939 travaille comme rapporteur au «Amt Schönheit der Arbeit» de Hanovre ▦ 1939-1944 rapporteur au «Deutsches Kunsthandwerk» (artisanat d'art allemand) près la Chambre du Reich chargée des arts plastiques.

Christopher Dresser 1834-1904
From 1847-1854 studied at the Central School of Design in London ▦ 1854 accredited as a lecturer by the Department of Science and Art ▦ from 1857 published widely on botany, decorative design, Oriental art and art theory ▦ 1859/60 received an honorary doctorate from the University of Jena ▦ 1862 deeply impressed by non-European arts and crafts at the International Exhibition in London, began designing for industry in the same year ▦ 1868 gave up teaching to concentrate on industrial design and set up a design studio ▦ 1876/77 travelled to America and Japan ▦ from 1878 he designed for the silverware manufacturers Hukin & Heath, Birmingham ▦ from 1879 art director of the newly founded Linthorpe Pottery in Middlesbrough and began designing for the silverware manufacturers Dixon & Sons, Sheffield ▦ from 1884 he designed for the silverware manufacturers Elkington & Co., Birmingham ▦ from around 1890 he designed for the newly founded Ault Pottery in Swadlincote

1847-1854 Studium an der Central School of Design, London ▦ ab 1854 Lehrauftrag im »Department of Science and Art«, South Kensington/London ▦ ab 1857 zahlreiche Veröffentlichungen zu den Themenbereichen Botanik, dekorative Kunst, ostasiatische Kunst und Kunsttheorie ▦ 1859/60 Ehrendoktor der Universität Jena ▦ 1862 Be-

160

such der Weltausstellung in London, starke Beeinflussung durch außereuropäisches Kunstgewerbe, Aufnahme der Entwurfstätigkeit für Industrieprodukte ▓ 1868 Aufgabe des Lehrauftrages zugunsten einer verstärkten Tätigkeit als Entwerfer für die Industrie, Aufbau eines Studios für Industriedesign ▓ 1876/77 Studienreise nach Amerika und Japan ▓ ab 1878 Entwurfstätigkeit für die Silberwarenfabrik Hukin & Heath, Birmingham ▓ ab 1879 künstlerische Leitung der neugegründeten Linthorpe Pottery, Middlesbrough, Beginn der Entwurfstätigkeit für die Silberwarenfabrik Dixon & Sons, Sheffield ▓ ab 1884 Entwurfsarbeit für die Silberwarenfabrik Elkington & Co., Birmingham ▓ ab ca. 1890 intensive Entwurfstätigkeit für die neugegründete Ault Pottery, Swadlincote

1847-1854 Etudes à la Central School of Design de Londres ▓ A partir de 1854 enseigne au «Department of Science and Art» dans South Kensington à Londres ▓ A partir de 1857 nombreuses publications sur la botanique, l'art décoratif, l'art asiatique et la théorie de l'art ▓ 1859/60 Docteur honoris causa de l'université de Jena ▓ visite l'Exposition universelle de Londres, très influencé par les arts décoratifs autres qu'européens, commence à créer pour l'industrie ▓ 1868 cesse l'enseignement pour se consacrer à la création industrielle, ouvre un studio de design industriel ▓ 1876/77 voyage d'études en Amérique et au Japon ▓ A partir de 1878 crée pour le fabricant d'objets en argent Hukin & Heath de Birmingham ▓ A partir de 1879 direction artistique de la poterie nouvellement créée Linthorpe Pottery à Middlesbrough, commence à travailler pour le fabricant d'argenterie Dixon & Sons de Sheffield ▓ à partir de 1890 grande activité de créateur pour la toute nouvelle Ault Pottery à Swadlincote

Henry Dreyfuss 1904-1972
Until 1922 he attended the Ethical Culture Arts High School, New York, where he took a course in stage design ▓ 1922 trained as a stage designer under Norman Bel Geddes, New York and worked on stage sets for musicals and plays ▓ travelled to France, Turin and Algeria ▓ 1927 worked as a stage designer in New York ▓ 1929 set up a major industrial design office in New York and designed typewriters, telephones, household articles, electrical appliances, tractors, trains, aircraft etc. in close collaboration with development engineers, and acted as artistic advisor to many major American companies ▓ 1952 taught engineering studies at the California Institute of Technology in Pasadena ▓ visiting professor at several American universities ▓ chairman of the council of the Industrial Designers Society of America ▓ numerous publications on design and technology

Bis 1922 Besuch der Ethical Culture Arts High School, New York: Kurs für Bühnenausstattung ▓ ab 1922 Ausbildung als Bühnenbildner bei Norman Bel Geddes, New York: Mitarbeit an der Bühnengestaltung von Musicals und Theateraufführungen ▓ Studienreisen nach Frankreich, Tunesien und Algerien ▓ ab 1927 wieder in New York als Bühnenbildner tätig ▓ ab 1929 Aufbau eines großen Büros für Industriedesign in New York: Entwürfe für Schreibmaschinen, Telefonapparate, Haushaltswaren, Elektroartikel, Traktoren, Züge, Flugzeuge u.a., enge Zusammenarbeit mit den Entwicklungsingenieuren, als künstlerischer Berater für zahlreiche amerikanische Großfirmen tätig ▓ ab 1952 Lehrauftrag für Ingenieurwissenschaften am California Institute of Technology, Pasadena ▓ Gastprofessuren an vielen amerikanischen Universitäten ▓ Vorsitzender des Rats der »Industrial Designers Society of America« ▓ zahlreiche Veröffentlichungen zu den Themenbereichen Design und Technik

Jusqu'en 1922 fréquente l'Ethical Culture Arts High School de New York: cours de décors de théâtre ▓ A partir de 1922 formation de scénographe chez Norman Bel Geddes à New York: collaboration à la réalisation de décors pour des musicals et des pièces de théâtre ▓ Voyages d'études en France, Tunisie et Algérie ▓ A partir de 1927 retour à New York comme créateur de décors ▓ A partir de 1929 ouvre un grand bureau de design industriel à New York: il conçoit des machines à écrire, des téléphones, des articles ménagers, des appareils électriques, des tracteurs, des trains, des avions etc., étroite collaboration avec des ingénieurs d'études, conseiller artistique de nombreuses grandes firmes américaines ▓ A partir de 1952 enseigne les sciences de l'ingénierie au California Institute of Technology à Pasadena ▓ Postes de professeur invité dans de nombreuses universités américaines ▓ Président du Conseil de la «Industrial Designers Society of America» ▓ Nombreuses publications sur le design et la technique

Wilhelm von Eiff 1890-1943
1904-1911 trained and worked at the Göppingen branch of the WMF metalware factory and apprenticed as a glass engraver ▓ 1906 attended evening classes at the Kolb & Gmelich school of art in Göppingen, 1908 journeyman's exam ▓ 1911 travelled to Italy, Austria and France ▓ 1911/12 worked as a glass engraver and stone cutter in Paris ▓ 1912/13 study trip to Austria ▓ 1914-1918 military service ▓ 1919-1921 set up a workshop for glass and stone cutting in Stuttgart ▓ 1921-1943 taught at the Kunstschule in Stuttgart, establishing and running the new department for glass and gem processing ▓ 1931 member of the German glass society »Deutsche Glastechnische Gesellschaft« and chairman of the glass finishing committee

1904-1911 Ausbildung und Arbeit in der Württembergischen Metallwarenfabrik, Filiale Göppingen: Lehre als Glasgraveur, ab 1906 Besuch der Abendkurse an der Zeichenschule Kolb & Gmelich, Göppingen, 1908 Gesellenprüfung, 1911 Studienreise nach Italien, Österreich und Frankreich ▓ 1911/12 als Glas- und Steingraveur in Paris tätig ▓ 1912/13 Studienreise nach Österreich ▓ 1914-1918 Kriegsdienst ▓ 1919-1921 Aufbau einer Werkstatt für Glas- und Steinschnitt in Stuttgart ▓ 1921-1943 Lehrauftrag an der Kunstgewerbeschule Stuttgart: Aufbau und

Leitung der neuen Fachabteilung für Glas- und Edelsteinbearbeitung ▓ ab 1931 Mitarbeit in der »Deutschen Glastechnischen Gesellschaft«: Vorsitz des Fachausschusses IV für Glasveredlung

1904-1911 Formation et travail à la filiale de Göppingen de la fabrique d'articles en métal du Würtemberg : apprentissage de graveur sur verre , à partir de 1906 suit les cours du soir de l'école de dessin Kolb & Gmelich à Göppingen, 1908 examen de compagnonnage , 1911 voyage d'études en Italie, en Autriche et en France ▓ 1911/12 travaille comme graveur sur verre et sur pierre à Paris ▓ 1912/13 voyage d'études en Autriche ▓ 1914-1918 service de guerre ▓ 1919-1921 création d'un atelier de gravure sur verre et sur pierre à Stuttgart ▓ 1921-1943 enseigne à l'Ecole des Arts décoratifs de Stuttgart: organisation et direction de la nouvelle section de verre et de métal ▓ à partir de 1931 collabore à la «Deutsche Glastechnische Gesellschaft»: président de la commission technique IV pour l'affinage du verre

Johannes (Jan) Eisenloeffel 1876-1957
From 1892-1896 attended the Rijksnormaalschool in Amsterdam, where he trained as a teacher of drawing ▓ from 1893-1896 trained at the metalware factory of W. Hoecker & Zoon, Amsterdam ▓ 1896/97 took a study trip to Russia: staying in Moscow and St. Petersburg, where he studied enamel and niello techniques at Fabergé ▓ from 1897-1902 on his return from Russia became head of the newly established metal department of the Amstelhoeck company, Amsterdam 1899 ▓ 1902 set up his own metalware company in Amsterdam together with J. C. Stoffels ▓ 1902-1913 founding member of the modern furnishings company »De Woning« in Amsterdam, through which he marketed his metalwork ▓ 1904-1907 designed for the silverware factory of Begeer, Utrecht ▓ 1908 worked with the

»Vereinigte Werkstätten für Kunst im Handwerk« (United Workshops) in Munich ▓ 1908 returned to Holland and set up a workshop at the Laren artists' colony near Amsterdam, producing metalwork

1892-1896 Besuch der Rijksnormaalschool, Amsterdam: Ausbildung zum Zeichenlehrer ▓ 1893-1896 Ausbildung im Atelier der Metallwarenfabrik W. Hoecker & Zoon, Amsterdam ▓ 1896/97 Studienreise nach Rußland: Aufenthalt in Moskau und St. Petersburg, Praktikum in der Firma Fabergé, St. Petersburg: Ausbildung in der Email- und Niellotechnik ▓ 1897-1902 Rückkehr aus Rußland, ab 1899 Leitung der neugegründeten Metallabteilung der Firma Amstelhoeck, Amsterdam ▓ 1902 Gründung einer eigenen Firma für Metallwaren in Amsterdam zusammen mit J. C. Stoffels ▓ 1902-1913 Mitbegründer der Vertriebsfirma für modernen Einrichtungsbedarf »De Woning« in Amsterdam: Vertrieb seiner Metallarbeiten ▓ 1904-1907 Entwurfstätigkeit für die Silberwarenfabrik Begeer, Utrecht ▓ 1908 Zusammenarbeit mit den »Vereinigten Werkstätten für Kunst im Handwerk«, München ▓ 1908 Rückkehr nach Holland, Aufbau einer Werkstatt in der Künstlerkolonie Laren bei Amsterdam, dort Herstellung von Metallarbeiten, zumeist mit Unikatcharakter

1892-1896 Etudes à la Rijksnormaalschool d'Amsterdam : formation de dessinateur ▓ 1893-1896 formation dans l'atelier de métaux W. Hoecker & Zoon à Amsterdam ▓ 1896/97 voyage d'études en Russie: séjour à Moscou et Saint-Pétersbourg, stage chez Fabergé à Saint-Pétersbourg, formation dans les techniques d'émail et de niellure ▓ 1897-1902 retour de Russie, à partir de 1899 direction de la section de métal nouvellement créée chez Amstelhoeck à Amsterdam ▓ 1902 fondation de sa propre entreprise d'articles métalliques avec J.C. Stoffels ▓ 1902-1913 co-fondateur de la société «De Woning» commercialisant des ameublements modernes: édite ses créations en métal ▓ 1904-1907 travaille de concepteur pour le fabricant d'objets en argent Begeer d'Utrecht ▓ 1908 coopération avec les «Vereinigte Werkstätten für Kunst im Handwerk» de Munich ▓ 1908 retour en Hollande, création d'un atelier dans la colonie d'artistes de Laren près d'Amsterdam, y fabrique des objets en métal qui ont le plus souvent un caractère de pièces uniques

Kay Fisker 1893-1965
1909-1911 apprentice mason ▓ until 1920 studied architecture at the academies of Copenhagen, Stockholm and London, trained at the architectural firms of Anton Rosen and Hack Kampmann in Copenhagen and Sigurd Lewerenz in Stockholm ▓ 1918-1926 editor of the Danish art periodical »Architekten« ▓ 1919-1963 taught architecture at the Academy in Copenhagen, working as freelance archi-

tect at the same time and designing interiors for passenger ships ▓ 1925 designed the Danish Pavilion for the »Exposition internationale des arts décoratifs et industriels modernes« in Paris ▓ from about 1925 designed for the silversmith A. Michelsen, Copenhagen

1909-1911 Lehre als Maurer ▓ bis 1920 Architekturstudium an den Akademien in Kopenhagen, Stockholm und London, praktische Tätigkeit in den Architekturbüros Anton Rosen und Hack Kampmann in Kopenhagen sowie Sigurd Lewerenz in Stockholm ▓ 1918-1926 Redaktion der dänischen Kunstzeitschrift »Architekten« ▓ 1919-1963 Lehrauftrag für Architektur an der Akademie in Kopenhagen, parallel dazu als selbständiger Architekt tätig, Entwurf von Inneneinrichtungen für Passagierschiffe ▓ 1925 Gestaltung des dänischen Pavillons für die »Exposition internationale des arts décoratifs et industriels modernes« in Paris ▓ ab ca. 1925 Entwurfstätigkeit für die Silberschmiede A. Michelsen, Kopenhagen

1909-1911 Apprentissage de maçon ▓ Jusqu'en 1920 études d'architecture dans les académies de Copenhague, de Stockholm et de Londres, travail pratique dans les cabinets d'architectes d'Anton Rosen et de Hack Kampmann à Copenhague ainsi que chez Sigurd Lewerenz à Stockholm ▓ 1918-1926 rédaction de la revue danoise «Architekten» ▓ 1919-1963 enseigne l'architecture à l'académie de Copenhague, travaille en même temps comme architecte indépendant, création d'intérieurs de paquebots ▓ 1925 réalise le pavillon danois pour l'Exposition internationale des arts décoratifs et industriels modernes de Paris ▓ A partir de 1925 travaille comme créateur pour l'orfèvrerie A. Michelsen de Copenhague

Hayno Focken 1905-1968
1924-1929 apprenticed to the Max Krüger lighting workshop in Berlin ▓ 1929-1932 studied at Burg Giebichenstein School of Applied Art in Halle and was apprenticed at the metal workshop of Karl Müller ▓ 1932-1968 ran a metal workshop in Lahr/Baden where he designed and produced numerous appliances and sculptures in steel and coloured metals

1924-1929 Lehre, vermutlich als Gürtler oder Ziseleur, in den Werkstätten für Beleuchtungskörper Max Krüger, Berlin ▓ 1929-1932 Studium an der Kunstgewerbeschule Burg Giebichenstein in Halle: Lehre in der Metallwerkstatt bei Karl Müller ▓ 1932-1968 Aufbau einer Werkstatt für Metallarbeiten in Lahr/Baden: Entwurf und Ausführung zahlreicher Geräte und Skulpturen in Edel- und Buntmetallen

1924-1929 Apprentissage, probablement comme ciseleur, à l'atelier d'appareils d'éclairage Max Krüger à Berlin ▓ 1929-1932 études à l'Ecole des Arts décoratifs Burg Giebi-

chenstein à Halle: apprentissage dans l'atelier de métal chez Karl Müller ▓ 1932-1968 création d'un atelier de travail sur métaux à Lahr dans le pays de Bade: conception et réalisation de nombreux objets et de sculptures dans des métaux précieux et colorés

Marguerite Friedlaender-Wildenhain 1896-1983
1917/18 studied at the Kunstgewerbeschule (School of Applied Art) in Berlin ▓ 1918/19 designed for the Rudolstadt porcelain manufactory in Thuringia ▓ 1919-1925 studied

at the Bauhaus in Weimar (basic course, apprenticeship at the ceramics workshop in Dornburg, journeyman's exam) ▓ 1925-1933 taught at Burg Giebichenstein School of Applied Art in Halle as director of the ceramics workshop, set up a porcelain workshop and worked closely with the Staatliche Porzellanmanufaktur (KPM) in Berlin ▓ 1926 master's exam ▓ 1928 study period in Höhr-Grenzhausen ▓ 1930 married Franz Rudolf Wildenhain ▓ 1933-1940 removed from the teaching staff by the Nazi regime, emigrated to Holland and set up the »Het Kruikje« ceramics workshop in Putten ▓ 1940-1942 taught at the College of Arts and Crafts/Oakland, Cal. as head of the ceramics workshop ▓ 1942-1949 established the »Pond Farm« in Guernville/Cal. and set up a ceramics workshop ▓ when the artists' colony broke up in 1949, she continued to run Pond Farm pottery on her own, holding annual summer workshops for young ceramics artists

1917/18 Studium an der Kunstgewerbeschule Berlin ▓ 1918/19 Entwurfstätigkeit für die Porzellanmanufaktur Rudolstadt/Thüringen ▓ 1919-1925 Studium am Bauhaus Weimar: Vorkurs, Lehre in der Keramikwerkstatt in Dornburg, Gesellenprüfung ▓ 1925-1933 Lehrauftrag an der Kunstgewerbeschule Burg Giebichenstein in Halle: Leitung der Keramikwerkstatt, Aufbau einer Porzellanwerkstatt, enge Zusammenarbeit mit der Staatlichen Porzellanmanufaktur (KPM) Berlin ▓ 1926 Meisterprüfung ▓ 1928 Studienaufenthalt in Höhr-Grenzhausen ▓ 1930 Heirat mit Franz Rudolf Wildenhain ▓ 1933-1940 Entlassung als Lehrkraft durch die Nationalsozialisten, Emigration nach Holland, Aufbau der Keramikwerkstatt »Het Kruikje« in Putten ▓ 1940-1942 Lehrauftrag am College of Arts and Crafts, Oakland/Cal.: Leitung der Keramikwerkstatt ▓ 1942-1949 Gründung der »Pond Farm« in Guernville/Cal.: Aufbau einer Keramikwerkstatt ▓ ab 1949 Auflösung der Künstlerkolonie, selbständige

Weiterführung der Keramikwerkstatt als »Pond Farm Pottery«, Leitung jährlicher Sommerkurse für junge Keramiker

1917/18 Etudes à l'Ecole des Arts décoratifs de Berlin ▓ 1918/19 travaille comme créatrice pour la manufacture de porcelaine de Rudolstadt en Thuringe ▓ 1919-1925 études au Bauhaus de Weimar: cours préliminaire, apprentissage à l'atelier de métal de Dornbourg, examen de compagnonnage ▓ 1925-1933 enseigne à l'école Burg Giebichenstein de Halle: direction de l'atelier de céramique, mise sur pied d'un atelier de porcelaine, étroite coopération avec la Staatliche Porzellanmanufaktur (manufacture de porcelaine) (KPM) de Berlin ▓ 1926 examen de maîtrise ▓ 1928 séjour à Höhr-Grenzhausen ▓ 1930 mariage avec Franz Rudolf Wildenhain ▓ 1933-1940 licenciement de son poste d'enseignante par les nationaux-socialistes, émigration en Hollande, création de l'atelier de céramique «Het Kruikje» à Putten ▓ 1940-1942 enseigne au College of Arts and Crafts d'Oakland/Cal.: direction de l'atelier de céramique ▓ 1942-1949 fonde la «Pond Farm» à Guernville/Cal.; création d'un atelier de céramique ▓ A partir de 1949 dissolution de la colonie d'artistes, dirige seule l'atelier appelé maintenant «Pond farm Pottery», donne des cours d'été à des jeunes céramistes

Hubert Griemert 1905-1990
1921-1925 studied painting and ceramics at the Kunstgewerbeschule (School of Applied Art) in Hildesheim ▓ 1925-1927 trained as a ceramics artist under Kurt Feuerriegel in Frohburg/Saxony ▓ 1927-1929 studied at the Staatliche Keramische Fachschule (state ceramics school) in Bunzlau ▓ 1930-1946 studied and worked at Burg Giebichenstein School of Applied Art in Halle: apprenticeship in the ceramics workshop, 1932 journeyman's exam, teaching assistantship in the ceramics workshop, 1935 master's exam, director of the ceramics class ▓ 1943-1945 military service ▓ 1947-1954 set up a ceramics workshop in Schötmar/Lippe ▓ 1950-1954 taught at the Werkkunstschule (School of Applied Art) in Krefeld as director of the ceramics class ▓ 1954-1970 gave master classes at the Staatliche Werkschule für Keramik (School of Ceramics) in Höhr-Grenzhausen ▓ 1971 settled in Lauf/Pegnitz

1921-1925 Studium der Malerei und Keramik an der Kunstgewerbeschule Hildesheim ▓ 1925-1927 Ausbildung als Keramiker bei Kurt Feuerriegel in Frohburg/Sachsen ▓ 1927-1929 Studium an der Staatlichen Keramischen Fachschule in Bunzlau ▓ 1930-1946 Studium und Arbeit an der Kunstgewerbeschule Burg Giebichenstein Halle: Lehre in der Keramikwerkstatt, 1932 Gesellenprüfung, als Hilfslehrer in der Keramikwerkstatt tätig, 1935 Meisterprüfung, Übernahme der Fachklasse für Keramik ▓ 1943-1945 Kriegsdienst

▓ 1947-1954 Aufbau einer Keramikwerkstatt in Schötmar/Lippe ▓ 1950-1954 Lehrauftrag an der Werkkunstschule Krefeld: Leitung der Keramikklasse ▓ 1954-1970 Lehrauftrag an der Staatlichen Werkschule für Keramik in Höhr-Grenzhausen: Leitung der Meisterklasse ▓ ab 1971 in Lauf/Pegnitz ansässig

1921-1925 Etude de la peinture et de la céramique à l'Ecole des Arts décoratifs de Hildesheim ▓ 1925-1927 formation de céramiste chez Kurt Feuerriegel à Frohburg en Saxe ▓ 1927-1929 études à l'Ecole technique de Céramique de Bunzlau ▓ 1930-1946 études et travail à l'Ecole des Arts décoratifs Burg Giebichenstein à Halle: apprentissage à l'atelier de céramique, 1932 examen de compagnonnage, enseignant auxiliaire à l'atelier de céramique, 1935 examen de maîtrise, prend la direction de la classe de céramique ▓ 1943-1945 service militaire ▓ 1947-1954 création d'un atelier de céramique à Schötmar/Lippe ▓ 1950-1954 enseigne à l'école d'art de Krefeld: direction de la classe de céramique ▓ 1954-1970 enseigne à l'Ecole nationale de Céramique de Höhr-Grenzhausen: direction de la classe de maîtrise ▓ Depuis 1971 est installé à Lauf/Pegnitz

Paul Haustein 1880-1944
1886/87 studied at the Kunstgewerbeschulen (School of Applied Art) in Dresden and Munich ▓ 1898/99 studied painting at the Akademie der Bildenden Künste (Fine Arts Academy) in Munich as master pupil of Johann Caspar Herterich, created graphic works for the magazine »Jugend« and lamp designs for the metalware manufacturer Seifert & Co. of Dresden-Löbtau ▓ from 1899-1903 worked at the »Vereinigte Werkstätten für Kunst im Handwerk« (United Workshops) in Munich, designing and producing several items for the metal and belt-making workshop ▓ 1903-1905 member of the Darmstadt artists' colony ▓ 1907/08 gave master classes for the Bavarian Board of Trade in Nuremberg ▓ 1905-1944 taught metalwork at the Kunstgewerbeschule (School of Applied Art) in Stuttgart, designed for the WMF metalware factory in Geislingen and the silverware manufacturer Bruckmann & Söhne in Heilbronn

1886/87 Studium an den Kunstgewerbeschulen Dresden und München ▓ 1898/99 Studium der Malerei an der Akademie der Bildenden Künste München: Meisterschüler von Johann Caspar Herterich, grafische Arbeiten für die Zeitschrift »Jugend«, Lampenentwürfe für die Metallwarenfabrik Seifert & Co., Dresden-Löbtau ▓ 1899-1903 Mitarbeit in den »Vereinigten Werkstätten für Kunst im Handwerk«, München: Entwurf und Ausführung zahlreicher Arbeiten in der Metall- und Gürtlereiwerkstatt ▓ 1903-1905 Mitglied der Darmstädter Künstlerkolonie ▓ 1907/08 Leitung der Mei-

sterkurse des Bayerischen Landesge-
werbeamtes in Nürnberg ▧ 1905-
1944 Lehrauftrag für Metallkunst
an der Kunstgewerbeschule Stuttgart, Entwurfstätigkeit für die Württembergische Metallwarenfabrik,
Geislingen, die Silberwarenfabrik
Bruckmann & Söhne, Heilbronn u.a.

1886/87 Etudes dans les écoles
d'arts décoratifs de Dresde et de
Munich ▧ 1898/98 étude de la peinture à l'Académie des Beaux-Arts de
Munich: élève de maîtrise de Johann Caspar Herterich, travaux graphiques pour la revue «Jugend»,
création de lampes pour l'entreprise
Seifert & Co. de Dresden-Löbtau
▧ 1899 -1903 travaille aux «Vereinigte Werkstätten für Kunst im
Handwerk»: création et réalisation
de nombreux objets à l'atelier de
métal ▧ 1903-1905 membre de la
colonie d'artistes de Darmstadt
▧ 1907/08 direction des cours de
maîtrise de l'inspection de l'artisanat et de l'industrie de Bavière à
Nuremberg ▧ 1905-1944 enseigne
le travail sur métal à l'Ecole des Arts
décoratifs de Stuttgart, crée pour la
fabrique d'articles en métal du Wurtemberg à Geißlingen, la firme
Bruckmann & Fils de Heilbronn etc.

Poul Henningsen 1894-1967
1908-1910 studied painting at the
Technical University of Copenhagen
▧ 1911-1914 studied architecture
at the Polytechnic of Copenhagen
▧ 1917-1921 art critic for the magazine »Klingen« ▧ 1921-1925 wrote
articles for the »Politiken« and
»Extra Bladet« newspapers ▧ from
1924 designed lamps and furnishings for the companies Louis Poulsen and Zeiss & Goertz, Copenhagen ▧ 1926-1928 published the
periodical »Kritisk Revy« ▧ 1929
music critic ▧ 1933-1943 wrote
scripts for various films and articles
for newspapers and periodicals in
Copenhagen ▧ 1943-1945 fled to
Sweden ▧ 1947 worked as a freelance journalist and editor in Den-
mark

1908-1910 Studium der Malerei an
der Technischen Universität, Kopenhagen ▧ 1911-1914 Studium der Architektur an der Polytechnischen
Lehranstalt, Kopenhagen ▧ 1917-
1921 als Kunstkritiker für die Zeitschrift »Klingen« tätig ▧ 1921-1925
als Journalist für die Zeitungen »Politiken« und »Extra Bladet« tätig
▧ ab 1924 Entwürfe für Leuchten
und Möbel, Ausführung der Entwürfe durch die Firmen Louis Poulsen
und Zeiss & Goertz, Kopenhagen
▧ 1926-1928 Herausgeber der Zeitschrift »Kritisk Revy« ▧ ab 1929
auch als Verfasser von Musik-Revu-
en tätig ▧ 1933-1943 als Drehbuch-
autor für verschiedene Filme und
als freier Journalist für verschiedene
Zeitungen und Zeitschriften in Kopenhagen tätig ▧ 1943-1945 Flucht
nach Schweden ▧ ab 1947 erneut
als freier Journalist und Herausgeber in Dänemark tätig

1908-1910 Etude de la peinture à
l'université technique de Copenhague ▧ 1911-1914 études d'architec-

ture à l'Institut polytechnique de Copenhague ▧ 1917-1921 travaille
comme critique d'art à la revue
«Klingen» ▧ 1921-1925 comme
journaliste au «Politiken» et à «Extra Bladet» ▧ A partir de 1924 crée
des lampes et des meubles, réalisation de ses créations par les firmes
Louis Poulsen et Zeiss & Goertz de
Copenhague ▧ 1926-1928 éditeur
de la revue «Kritisk Revy» ▧ A partir de 1929 travaille aussi comme
compositeur de revues musicales
▧ 1933-1943 comme scénariste de
divers films et comme journaliste indépendant pour différents journaux
et revues ▧ 1843-1945 fuit en Suède ▧ A partir de 1947 revient au Da-
nemark et travaille à nouveau comme journaliste et éditeur

Karl Heubler 1884-1961
Trained as an engraver and metal
sculptor ▧ studied at the Kunstgewerbeschulen (Schools of Applied Art) in Düsseldorf and the
Städtische Handwerker- und Kunstgewerbeschule in Hanover ▧ 1905-
1943 taught at the Reimann School
(and subsequently at the »Kunst
und Werk – Privatschule für Gestaltung«) in Berlin, giving classes in metalwork and directing the metal
workshop, creating numerous designs in precious and coloured metal-
s ▧ after 1945 designed jewellery
for the Rua company in Berlin

Ausbildung als Ziseleur und Metallbildhauer ▧ Studium an der Kunstgewerbeschule Düsseldorf und der
Städtische Handwerker- und Kunstgewerbeschule Hannover ▧ 1905-
1943 Lehrauftrag an der Reimann-
Schule (später am Nachfolgeinstitut
»Kunst und Werk – Privatschule für
Gestaltung«) in Berlin: Leitung der
Klasse für Metallarbeiten und der
Metallwerkstatt, zahlreiche Entwürfe für Arbeiten in Edel- und Buntmetallen ▧ nach 1945 Schmuckentwürfe für die Firma Rua, Berlin

Apprentissage de ciseleur et de graveur sur métaux ▧ Etudes à l'Ecole
des Arts décoratifs de Düsseldorf et
à l'Ecole municipale d'Artisanat et
d'Arts décoratifs de Hanovre
▧ 1905-1943 enseigne à l'école Reimann (plus tard à l'école qui lui suc-
cédera: «Kunst und Werk – Privatschule für Gestaltung») à Berlin: direction de la classe de métal et de
l'atelier correspondant, nombreuses
créations sur métaux précieux et colorés ▧ Après 1945 devient créateur
de bijoux pour la firme Rua de Berlin

Margarete Heymann-Marks 1899
Studied at the Kunstgewerbeschule
(School of Applied Art) in Cologne
and the Academy in Düsseldorf
▧ 1920/21 studied at the Bauhaus
in Weimar (basic course and trial semester in the ceramics workshop in
Dornburg) ▧ 1921 worked in a ceramics workshop in Frechen and
gave a pottery course for children
at the Kunstgewerbeschule (School
of Applied Art) in Cologne ▧ 1922
appointed artistic advisor to the Velten-Vordamm pottery factory
▧ 1923-1932 set up the »Hael –
Werkstätten für künstlerische Ker-

amik« in Marwitz near Velten and
designed for the Rosenthal porcelain manufactory in Selb ▧ 1935-
1939 emigrated to England, designed for the Minton Factory in
Stoke-on-Trent, taught ceramics at
the Burslem School of Art in Stoke-
on-Trent and designed tableware
(»Greta Pottery«) for Ridgway of
Shelton near Stoke-on-Trent 1945
set up a ceramics workshop in London and produced ceramic wall
paintings and »studio pottery«

Studium an der Kunstgewerbeschule Köln und der Kunstakademie Düsseldorf ▧ 1920/21 Studium am Bauhaus Weimar: Vorkurs, Probeseme-
ster in der Keramikwerkstatt in
Dornburg ▧ 1921 Arbeit in einer Keramikwerkstatt in Frechen, Leitung
eines Töpferkurses für Kinder an
der Kunstgewerbeschule Köln
▧ 1922 künstlerische Mitarbeit im
Werk Velten der Steingutfabriken
Velten-Vordamm ▧ 1923-1932 Aufbau der »Hael-Werkstätten für
künstlerische Keramik« in Marwitz
bei Velten, Entwurfstätigkeit für die
Rosenthal-Porzellanmanufaktur,
Selb ▧ 1935-1939 Emigration nach
England, Entwurfstätigkeit für die
Minton-Factory in Stoke-on-Trent,
Lehrauftrag für Keramik an der
Burslem School of Art, Stoke-on-
Trent, Entwurf von Geschirren unter
der Bezeichnung »Greta-Pottery«
für die Steingutfabrik Ridgway, Shel-
ton bei Stoke-on-Trent ▧ ab 1945
Aufbau einer Keramikwerkstatt in
London: Ausführung von kerami-
schen Wandbildern und von »studio
pottery«

Etudes à l'Ecole des Arts décoratifs
de Cologne et à l'Académie de Düsseldorf ▧ 1920/21 études au Bauhaus de Weimar: cours préliminaire,
semestre d'essai à l'atelier de céramique de Dornbourg ▧ 1921 travaille dans un atelier de céramique de
Frechen, direction d'un cours de poterie pour enfants à l'école des arts
décoratifs de Cologne ▧ 1922 collaboration artistique à l'usine de grès
de Velten-Vordamm ▧ 1923-1932
création des »Hael-Werkstätten für
künstlerische Keramik» à Marwitz
près de Velten, activité de créatrice
pour la manufacture de porcelaine
Rosenthal, Selb ▧ 1935-1939 émigre en Angleterre, travaille comme
conceptrice pour la Minton-Factory
de Stoke-on-Trent, enseigne la céramique à la Burslem School of Art de
la ville, crée des vaisselles sous le
nom de «Greta-Pottery» pour la
gresserie Ridgway à Shelton près de
Stoke-on-Trent ▧ A partir de 1945
ouvre un atelier à Londres: réalisation de céramiques murales et de
«studio pottery»

Josef Hillerbrand 1892-1981
Trained as a painter ▧ studied at
the Kunstgewerbeschule in Munich
▧ 1922-1960 taught at the Kunstgewerbeschule (later at the
Academy of Fine Arts) in Munich,
giving classes in applied painting, interior design and textile design
▧ from the 1920s, worked closely
with the Deutsche Werkstätten, designing wallpaper, textiles, metal, ce-

ramics, glass, glass painting, furniture etc. ▧ also worked as an architect

Lehre als Maler ▧ Studium an der
Kunstgewerbeschule München
▧ 1922-1960 Lehrauftrag an der
Kunstgewerbeschule (später am
Nachfolgeinstitut der Staatsschule
für Angewandte Kunst bzw. der
Akademie der Bildenden Künste),
München: Klassen für angewandte
Malerei, Raumgestaltung und Textilentwurf ▧ ab den 1920er Jahren intensive Zusammenarbeit mit den
Deutschen Werkstätten: Entwürfe
für Tapeten, Textilien, Metall, Keramik, Glas, Hinterglasbilder, Möbel
etc. ▧ auch als Architekt tätig

Formation de peintre ▧ Etudes à l'E-
cole des Arts décoratifs de Munich
▧ 1922-1960 chargé de cours à l'é-
cole (deviendra plus tard Ecole des
Arts appliqués et plus tard encore
l'Académie des Beaux-Arts) : classes
de peinture appliquée, conception
de l'espace et création de textiles
▧ A partir des années vingt collaboration intensive avec les Ateliers allemands: création de papiers muraux,
de textiles, d'objets en métal, de céramique, de verre, de tableaux sous
verre, de meubles etc. ▧ Travaille
aussi comme architecte

Josef Hoffmann 1870-1956
1887-1891 studied architecture at
the Höhere Staatsgewerbeschule in
Brünn ▧ 1892-1895 studied architecture at the Kunstgewerbeschule
(School of Applied Arts) in Vienna
▧ 1895/96 founder member of the
»Siebenerclub« (Club of Seven) artists' group, travelled to Italy with Joseph Maria Olbrich ▧ 1897 worked
in the architecture practice of Otto
Wagner in Vienna, co-founder of
the Vienna Secession ▧ 1899-1936
taught at the Kunstgewerbeschule
in Vienna, giving classes in architecture, metalwork, enamelling and design ▧ 1900 travelled to England,
where he met Charles Robert Ashbee and Charles Rennie Mackintosh
▧ 1903-1932 founder member and
artistic director of the Wiener Werkstätte, established a major architecture practice in Vienna and produced numerous important architectural designs at home and abroad
▧ 1904 designed the Purkersdorf Sanatorium near Vienna ▧ 1905-1911
designed the Palais Stoclet in
Brussels ▧ 1907 founder member of
the Deutscher Werkbund ▧ 1912
founder member and, until 1920,
chairman of the Austrian Werkbund
▧ from 1920 municipal architect of
the City of Vienna

1887-1891 Studium an der Bauabteilung der Höheren Staatsgewerbeschule in Brünn ▧ 1892-1895 Studium an der Akademie der Bildenden
Künste Wien: Spezialschule für Architektur ▧ 1895/96 Gründungsmitglied der Künstlergemeinschaft »Siebenerclub«, Studienreise mit Joseph
Maria Olbrich nach Italien ▧ 1897
Mitarbeit im Architekturbüro Otto
Wagner in Wien, Mitbegründer der
Wiener Secession ▧ 1899-1936 Lehrauftrag an der Kunstgewerbeschule

Wien: Fachklassen für Architektur, Metallarbeit, Emailarbeit und Kunstgewerbe ▦ 1900 Studienreise nach England, dort Begegnung mit Charles Robert Ashbee und Charles Rennie Mackintosh ▦ 1903-1932 Gründungsmitglied und künstlerischer Direktor der Wiener Werkstätte, Aufbau eines großen Architekturbüros in Wien, zahlreiche bedeutende Architekturentwürfe für das In- und Ausland ▦ 1904 Planung des Sanatoriums Purkersdorf bei Wien ▦ 1905-1911 Planung des Palais Stoclet in Brüssel ▦ 1907 Gründungsmitglied des Deutschen Werk-

bundes ▦ 1912 Gründungsmitglied und bis 1920 Vorsitzender des Österreichischen Werkbundes ▦ ab 1920 Baurat der Stadt Wien

1887-1891 Etudes en classe de construction à l'Ecole d'Etat des Arts décoratifs à Brünn ▦ 1892-1895 études à l'Académie des Beaux-Arts de Vienne: Ecole spéciale d'architecture ▦ 1895/96 membre fondateur de la communauté d'artistes «Siebenerclub», voyage d'études en Italie avec Joseph Maria Olbrich ▦ 1897 collabore au cabinet d'architecte d'Otto Wagner à Vienne, co-fondateur de la Sécession viennoise ▦ 1899-1936 chargé de cours à l'Ecole d'Arts décoratifs de Vienne: classes d'architecture, de métal, d'émail et d'art appliqué ▦ 1900 voyage en Angleterre, rencontre Charles Robert Ashbee et Charles Rennie Mackintosh ▦ 1903-1932 membre fondateur et directeur artistique de la Wiener Werkstätte, création d'un grand cabinet d'architecte à Vienne, nombreuses et importantes réalisations architecturales dans le pays et à l'étranger ▦ 1904 projet du sanatorium de Purkersdorf près de Vienne ▦ 1905-1911 plans du Palais Stoclet à Bruxelles ▦ 1907 membre fondateur du Werkbund allemand ▦ 1912 membre fondateur et jusqu'en 1920 président du Werkbund autrichien ▦ A partir de 1920 conseiller du service d'urbanisme de la ville de Vienne

Patriz Huber 1878-1902
Until 1897 studied at the School of Applied Arts in Mainz and attended his father's classes ▦ 1897/98 studied at the Kunstgewerbeschule in Munich, entered several competitions, drew up graphic designs for the publisher Alexander Koch in Darmstadt ▦ 1899-1902 member of the Darmstadt artists' colony, produced architectural designs, interior designs and craft designs ▦ 1902 left the Darmstadt artists' colony, established a design and architecture practice »Atelier Patriz Huber« in Berlin-Charlottenburg, designed the interior of the Hirschwald House in Berlin, interior designs, plans for a villa colony in Posen, committed suicide in Berlin the same year

Bis 1897 Besuch der Kunstgewerbeschule Mainz: Unterricht in der Klasse seines Vaters ▦ 1897/98 Studium an der Kunstgewerbeschule München, Teilnahme an zahlreichen Wettbewerben, grafische Entwürfe für den Alexander Koch Verlag, Darmstadt ▦ 1899-1902 Mitglied der Darmstädter Künstlerkolonie: Entwürfe für Architektur, Inneneinrichtungen und Kunstgewerbe ▦ 1902 Austritt aus der Künstlerkolonie Darmstadt, Gründung des Ent-

wurfs- und Architekturbüros »Atelier Patriz Huber« in Berlin-Charlottenburg: Gestaltung von Räumen für das Kunstgewerbehaus Hirschwald in Berlin, Entwürfe für Innenarchitektur, Planungsauftrag für eine Villenkolonie in Posen, noch im selben Jahr Freitod in Berlin

Jusqu'en 1897 fréquentation de l'Ecole des Arts décoratifs de Mayence: enseignement dans la classe de son père ▦ 1897/98 études à l'Ecole des Arts décoratifs de Munich, participation à de nombreux concours, créations graphiques pour la maison d'édition Alexander Koch de Darmstadt ▦ 1899-1902 membre de la colonie d'artistes de la colline Sainte-Mathilde à Darmstadt: projets d'architecture, agencement d'intérieurs et arts décoratifs ▦ 1902 quitte la colonie d'artistes, ouvre un cabinet d'architecte et de création, l'«Atelier Patriz Huber» à Berlin-Charlottenbourg: agencement et aménagement de pièces pour la maison d'arts décoratifs Hirschwald de Berlin, projets de décoration intérieure, commande de plans pour un groupe de villas à Posen, se suicide la même année

Georg Kleemann 1863-1932
Studied at the Kunstgewerbeschule (School of Applied Arts) in Munich ▦ taught in the Spieß design studio, giving classes in ceramic design, wallpaper design and book design ▦ from 1887 taught at the Staatliche Fachschule für Edelmetall (Precious Metals Trade School) in Pforzheim as director of the design class ▦ from 1901 designed for the jewellery maker Theodor Fahrner in Pforzheim

Studium an der Kunstgewerbeschule München ▦ Lehre im Entwurfsatelier Spieß: Entwürfe für Keramik, Tapeten und Buchausstattung ▦ ab 1887 Lehrauftrag an der Staatlichen Fachschule für Edelmetall, Pforzheim: Leitung der Entwurfsklasse ▦ ab 1901 Entwurfstätigkeit für die Schmuckwarenfirma Theodor Fahrner, Pforzheim

Etudes à l'Ecole des Arts décoratifs de Munich ▦ apprentissage dans l'atelier de création Spieß: modèles de céramiques, de papiers muraux et de présentation de livres ▦ à partir de 1887 enseigne à l'Ecole d'Etat de métaux précieux de Pforzheim: direction de la classe de conception ▦ à partir de 1901 activité de création pour le fabricant de bijoux Theodor Fahrner de Pforzheim

Archibald Knox 1864-1933
1878-1883 teacher at St. Barnabas Elementary School on the Isle of Man, ▦ 1878-1884 attended the Douglas School of Art, Isle of Man where he studied historic ornamental theory in depth ▦ 1884-1888 taught at the Douglas School of Art ▦ 1892-1896 worked in the architectural offices of Baillie Scott, met Arthur Lasenby, founder of Liberty & Co. in London ▦ 1897-1899 taught at Redhill School of Art in London, designed silverware for Liberty & Co. ▦ 1899 became design master at Kingston-upon-Thames Art School in London ▦ 1900 returned to Isle of Man, continued designing for Liberty & Co. ▦ 1904-1912 taught at Kingston-upon-Thames Art School ▦ 1912 emigrated to the USA, where his business ventures in Philadelphia and New York failed ▦ 1913 returned from USA to Isle of Man ▦ 1914-1918 worked as censor in a POW camp on the Isle of Man ▦ 1920-1927 taught at Douglas High School, Isle of Man

1878-1883 Lehrer an der St. Barnabas Elementary School auf der Isle of Man ▦ 1878-1884 Studium an der Douglas School of Art, Isle of Man: intensive Auseinandersetzung mit historischer Ornamentlehre ▦ 1884-1888 Lehrauftrag an der Douglas School of Art ▦ 1892-1896 Beschäftigung im Architekturbüro von Baillie Scott, Kontaktaufnahme mit Arthur Lasenby, dem Gründer der Firma Liberty & Co. in London ▦ 1897-1899 Lehrauftrag an der Redhill School of Art in London, Aufnahme der Entwurfstätigkeit von Silberwaren für die Firma Liberty & Co. ▦ 1899 als »Design Master« an der Kingston-upon-Thames Art School in London tätig ▦ 1900 Rückkehr auf die Isle of Man, weiterhin als Entwerfer für Liberty & Co. tätig ▦ 1904-1912 erneuter Lehrauftrag an der Kingston-upon-Thames Art School ▦ 1912 Emigration in die USA: vergebliche Versuche der Existenzgründung in Philadelphia und New York ▦ 1913 Rückkehr aus den USA auf die Isle of Man ▦ 1914-1918 als Zensor in einem Kriegsgefangenenlager auf der Isle of Man tätig ▦ 1920-1927 Lehrauftrag an der Douglas High School, Isle of Man

1878-1883 Instituteur à la St Barnabas Elementary School de l'île de Man ▦ 1878-1884 études à la Douglas School of Art de l'île: étude intensive des principes historiques de l'ornement ▦ 1884-1888 chargé de cours à la Douglas School of Art ▦ 1892-1896 employé dans l'étude d'architecte Baillie Scott, rencontre avec Arthur Lasenby, fondateur de la société Liberty & Co. à Londres ▦ 1897-1899 poste d'enseignant à la Redhill School of Art à Londres, créations d'objets en argent pour le compte de la firme Liberty & Co. ▦ 1899 chargé de cours en tant que «maître du design» à la Kingston-upon-Thames Art School de Londres ▦ 1900 retour sur l'île de Man, continue de créer pour Liberty & Co. ▦ 1904-1912 enseigne à nouveau à la Kingston-upon-Thames Art School ▦ 1912 émigre aux Etats-Unis: essaie vainement de se forger une nouvelle existence à Philadelphie et à New York ▦ 1913 s'installe sur l'île de Man à son retour des USA ▦ 1914-1918 travaille comme surveillant dans un camp de prisonniers de guerre installé sur l'île ▦ 1920-1927 enseignant à la Douglas High School de l'île de Man

Otto Lindig 1895-1966
1909-1911 attended drawing and sculpting classes in Lichte/Thuringia ▦ 1911-1913 taught sculpture at the Bechstein Atelier in Ilmenau ▦ 1913-1915 studied at the Großherzoglich Sächsische Kunstgewerbeschule (School of Applied Arts) in Weimar ▦ 1915-1918 studied at the Großherzoglich Sächsische Hochschule für Bildende Kunst (School of Fine Arts) in Weimar, where he attended sculpture classes by Richard Engelmann ▦ 1917 final exam, set up his own studio ▦ 1918 military service ▦ 1919-1925 studied at the Bauhaus in Weimar (basic course, apprenticeship in the ceramics workshop in Dornburg), 1922 journeyman's exam, later head of technical and commercial division of the ceramics workshop, designs for Aelteste Volkstedter Porzellanfabrik and the Staatliche Porzellanmanufaktur Berlin ▦ 1926-1930 master's exam, head of the ceramics workshop at the Staatliche Bauhochschule Weimar in Dornburg, produced designs for the Staatliche Majolika-Manufaktur in Karlsruhe ▦ from 1930 continued to run the Dornburg ceramics workshop independently ▦ 1947-1960 taught ceramics master classes at the Art School in Hamburg (then known as the Landeskunstschule, later the Hochschule für Bildende Künste)

1909-1911 Besuch der Zeichen- und Modellierschule in Lichte/Thüringen ▦ 1911-1913 Lehre als Bildhauer im Atelier Bechstein, Ilmenau ▦ 1913-1915 Studium an der Großherzoglich Sächsischen Kunstgewerbeschule Weimar ▦ 1915-1918 Studium an der Großherzoglich Sächsischen Hochschule für Bildende Kunst, Weimar: Bildhauerklasse Richard Engelmann ▦ 1917 Diplomprüfung und Einrichtung eines Ateliers ▦ 1918 Kriegsdienst ▦ 1919-1925 Studium am Bauhaus Weimar: Vorkurs, Lehre in der Keramikwerkstatt in Dornburg, 1922 Gesellenprüfung, später technische und kaufmännische Leitung der Keramikwerkstatt, Entwurfstätigkeit für die Aelteste Volkstedter Porzellanfabrik und die Staatliche Porzellanmanufaktur Berlin ▦ 1926-1930 Meisterprüfung, Leitung der keramischen Lehrwerkstatt der Staatlichen Bauhochschule Weimar in Dornburg, Entwurfstätigkeit für die Staatliche Majolika-Manufaktur Karlsruhe ▓ ab 1930 selbständige Weiterführung der Dornburger Keramikwerkstatt ▓ 1947-1960 Lehrauftrag an der Landeskunstschule (später Hochschule für Bildende Künste), Hamburg: Leitung der Meisterklasse für Keramik

1909-1811 Fréquente de l'école de dessin et de modelage de Lichte en Thuringe ▓ 1911-1913 apprentissage de sculpteur à l'atelier Bechstein à Ilmenau ▓ 1913-1915 études à

Großherzoglich Sächsische Kunstgewerbeschule de Weimar ▓ 1915-1918 études à Großherzoglich Sächsische Hochschule für Bildende Kunst à Weimar: classe de sculpture de Richard Engelmann ▓ 1917 diplôme et création d'un atelier ▓ 1918 service militaire ▓ 1919-1925 études au Bauhaus de Weimar: cours préliminaire, apprentissage dans l'atelier de céramique à Dornbourg, 1922 examen de compagnonnage, plus tard direction technique et commerciale de l'atelier, créations pour deux fabriques de porcelaines, l'Aelteste Volkstedter Porzellanfabrik et la Staatliche Porzellanmanufaktur de Berlin ▓ 1926-1930 examen de maîtrise, direction de l'atelier de la Staatliche Bauhochschule de Weimar à Dornbourg, crée pour la manufacture Majolika de Karlsruhe ▓ A partir de 1930 dirige sans interruption l'atelier de céramique de Dornbourg ▓ 1947-1960 enseigne à l'Ecole d'art du Land (plus tard transformée en Ecole des Beaux-Arts) de Hambourg: direction de la classe de céramique, cours de maîtrise

Adolf Loos 1870-1933
1887/88 attended the building construction department of the Gewerbeschule (Trade School) in Reichenberg ▓ 1890-1893 studied architecture at the Technische Hochschule (Polytechnic) in Dresden ▓ 1893-1896 undertook various jobs in the USA, went to the 1883 International Exhibition in Chicago, visited several American cities ▓ 1896/97 returned to Austria, worked for the architect Carl Mayreder in Vienna ▓ from 1897 published numerous critical articles on architecture, art, culture and lifestyle, worked as an independent architect in Vienna ▓ 1899 designed the »Café Museum« in Vienna ▓ 1903 established the periodical »Das Andere« ▓ 1908 published his famous essay on »Ornament und Verbrechen« (Ornament and Crime) ▓ 1909 designed the »Kärtner Bar« ▓ 1910/11 designed and built the »Hauses am Michaelerplatz« ▓ 1912-1914 established his own school of architecture

▓ 1916/17 military service ▓ 1920-1922 chief municipal architect for housing development in Vienna ▓ 1922-1927 emigrated to France, where he continued to work as an architect, numerous lecture trips ▓ 1928 returned to Vienna

1887/88 Besuch der Staats-Gewerbeschule in Reichenberg: Bautechnische Abteilung ▓ 1890-1893 Architekturstudium an der Technischen Hochschule Dresden ▓ 1893-1896 Aufenthalt in den USA, dort in verschiedenen Berufen tätig, Besuch der Weltausstellung 1883 in Chica-

go, Besichtigung zahlreicher amerikanischer Großstädte ▓ 1896/97 Rückkehr nach Österreich, in der Firma des Baumeisters Carl Mayreder in Wien tätig ▓ ab 1897 Verfasser zahlreicher kritischer Artikel über Architektur, Kunst, Kultur und Lebensform, als selbständiger Architekt in Wien tätig ▓ 1899 Gestaltung des »Café Museum« in Wien ▓ 1903 Gründung der Zeitschrift »Das Andere« ▓ 1908 Veröffentlichung des berühmten Aufsatzes »Ornament und Verbrechen« ▓ 1909 Gestaltung der »Kärtner Bar« ▓ 1910/11 Planung und Ausführung des »Hauses am Michaelerplatz« ▓ 1912-1914 Gründung einer eigenen Bauschule ▓ 1916/17 Kriegsdienst ▓ 1920-1922 Chefarchitekt des Siedlungsamtes der Gemeinde Wien ▓ 1922-1927 Emigration nach Frankreich, weiterhin als Architekt tätig, zahlreiche Vortragsreisen ▓ 1928 Rückkehr nach Wien

1887/88 Etudes à l'Ecole d'Artisanat de Reichenberg: section techniques de construction ▓ 1890-1893 études à l'Université technique de Dresde ▓ 1893-1896 séjour aux Etats-Unis, gagne sa vie par des petits emplois, visite l'Exposition universelle de Chicago et de nombreuses grandes villes américaines ▓ 1896/97 retour en Autriche, travaille brièvement chez l'architecte Carl Mayreder de Vienne ▓ A partir de 1897 écrit de nombreux articles critiques sur l'architecture, l'art, la culture et le mode d'existence, s'installe à son compte comme architecte à Vienne ▓ 1899 Conception du «Café Museum» de Vienne ▓ 1903 fondateur de la revue «Das Andere» ▓ 1908 publication du fameux article «Ornament und Verbrechen» (ornement et crime) ▓ 1909 agencement du «Kärtner Bar» ▓ 1910/11 agencement et réalisation de «Haus am Michaelerplatz» ▓ 1912-1914 fonde sa propre école de construction ▓ 1916/17 service de guerre ▓ 1920-1922 architecte en chef du bureau des lotissements de Vienne ▓ 1922-1927 émigre en France, continue ses activités d'architecte et voyage beaucoup comme conférencier ▓ 1928

retour à Vienne

Charles Rennie Mackintosh 1868-1928
From 1884 entered the architecture office of John Hutchinson in Glasgow as an articled pupil and enroled in evening classes at Glasgow School of Art, where he worked closely with Herbert MacNair and the Macdonald sisters (The Glasgow Four) ▓ 1889-1913 employed in the architecture offices of Honeyman & Keppie, becoming a partner in 1904 ▓ 1896-1899 designed and built the new Glasgow School of Art, in-

cluding interior design ▓ 1897-1917 designed a chain of »Glasgow tea rooms« for Miss Cranston ▓ 1900 took part in the 8th Vienna Secession Exhibition ▓ 1902-1904 designed and built »Hill House« in Helensburgh ▓ 1907-1909 designed and built the west wing of Glasgow School of Art ▓ from 1914/15 freelance designer and architect in London ▓ from 1920 gave up architecture and design, and moved to Port de Vendres, France, where he dedicated himself to painting

Ab 1884 Ausbildung im Architekturbüro John Hutchinson in Glasgow, Besuch der Abendklassen an der Glasgow School of Art: enge Zusammenarbeit mit Herbert MacNair und den Geschwistern Macdonald (bekannt als »The Glasgow Four«) ▓ 1889-1913 im Architekturbüro Honeyman & Keppie tätig, ab 1904 als gleichberechtigter Partner ▓ 1896-1899 Planung und Ausführung des Neubaus der Glasgow School of Art, Entwurf der gesamten Inneneinrichtung ▓ 1897-1917 Gestaltung der »Glasgow tea rooms« für Miss Cranston ▓ 1900 Beteiligung an der VIII. Ausstellung der Wiener Secession ▓ 1902-1904 Planung und Ausführung des »Hill House« in Helensburgh ▓ 1907-1909 Entwurf und Ausführung des West-Flügels der Glasgow School of Art ▓ ab 1914/15 als freischaffender Architekt und Entwerfer in London tätig ▓ ab 1920 Aufgabe der Tätigkeit als Architekt und Entwerfer, Übersiedlung nach Port de Vendres, Frankreich, dort ausschließliche Beschäftigung mit der Malerei

A partir de 1884 formation chez l'architecte John Hutchinson à Glasgow, école du soir à la Glasgow School of Art: étroite collaboration avec Herbert MacNair et les frères Macdonald (bien connus sous le nom de «Glasgow Four») ▓ 1889-1913 travaille dans l'étude d'architectes Honeyman & Keppie; à partir de 1904 comme parternaire à part entière ▓ 1896-1899 plans et réalisation du nouveau bâtiment de la Glasgow School of Art, conception

de l'ensemble du mobilier ▓ 1897-1917 Agencement des «Glasgow tea rooms» pour Miss Cranston ▓ 1900 participation à la 8ème Exposition de la Sécession viennoise ▓ 1902-1904 plans et réalisation de la «Hill Hause» d'Helensburgh ▓ 1907-1909 conception et réalisation de l'aile ouest de la Glasgow School of Art ▓ A partir de 1914/15 travaille comme architecte et créateur indépendant à Londres ▓ A partir de 1920 abandonne ses activités et s'installe à Port-Vendres en France, se consacre désormais à la peinture

Gerhard Marcks 1989-1981
From 1907 taught himself sculpture ▓ 1908-1912 workshop with sculptor Richard Scheibe in Berlin ▓ 1914-1918 military service ▓ 1918/19 taught at the Kunstgewerbeschule (School of Applied Arts) in Berlin, 1919 member of the Arbeitsrat für Kunst (Working Council for Art) in Berlin ▓ 1919-1924 taught at the Bauhaus in Weimar and was artistic director of the ceramics workshop in Dornburg ▓ 1925-1933 taught at Burg Giebichenstein School of Applied Arts in Halle as director of the sculpture workshop ▓ 1933 dismissed from the teaching staff by the National Socialist regime, moved to Niehagen near Wustrow/Mecklenburg ▓ from 1936 freelance artist in Berlin, banned from exhibitions ▓ 1943 his atelier in Berlin-Nikolassee was destroyed ▓ 1946-1950 taught sculpture classes at the Landeskunstschule (Art School) in Hamburg ▓ from 1950 freelance artist in Cologne

Ab 1907 Beschäftigung mit der Bildhauerei als Autodidakt ▓ 1908-1912 Werkstattgemeinschaft mit dem Bildhauer Richard Scheibe in Berlin ▓ 1914-1918 Kriegsdienst ▓ 1918/19 Lehrauftrag an der Kunstgewerbeschule Berlin, 1919 Mitglied im Geschäftsausschuß »Arbeitsrat für Kunst« in Berlin ▓ 1919-1924 Lehrauftrag am Bauhaus Weimar: künstlerische Leitung der Keramikwerkstatt in Dornburg ▓ 1925-1933 Lehrauftrag an der Kunstgewerbeschule Burg Giebichenstein in Halle: Leitung der Werkstatt für Plastik ▓ 1933 Entlassung als Lehrkraft durch die Nationalsozialisten, Übersiedlung nach Niehagen bei Wustrow/Mecklenburg ▓ ab 1936 als freischaffender Künstler in Berlin tätig, Ausstellungsverbot ▓ 1943 Zerstörung seines Ateliers in Berlin-Nikolassee ▓ 1946-1950 Lehrauftrag an der Landeskunstschule Hamburg: Klasse für Bildhauerei ▓ ab 1950 als freischaffender Künstler in Köln tätig

A partir de 1907 premiers travaux

plastiques en autodidacte ▓ 1908-1912 atelier commun avec le sculpteur Richard Scheibe à Berlin ▓ 1914-1918 service de guerre ▓ 1918/19 chargé de cours à l'Ecole des Arts décoratifs de Berlin, 1919 membre de la commission des affaires courantes du «Conseil ouvrier pour l'Art» à Berlin ▓ 1919-1924 enseigne au Bauhaus de Weimar: direction artistique de l'atelier de céramique à Dornbourg ▓ 1925-1933 enseignant à l'Ecole des Arts décoratifs de Burg Giebichenstein à Halle : direction de l'atelier d'art plastique ▓ 1933 révoqué par les nationaux-socialistes, il s'installe à Niehagen près de Wustrow dans le Land de Mecklenbourg ▓ A partir de 1936 travaille comme artiste libre à Berlin, interdit d'exposition ▓ 1943 destruction de son atelier à Berlin-Nikolassee ▓ 1946-1950 nommé à la Landeskunstschule de Hambourg: classe de sculpture ▓ A partir de 1950 travaille à Cologne à de nombreux projets

Emanuel Josef Margold 1889-1962
Trained as a carpenter at the Fachschule für Holzbearbeitung (Woodworking Trade College) in Königsberg/Eger ▓ studied at the Kunstgewerbeschule (School of Applied Arts) in Mainz ▓ from 1906 studied at the Kunstgewerbeschule in Vienna, attending architecture classes by Josef Hoffmann, exhibition design, architecture and design ▓ 1909/10 assistant to Josef Hoffmann in his architecture master classes at the Kunstgewerbeschule in Vienna and employee in his architecture office, member of the Wiener Werkstätte, designer for the porcelain manufacturer Josef Böck, Vienna ▓ from 1911 member of the Darmstadt artists' colony, several architectural plans, interior designs and design work ▓ from 1912 designed biscuit tins, shop fittings, window decorations etc. for the biscuit factory of Hermann Bahlsen in Hanover ▓ 1914-1918 military service ▓ from 1929 freelance architect in Berlin

Ausbildung als Schreiner an der Fachschule für Holzbearbeitung in Königsberg/Eger ▓ Studium an der Kunstgewerbeschule Mainz ▓ ab 1906 Studium an der Kunstgewerbeschule Wien: Fachklasse für Architektur unter Josef Hoffmann, Ausstellungsgestaltung, Entwürfe für Architektur und Kunstgewerbe ▓ 1909/10 Assistent von Josef Hoffmann in der Meisterklasse für Architektur an der Kunstgewerbeschule Wien und Mitarbeit in dessen Architekturbüro, Mitarbeiter der Wiener Werkstätte, Entwurfstätigkeit für die Porzellanmanufaktur Josef Böck, Wien ▓ ab 1911 Mitglied der Darmstädter Künstlerkolonie: zahlreiche Entwürfe für Architektur, Innenarchitektur und Kunstgewerbe ▓ ca. 1912 Zusammenarbeit mit der Keks-Fabrik Hermann Bahlsen, Hannover: Entwürfe für Keksdosen, Ladeneinrichtungen, Schaufensterdekorationen u.a. ▓ 1914-1918 Kriegsdienst ▓ ab 1929 als selbständiger Architekt in Berlin tätig

Il reçoit tout d'abord une formation de menuisier à la Fachschule für Holzbearbeitung de Königsberg-Eger ▓ Etudie à la Kunstgewerbeschule de Mayence ▓ A partir de 1906 à l'Ecole des Art décoratifs de Vienne; classe d'architecture et d'arts décoratifs ▓ 1909/10 assistant de Josef Hoffmann dans la classe de maîtrise et collaboration dans son cabinet d'architecte, membre des Wiener Werkstätte, «Glasgow tea rooms» activité créatrice pour la manufacture de porcelaine Josef Böck à Vienne ▓ A partir de 1911 membre de la colonie d'artistes de Darm-

stadt: nombreuses créations en architecture, décoration intérieure et arts décoratifs ▓ A partir de 1912 coopération avec la firme Hermann Bahlsen de Hanovre, créations de boîtes à biscuits, d'intérieurs de magasins, de décoration de vitrines etc. ▓ 1914-1918 service militaire ▓ A partir de 1929 travaille comme architecte indépendant à Berlin

Ludwig Mies van der Rohe 1886-1969
1900-1904 trained as designer of stucco decoration and ornamentation in Aachen ▓ 1904/05-1907 worked in Bruno Paul's design and architecture office in Berlin, and studied at the Kunstgewerbeschule (School of Applied Arts) in Berlin ▓ 1908-1911 architect in the office of Peter Behrens in Berlin ▓ from 1912 set up an architecture practice in Berlin ▓ 1914-1918 military service ▓ 1921-1924 four ideal designs for villas, highrises and office buildings ▓ 1921-1925 organised exhibitions by the Novembergruppe ▓ 1926/27 directed the Werkbund exhibition »Die Wohnung« (The Home) in Stuttgart, for which he designed tubular steel furniture ▓ 1929 designed the German Pavilion for the International Exhibition in Barcelona ▓ 1930-1933 director of the Bauhaus in Dessau and Berlin, where he taught architecture ▓ from 1933 freelance architect in Berlin ▓ 1937 emigrated to the USA ▓ from 1938 set up a major architecture office in Chicago, taught at the Armour Institute (later Illinois Institute of Technology), Chicago, appointed director of the department of architecture

1900-1904 Ausbildung als Stuck- und Ornamentzeichner in Aachen ▓ 1904/05-1907 im Entwurfs- und Architekturbüro von Bruno Paul in Berlin tätig, gleichzeitig Studium an der Kunstgewerbeschule Berlin ▓ 1908-1911 als Architekt im Büro von Peter Behrens in Berlin tätig ▓ ab 1912 Aufbau eines eigenen Architekturbüros in Berlin ▓ 1914-1918 Kriegsdienst ▓ 1921-1924 Entwicklung von vier maßgeblichen

Idealentwürfen für Villen, Hochhäuser und Bürobauten ▓ 1921-1925 Organisator von Ausstellungen der Novembergruppe ▓ 1926/27 Leitung der Werkbundausstellung »Die Wohnung« in Stuttgart, in diesem Zusammenhang Entwurf von Stahlrohrmöbeln ▓ 1929 Planung des Deutschen Pavillons auf der Weltausstellung in Barcelona ▓ 1930-1933 Direktor des Bauhauses Dessau und Berlin: Architekturunterricht ▓ ab 1933 wieder in Berlin als freier Architekt tätig ▓ 1937 Emigration in die USA ▓ ab 1938 Aufbau eines großen Architekturbüros in Chicago, Lehrauftrag am Armour Institute (später Illinois Institute of Technology), Chicago: Direktor der Architekturabteilung

1900-1904 Formation de dessinateur de stucs et d'ornements à Aix-la-Chapelle ▓ 1904/05-1907 travaille chez Bruno Paul, à côté, études à l'Ecole des Arts décoratifs de Berlin ▓ 1908-1911 collaborateur du bureau d'architecte de Peter Behrens ▓ A partir de 1912 architecte indépendant à Berlin ▓ 1914-1918 service de guerre ▓ 1921-1924 crée quatre projets idéaux de villas, d'immeubles de bureaux et de buildings ▓ 1921-1925 organise les expositions du Novembergruppe ▓ 1926/27 direction de l'exposition du Werkbund «Die Wohnung» à Stuttgart, crée à cette occasion des meubles tubulaires en acier ▓ 1929 construction du pavillon allemand de l'Exposition universelle de Barcelone ▓ 1930-1933 directeur du Bauhaus de Dessau et de Berlin: cours d'architecture ▓ A partir de 1933 de nouveau architecte indépendant à Berlin ▓ 1937 émigre aux Etats-Unis ▓ A partir de 1938 grande étude d'architecte à Chicago, donne aussi des cours au Armour Institute (plus tard Illinois Institute of Technology) de Chicago: direction de la section d'architecture

Christian Ferdinand Morawe 1865-1931
Studied at the Art School in Breslau ▓ 1896 worked as an art dealer, painter and writer in Munich ▓ from 1900 he lived in Darmstadt ▓ 1901-1904 he designed for the jewellery maker Theodor Fahrner in Pforzheim ▓ from 1902 he worked in Berlin, where he taught at the Art School until 1910, later becoming director of the State Artisanal Skills Courses in Berlin, before returning to teach at the Art School around 1930

Studium an der Kunstschule Breslau ▓ 1896 als Kunsthändler, Maler und Kunstschriftsteller in München tätig ▓ ab 1900 in Darmstadt ansässig ▓ 1901-1904 Entwurfstätigkeit für die Schmuckwarenfabrik Theodor Fahrner, Pforzheim ▓ ab 1902 in Berlin tätig: bis 1910 Lehrauftrag an der Kunstschule Berlin, später Leitung der Staatlichen Handfertigkeitskurse in Berlin, ab ca. 1930 erneuter Lehrauftrag an der Staatlichen Kunstschule Berlin

Etudes à l'école d'art de Breslau

▓ 1896 travaille comme marchand d'art, peintre et écrivain de l'art à Munich ▓ S'installe en 1900 à Darmstadt ▓ 1901-1904 travail de créateur pour le fabricant de bijoux Theodor Fahrner de Pforzheim ▓ s'installe en 1902 à Berlin: jusqu'en 1910 chargé de cours à l'Ecole des Beaux-Arts de Berlin, plus tard directeur des Cours d'Etat d'habileté manuelle, à partir de 1930 nouveau poste d'enseignant à l'Ecole des Beaux-Arts de Berlin

Koloman Moser 1868-1918
1885-1892 studied at the Akademie

der Bildenden Künste (Fine Arts Academy) in Vienna, where he contributed to the graphic design of the magazines »Wiener Mode« and »Meggendorfers Humoristische Blätter« ▓ 1986 attended classes by Professor Franz Rumpler at the Allegemeine Malerschule (Painting School) in Vienna ▓ 1892-1895 studied at the Kunstgewerbeschule (School of Applied Arts) in Vienna, taught drawing to the children of Archduke Karl Ludwig ▓ 1894 co-founder of the »Club of Seven« group of artists ▓ from 1895 freelance graphic artist, contributing to numerous portfolios and books ▓ 1897 co-founder of the Vienna Secession ▓ from 1898 co-editor of the magazine »Ver Sacrum«, initial design work ▓ 1899-1918 taught painting and drawing classes at the Kunstgewerbeschule (School of Applied Arts) in Vienna ▓ 1901 co-founder of the »Wiener Kunst im Haus« group of artists ▓ 1903 co-founder of the Wiener Werkstätte, artistic director with Josef Hoffmann until 1907 ▓ 1904-1906 designed glass windows for the Am Steinhof church (architect Otto Wagner) ▓ 1907 left the Wiener Werkstätte, dedicated himself to painting

1885-1892 Studium an der Akademie der Bildenden Künste, Wien, Mitarbeit an der grafischen Gestaltung der Zeitschriften »Wiener Mode« und »Meggendorfers Humoristische Blätter« ▓ 1886 Besuch der Allgemeinen Malerschule in Wien unter der Leitung von Prof. Franz Rumpler ▓ 1892-1895 Studium an der Kunstgewerbeschule Wien, als Zeichenlehrer für die Kinder von Erzherzog Karl Ludwig tätig ▓ 1894 Mitbegründer der Künstlervereinigung »Siebenerclub« ▓ ab 1895 als freischaffender Grafiker an der künstlerischen Gestaltung von zahlreichen Mappenwerken und Büchern beteiligt ▓ 1897 Mitbegründer der Wiener Secession ▓ ab 1898 Mitherausgeber der Zeitschrift »Ver Sacrum«, erste Entwurfstätigkeit für Kunstgewerbe ▓ 1899-1918 Lehrauftrag an der Kunstgewerbeschule

Wien: Fachklasse für Malerei und Zeichnen ▩ 1901 Mitbegründer der Künstlervereinigung »Wiener Kunst im Haus« ▩ 1903 Mitbegründer der Wiener Werkstätte, bis 1907 zusammen mit Josef Hoffmann deren künstlerischer Direktor ▩ 1904-1906 Mitarbeit an der Kirche am Steinhof (Otto Wagner): Entwurf der Glasfenster ▩ 1907 Austritt aus der Wiener Werkstätte, in der Folgezeit ausschließliche Beschäftigung mit der Malerei

1885-1892 Etudes à l'Académie des Beaux-Arts de Vienne, collabore à la présentation graphique de la revue «Wiener Mode» et des «Meggendorfers Homoristische Blätter» ▩ 1886 fréquente l'Ecole générale des peintres de Vienne dirigée par Hans Rumpler ▩ 1892-1895 études à l'Ecole des Arts décoratifs de Vienne, professeur de dessin des enfants de l'archiduc Karl Ludwig ▩ 1894 cofondateur de l'association d'artistes «Siebenerclub» ▩ A partir de 1895 participe en tant que graphiste indépendant à la conception de nombreux albums et de livres ▩ 1897 cofondateur de la Sécession Viennoise ▩ A partir de 1898 co-éditeur de la revue «Ver Sacrum», sa première activité de création dans le domaine des arts décoratifs ▩ 1899-1918 enseigne à l'Ecole des Arts décoratifs de Vienne dont il dirige la classe de peinture et de dessin ▩ 1901 co-fondateur de l'association d'artistes «Wiener Kunst im Haus» ▩ 1903 cofondateur de la Wiener Werkstätte dont il est jusqu'en 1907 le co-directeur artistique avec Josef Hoffmann ▩ 1904-1906 collabore aux travaux de construction de l'église Am Steinhof (plans d'Otto Wagner): conception des vitraux ▩ 1907 quitte la Wiener Werkstätte et se consacre ensuite à la peinture

Albin Müller 1871-1941
1887-1890 apprentice carpenter in his parents' workshop in Dittersbach/Erzgebirge, travelling journeyman ▩ 1891-1897 furniture designer and interior designer in the furniture factory of Heinrich Rauch in Mainz, and the furniture factory of Fr. Hege in Bromberg/Posen ▩ 1897-1900 studied at the Kunstgewerbeschule (School of Applied Arts) in Mainz and the Akademie der Bildenden Künste (Fine Arts Academy) in Dresden, worked as furniture designer in the furniture factory of Heinrich Pallenberg in Cologne ▩ 1900-1906 taught interior design and architectural form theory at the Kunstgewerbeschule in Magdeburg, autodidactic study of architecture, intensive design work ▩ 1906-1914 member of the Darmstadt artists' colony, prolific work in the fields of architecture, interior decoration and design ▩ 1907-1911 taught interior design at the Grand Ducal Studio of Applied Art ▩ from 1914 he attempted in vain to revive the artists' colony in Darmstadt, and worked in Darmstadt as freelance architect, painter and publisher

1887-1890 Lehre als Tischler im Betrieb der Eltern in Dittersbach/Erzgebirge, Gesellen- und Wanderjahre ▩ 1891-1897 als Möbelzeichner und Innenarchitekt bei der Möbelfabrik Heinrich Rauch in Mainz und bei der Möbelfabrik Fr. Hege in Bromberg/Posen tätig ▩ 1897-1900 Studium an der Kunstgewerbeschule Mainz und der Akademie der Bildenden Künste, Dresden, als Möbelzeichner in der Möbelfabrik Heinrich Pallenberg in Köln tätig ▩ 1900-1906 Lehrauftrag für Raumkunst und architektonische Formenlehre an der Kunstgewerbeschule Magdeburg, autodidaktische Beschäftigung mit der Architektur, intensive

Entwurfstätigkeit für Kunstgewerbe ▩ 1906-1914 Mitglied der Darmstädter Künstlerkolonie: intensive Entwurfstätigkeit für Architektur, Innenarchitektur und Kunstgewerbe ▩ 1907-1911 Lehrauftrag für Raumkunst an den Großherzoglichen Lehrateliers für angewandte Kunst ▩ ab 1914 vergebliche Bemühungen zur Wiederbelebung der Künstlerkolonie Darmstadt, als freischaffender Architekt, Maler und Publizist in Darmstadt tätig

1887-1890 Formation de menuisier dans l'atelier familial à Dittersbach dans les Monts métallifères, compagnon et années de voyage ▩ 1891-1897 travaille comme dessinateur concepteur de meubles et architecte décorateur chez le fabricant de meubles Heinrich Rauch à Mayence et chez Fr. Hege à Bromberg/Posen ▩ 1897-1900 études à l'Ecole des Arts décoratifs de Mayence et à l'Académie des Beaux-Arts de Dresde, travaille aussi comme dessinateur concepteur à Cologne chez le fabricant Heinrich Pallenberg ▩ 1900-1906 nommé professeur à l'Ecole des Arts décoratifs de Magdebourg: classe d'aménagement d'intérieurs et des formes architectoniques, s'occupe d'architecture en autodidacte, période d'intense activité créatrice en art décoratif ▩ 1906-1914 membre de la colonie d'artistes de Darmstadt: période d'intense activité créatrice en architecture, décoration intérieure et art décoratif ▩ 1907-1911 enseigne l'art de la décoration intérieure aux Ateliers d'arts décoratifs du Grand-Duché ▩ A partir de 1914 efforts vains de redonner vie à la colonie d'artistes de la colline Sainte-Mathilde, travaille à Darmstadt comme architecte indépendant, peintre et publiciste

Karl Müller 1888-1972
1903-1907 apprentice enchaser with the firm of Viktor Matzner in Berlin ▩ 1907-1909 assistant to the sculptor and carver Otto Rohloff and in other workshops in Berlin ▩ 1909-1915 studied at the Kunstgewerbeschule (School of Applied Arts) in Berlin, where he attended metal engraving classes ▩ 1915-1918 military service ▩ 1919/20 studied at the Akademie der Künste (Academy of Arts) in Berlin, where he was a master pupil of Hugo Lederer's ▩ 1920-1922 self-employed in Berlin ▩ 1923-1958 taught at the Burg Giebichenstein School of Applied Arts in Halle, director of the metal workshop, design work, produced several works in precious and coloured metals ▩ from 1958 freelance metal sculptor, studio at Burg Giebichenstein in Halle

1903-1907 Lehre als Ziseleur bei der

Firma Viktor Matzner, Berlin ▩ 1907-1909 Gehilfe bei dem Bildhauer und Ziseleur Otto Rohloff und in anderen Werkstätten in Berlin ▩ 1909-1915 Studium an der Kunstgewerbeschule Berlin: Fachklasse für Metallzeichnen ▩ 1915-1918 Kriegsdienst ▩ 1919/20 Studium an der Akademie der Künste, Berlin: Meisterschüler von Hugo Lederer ▩ 1920-1922 in Berlin selbständig tätig ▩ 1923-1958 Lehrauftrag an der Kunstgewerbeschule Burg Giebichenstein in Halle, Leitung der Metallwerkstatt, Entwurf und Ausführung zahlreicher Arbeiten in Edel- und Buntmetallen ▩ ab 1958 als freischaffender Metallbildhauer tätig, Atelier in den Räumen der Burg Giebichenstein in Halle

1903-1907 Apprentissage de ciseleur à l'atelier de Viktor Matzner à Berlin ▩ 1907-1909 commis chez le sculpteur et ciseleur Otto Rohloff et dans d'autres ateliers de Berlin ▩ 1909-1915 études à l'Ecole d'Arts décoratifs de Berlin: classe de dessin sur métal 1915-1918 service de guerre ▩ 1919/20 étudie à l'Académie des Beaux-Art de Berlin: élève de classe de maîtrise de Hugo Lederer ▩ 1920-22 s'installe à son compte à Berlin ▩ 1923-1958 enseigne à l'Ecole des Arts décoratifs de Burg Giebichenstein à Halle, direction de l'atelier de métal, conception et réalisation de nombreux objets en métaux précieux et colorés ▩ A partir de 1958 se consacre à la sculpture, son atelier se trouve dans les locaux de l'école de Burg Giebichenstein

Eckart Muthesius 1904-1989
Studied at the Vereinigte Staatsschulen für freie und angewandte Kunst (United Schools of Free and Applied Arts) in Berlin ▩ studied architecture at the Polytechnic in London ▩ worked in the architecture practice of James & Yerbury and Raymond Urwin in London ▩ master pupil in the studio of his father, Hermann Muthesius, in Berlin ▩ 1929 met the future Maharaja of Indore, Yeshwant Rao Holkar Bahadur, in Oxford ▩ from 1930 he designed the palace for the Maharaja of Indore, including the interior decor and fittings ▩ 1936-1939 head of the urban development and urban renewal department and architectural advisor to the State of Indore ▩ returned to Berlin on the outbreak of war, and worked as a freelance architect in Berlin

Studium an den Vereinigten Staatsschulen für freie und angewandte Kunst Berlin ▩ Architekturstudium am Polytechnikum, London ▩ in den Architekturbüros von James & Yerbury und Raymond Urwin in London tätig ▩ Meisterschüler im Atelier seines Vaters (Hermann Muthesius) in Berlin ▩ 1929 Bekanntschaft mit dem späteren Maharadscha von Indore Yeshwant Rao Holkar Bahadur in Oxford ▩ ab 1930 Planung des Palastes für den Maharadscha von Indore: Entwurf und Zusammenstellung der Inneneinrichtung ▩ 1936-1939 Leitung der Stadtbau- und Sanierungsbehörde sowie beratender Architekt des Staates Indore ▩ Rückkehr nach Berlin bei Kriegsausbruch, ab 1939 als selbständiger Architekt in Berlin tätig

Il étudie aux Vereinigte Staatsschulen für freie und angewandte Kunst de Berlin ▩ Etudes d'architecture à l'Ecole polytechnique de Londres ▩ travaille dans l'étude d'architectes James & Yerbury et dans celle de Raymond Urwin ▩ élève de classe de maîtrise dans l'atelier de son père (Hermann Muthesius) à Berlin ▩ 1929 rencontre le futur maharajah d'Indore Yeshwant Rao Holkar Bahadur, à Oxford ▩ à partir de 1930 plans du palais du maharadjah: conception et constitution de l'équipement intérieur ▩ 1936-1939 direction des services de planification et d'assainissement urbains, architecte conseiller de l'Etat d'Indore ▩ Retour à Berlin à l'éclatement de la guerre, à partir de 1939 travaille comme architecte indépendant

Joseph Maria Olbrich 1867-1908
1882-1886 studied architecture at the Staatsgewerbeschule (State School of Arts and Crafts) in Vienna ▩ 1886-1890 architect and head of construction for the contractor August Bartel in Troppau ▩ 1890-1893 studied at the Akademie der Bildenden Künste (Fine Arts Academy) in Vienna, where he attended architecture classes by Carl von Hasenauer ▩ from 1893 he worked in the architecture office of Otto Wagner in Vienna ▩ 1897 founder member of the Vienna Secession, designed the Secession exhibition building ▩ 1899-1908 member of the Darmstadt artists' colony, artistic director of the artists' colony, prolific output in the fields of architecture, interior decor and design: houses and exhibition buildings on the Mathildenhöhe in Darmstadt, furniture, silverware, pewterware, glass, ceramics and textiles ▩ 1907/08 set up an architecture office in Düsseldorf, designed the Tietz department store

1882-1886 Architekturstudium an der Staatsgewerbeschule Wien ▩ 1886-1890 als Architekt und Bau-leiter für den Bauunternehmer August Bartel in Troppau tätig ▨ 1890-1893 Studium an der Akademie der Bildenden Künste, Wien: Architekturklasse Carl von Hasenauer ▨ ab 1893 Mitarbeiter im Architekturbüro von Otto Wagner in Wien ▨ 1897 Gründungsmitglied der Wiener Secession, Entwurf des »Sezessions-Gebäudes« ▨ 1899-1908 Mitglied der Darmstädter Künstlerkolonie, künstlerische Leitung der Künstlerkolonie, intensive Entwurfstätigkeit für Architektur, Innenarchitektur und Kunstgewerbe: Wohn- und Ausstellungsbauten auf der Mathil-

denhöhe in Darmstadt, Entwürfe für Möbel, Silber, Zinn, Glas, Keramik und Textil ▨ 1907/08 Aufbau eines Architekturbüros in Düsseldorf, Planung des Warenhauses Tietz

1882-1886 Etudes d'architecture à l'Ecole nationale d'Arts décoratifs de Vienne ▨ 1886-1890 travaille comme architecte et directeur des travaux dans l'entreprise de construction August Bartel à Troppau ▨ 1890-1893 études à l'Académie des Beaux-Arts de Vienne, en classe d'architecture sous la direction de Carl von Hasenauer ▨ A partir de 1893 collaborateur de l'architecte Otto Wagner à Vienne ▨ 1897 Membre fondateur de la Sécession viennoise, conception du bâtiment de la Sécession ▨ 1899-1908 membre de la colonie d'artistes de Darmstadt, directeur artistique de la colonie, grande activité créatrice en architecture, aménagement intérieur et art décoratif: maisons et locaux d'exposition sur la colline Sainte-Mathilde, créations de meubles, d'objets en argent, en étain ou en verre, de céramiques et de textiles ▨ 1907/08 ouvre une étude d'architecte à Düsseldorf et réalise le grand magasin Tietz de la ville

Nora Ortlieb 1904-1984
Business studies ▨ 1924-1943 studied and worked at the Kunstgewerbeschule (School of Applied Arts) in Stuttgart: glass-cutting apprenticeship in Wilhelm von Eiff's department, 1926 exam, visited master classes, 1933 master's exam, then freelance work ▨ from 1933 member of the specialist glass-finishing committee of the «Deutsche Glastechnische Gesellschaft» (German Glass Society) ▨ from 1943 set up her own workshop in Stuttgart-Werfmershalde ▨ 1947-1969 worked for Marianne Schoder, Stuttgart-Degerloch ▨ 1969-1977 designed for Erwin Barthel, Gingen

Kaufmännische Ausbildung ▨ 1924-1943 Studium und Arbeit an der Kunstgewerbeschule Stuttgart: Lehre als Glasschneiderin in der Abteilung Wilhelm von Eiff, 1926 Gesel-

lenprüfung, Besuch der Meisterklasse, 1933 Meisterprüfung, danach freie Mitarbeit ▨ ab 1933 für die »Deutsche Glastechnische Gesellschaft« tätig: Fachausschuß für Glasveredlung ▨ ab 1943 Aufbau einer eigenen Werkstatt in Stuttgart-Werfmershalde ▨ 1947-1969 Mitarbeit in der Werkstatt Marianne Schoder, Stuttgart-Degerloch ▨ 1969-1977 Entwurfstätigkeit für die Firma Erwin Barthel, Gingen

Formation commerciale ▨ 1924-1943 étudie et travaille à l'Ecole des arts décoratifs de Stuttgart: apprentissage comme graveuse sur verre dans la classe de Wilhelm von Eiff, 1926 examen de compagnonnage, entre en classe de maîtrise, 1933 examen de maîtrise, ensuite artisan indépendant ▨ A partir de 1933 entre à la «Deutsche Glastechnische Gesellschaft», membre de la commission d'affinage du verre ▨ à partir de 1943 crée son propre atelier à Stuttgart-Werfmershalde ▨ 1947-1969 collabore avec Marianne Schoder qui a un atelier à Stuttgart-Degerloch ▨ 1969-1977 travaille comme concepteur pour l'entreprise Erwin Barthel de Gingen

Jacobus Johannes Pieter Oud 1890-1963
1904-1907 attended the Quellinus school of decorative art in Amsterdam ▨ 1907/08 assistant in the architecture practice of Cuijpers & Stuijt in Amsterdam ▨ 1909/10 studied at the state school of drawing in Amsterdam ▨ 1910-1912 guest student at the polytechnic in Delft, 1911 assistant in the studio of Theodor Fischer in Munich ▨ 1912-1918 self-employed architect in Purmerend, later Leiden ▨ from 1916 contact and collaboration with Theo van Doesburg, founder member of the »De Sphinx« artists' club ▨ 1917 founder member of the »De Stijl« group of artists ▨ 1918-1933 appointed municipal architect of Rotterdam, moved to Rotterdam, continued to work as a freelance architect, intensive contacts with the international architecture scene ▨ 1920 founder member of the »Opbouw« group of artists' in Rotterdam ▨ 1921 left the »De Stijl« group, visited the Bauhaus in Weimar ▨ 1927 took part in the Werkbund exhibition in Stuttgart ▨ from 1933 set up an architecture and design studio in Hillegersberg ▨ 1954 honorary doctorate from the Polytechnic of Delft, moved to Wassenaar

1904-1907 Besuch der Schule für dekorative Kunst »Quellinus«, Amsterdam ▨ 1907/08 Assistent im Architekturbüro Cuijpers & Stuijt, Amsterdam ▨ 1909/10 Studium an der Staatsschule für Zeichenunterricht, Amsterdam ▨ 1910-1912 Studium als Gasthörer an der Technischen Hochschule Delft, 1911 Assistent im Atelier von Theodor Fischer, München ▨ 1912-1918 als selbständiger Architekt in Purmerend, später in Leiden tätig ▨ ab 1916 Kontakt und Zusammenarbeit mit Theo van Doesburg, Gründungsmitglied des

Künstlerklubs »De Sphinx« ▨ 1917 Gründungsmitglied der Künstlergruppe »De Stijl« ▨ 1918-1933 Ernennung zum Rotterdamer Stadtbaumeister, Übersiedlung nach Rotterdam, weiterhin als freier Architekt tätig, intensiver Kontakt zu der internationalen Architekturszene ▨ 1920 Gründungsmitglied der Künstlergruppe »Opbouw« in Rotterdam ▨ 1921 Austritt aus der »De Stijl«-Gruppe, Besuch des Weimarer Bauhauses ▨ 1927 Teilnahme an der Stuttgarter Werkbundausstellung ▨ ab 1933 Aufbau eines Architektur- und Entwurfsateliers in Hillegersberg ▨ 1954 Ehrendoktor der Technischen Hochschule Delft, Übersiedlung nach Wassenaar

1904-1907 étude à l'école d'art décoratif «Quellimus» à Amsterdam ▨ 1907/08 travail d'assistant à l'étude d'architecte Cuijpers & Stuijt à Amsterdam ▨ 1909/10 étudie à l'école de dessin d'Amsterdam ▨ 1910-1912 étudie comme auditeur libre à l'Ecole technique supérieure de Delft ▨ 1911 assistant dans l'atelier de Theodor Fischer à Munich ▨ 1912-1918 s'installe à son compte comme architecte à Purmerend, plus tard à Leiden ▨ A partir de 1916 collabore avec Theo van Doesburg, membre fondateur du club d'artistes «De Sphinx» ▨ 1917 membre fondateur du groupe «De Stijl» ▨ 1918-1933 nommé architecte municipal de la ville de Rotterdam, s'installe dans cette ville, continue à travailler comme architecte indépendant, contacts étroits avec le milieu des architectes au niveau international ▨ 1920 membre fondateur du groupe «Opbouw» à Rotterdam ▨ 1921 quitte le «De Stijl», visite le Bauhaus de Weimar ▨ 1927 participe à l'exposition du Werkbund à Stuttgart ▨ à partir de 1933 ouvre un atelier d'architecture et de création à Hillegersberg ▨ 1954 docteur honoris causa de l'Ecole technique supérieure de Delft, s'installe à Wassenaar

Bruno Paul 1874-1968
1886-1894 studied at the Kunstgewerbeschule (School of Applied Art) in Dresden ▨ 1894-1907 studied at the Akademie der Bildenden Künste (Fine Arts Academy) in Munich, produced caricatures and drawings for the Munich magazines »Jugend« and »Simplicissimus« ▨ 1898 co-founder of the «Vereinigte Werkstätten für Kunst im Handwerk» in Munich: interior decor and design work ▨ 1907 founder member of the Deutscher Werkbund, first architectural designs ▨ 1907-1932 director of the Kunstgewerbeschule in Berlin (from 1924 United State Schools of Free and Applied Arts), set up an architecture office and produced architectural and interior designs ▨ 1932 gave master classes at the Akademie der Bildenden Künste in Berlin, architectural advisor to the Maharaja of Mysore Colombo ▨ 1933 forced into retirement by the National Socialists ▨ from 1933 freelance architect in Berlin, Lehnitz/Oranienburg, Hanau, Frankfurt a. M. and Düsseldorf

1886-1894 Studium an der Kunstgewerbeschule Dresden ▨ 1894-1907 Studium an der Akademie der Bildenden Künste, München, Karikaturen und Zeichnungen für die Münchener Zeitschriften »Jugend« und »Simplicissimus« ▨ 1898 Mitbegründer der »Vereinigten Werkstätten für Kunst im Handwerk«, München: Entwürfe für Innenarchitektur und Kunstgewerbe ▨ 1907 Gründungsmitglied des Deutschen Werkbundes, erste Architekturentwürfe ▨ 1907-1932 Direktor der Berliner Kunstgewerbeschule (ab 1924 Vereinigte Staatsschulen für freie und an-

gewandte Kunst), Aufbau eines Architekturbüros: Entwurfstätigkeit für Architektur und Innenarchitektur ▨ 1932 Leitung eines Meisterateliers an der Akademie der Bildenden Künste, Berlin, als beratender Architekt des Maharadschas von Mysore/Colombo tätig ▨ 1933 Versetzung in den Ruhestand durch die Nationalsozialisten ▨ ab 1933 als freischaffender Architekt in Berlin, Lehnitz/Oranienburg, Hanau, Frankfurt a.M. und Düsseldorf tätig

1886-1894 études à l'Ecole des Arts décoratifs de Dresde ▨ 1894-1907 études à l'Académie des Beaux-Arts de Munich, caricatures et dessins pour les revues munichoises «Jugend» et «Simplicissmus» ▨ 1898 cofondateur des «Vereinigte Werkstätten für Kunst im Handwerk» de Munich: créations d'agencement intérieur et d'art décoratif ▨ 1907 membre fondateur du Werkbund allemand, premières créations architecturales ▨ 1907-1932 directeur de l'Ecole des Arts décoratifs de Berlin (à partir de 1924 Ecoles réunies d'art libre et appliqué), monte une étude d'architecte: création pour l'architecture et la décoration intérieure ▨ 1932 direction d'un atelier de maîtrise à l'Académie des Beaux-Arts de Berlin, architecte conseiller du maharadjah de Mysore à Colombo ▨ 1933 mise en retraite d'office par les nationaux-socialistes ▨ A partir de 1933 architecte indépendant à Berlin, Lehnitz/Oranienbourg, Hanau, Francfort et Düsseldorf

Michael Powolny 1871-1954
1885-1891 trained as a potter at his father's company in Judenburg/Steiermark and at the Sommerhuber company in Steyr, Austria ▨ 1891-1894 studied at the Fachschule für »Thonindustrie« (Pottery Trade School) in Znaim ▨ 1894-1901 studied at the Kunstgewerbeschule (School of Applied Arts) in Vienna ▨ 1901-1903 freelance sculptor in Vienna, from 1901 member of the applied-arts association »Wiener Kunst im Haus« ▨ 1903-1906 assistant to Franz Metzner at

the Kunstgewerbeschule in Vienna in the sculpture department ▦ 1906 founded the Vienna ceramics workshops together with Berthold Löffler and Gustav Lang, collaboration with the Wiener Werkstätte (Vienna Workshop) ▦ 1907/08 member of the »Hagenbund« group of artists ▦ 1909-1936 taught at the Kunstgewerbeschule in Vienna: built up and directed the ceramics workshop, later director of the glass workshop and the sculpture class ▦ 1925-1927 artistic advisor to the Augarten porcelain factory in Vienna ▦ 1937-1939 taught at the

Frauenakademie in Vienna ▦ from 1939 freelance sculptor in Vienna

1885-1891 Ausbildung als Hafner im Betrieb seines Vaters in Judenburg/Steiermark und in der Firma Sommerhuber, Steyr/Oberösterreich ▦ 1891-1894 Studium an der Fachschule für »Thonindustrie«, Znaim ▦ 1894-1901 Studium an der Kunstgewerbeschule Wien ▦ 1901-1903 als freischaffender Bildhauer in Wien tätig, ab 1901 Mitglied der kunstgewerblichen Vereinigung »Wiener Kunst im Haus« ▦ 1903-1906 als Assistent von Franz Metzner an der Kunstgewerbeschule Wien tätig: Allgemeine Modellierabteilung ▦ 1906 zusammen mit Berthold Löffler und Gustav Lang Gründung der Werkstätte »Wiener Keramik«, Zusammenarbeit mit der Wiener Werkstätte ▦ 1907/08 Mitglied in der Künstlervereinigung »Hagenbund« ▦ 1909-1936 Lehrauftrag an der Kunstgewerbeschule Wien: Aufbau und Leitung der Keramikwerkstatt, später Leitung der Werkstätte für Glasbearbeitung und der Fachklasse für Bildhauerei ▦ 1925-1927 als künstlerischer Beirat der Porzellanmanufaktur Augarten in Wien tätig ▦ 1937-1939 Lehrauftrag an der Wiener Frauenakademie ▦ ab 1939 als freier Bildhauer in Wien tätig

1885-1891 formation de potier à l'atelier paternel à Judenbourg dans le Steiermark et dans l'entreprise Sommerhuber à Steyr en Autriche ▦ 1891-1894 études à l'Ecole professionnelle «d'industrie de l'argile» à Znaim ▦ 1894-1901 études à l'Ecole des Arts décoratifs de Vienne ▦ 1901-1903 travaille à Vienne comme sculpteur indépendant, à partir de 1901 membre de l'Union des arts décoratifs «Wiener Kunst im Haus» ▦ 1903-1906 assistant de Franz Metzner à l'Ecole des Arts décoratifs de Vienne: atelier général de modelage ▦ 1906 fondation avec Berthold Löffler et Gustav Lang des Ateliers de «Céramique viennoise», coopération avec les Ateliers viennois ▦ 1907/08 membre de l'associa-

tion d'artistes «Hagenbund» ▦ 1909-1936 enseigne à l'Ecole des Arts décoratifs de Vienne: création et direction de l'atelier de céramique, plus tard direction de l'atelier de verre et de la classe de sculpture ▦ 1925-1927 conseiller artistique de la manufacture de porcelaine Augarten ▦ 1937-1939 enseigne à l'Académie viennoise réservée aux femmes ▦ A partir de 1939 travaille comme sculpteur indépendant à Vienne

Otto Prutscher 1880-1949 (School of Applied Arts)
Attended a woodworking-trade school ▦ 1898-1901 studied at the Kunstgewerbeschule in Vienna ▦ 1901-1903 freelance architect in Vienna, interior decor and design work ▦ 1903-1907 assistant at the Graphic Arts Institute in Vienna ▦ from 1908 designed for the Wiener Werkstätte (Vienna Workshop) ▦ 1909-1939 taught at the Kunstgewerbeschule in Vienna, head of the open-drawing class, freelance work as architect and designer ▦ 1918 appointed educational inspector in Vienna ▦ 1939 dismissed from the teaching staff of the Kunstgewerbeschule in Vienna by the National Socialists ▦ 1945/46 taught at the Kunstgewerbeschule in Vienna, head of the open-drawing class

Besuch einer Fachschule für Holzindustrie ▦ 1897-1901 Studium an der Kunstgewerbeschule Wien ▦ 1901-1903 als freischaffender Architekt in Wien tätig: Entwurfstätigkeit für Innenarchitektur und Kunstgewerbe ▦ 1903-1907 Assistent an der grafischen Lehr- und Versuchsanstalt in Wien ▦ ab ca. 1908 Entwurfstätigkeit für die Wiener Werkstätte ▦ 1909-1939 Lehrauftrag an der Kunstgewerbeschule Wien: Leitung des offenen Zeichensaales für Gewerbetreibende, gleichzeitig selbständige Tätigkeit als Architekt und Entwerfer ▦ 1918 Ernennung zum Fachinspektor des Fortbildungswesens in Wien ▦ 1939 Entlassung als Lehrkraft der Kunstgewerbeschule in Wien durch die Nationalsozialisten ▦ 1945/46 erneuter Lehrauftrag an der Kunstgewerbeschule in Wien: Leitung des offenen Zeichensaales

Formation dans une école professionnelle de l'industrie du bois ▦ 1897-1901 études à l'Ecole des Arts décoratifs de Vienne ▦ 1901-1903 travaille comme architecte indépendant: création pour la décoration intérieure et les arts décoratifs ▦ 1903-1907 assistant à l'Institut de Recherche et d'Enseignement graphique de Vienne ▦ A partir de 1908 poursuit son travail de création aux Ateliers viennois ▦ 1909-1939 enseigne à l'Ecole des Arts décoratifs de Vienne: direction de la salle de dessin ouverte aux artisans, à côté, toujours ses activités d'architecte et de créateur ▦ 1939 révoqué par les nationaux-socialistes ▦ 1945/46 retrouve son poste d'enseignant à l'Ecole des Arts décoratifs de Vienne: direction de la sal-

le de dessin ouverte

Hans Przyrembel 1900-1945
From 1915 apprentice locksmith in Leipzig ▦ 1918 military service ▦ until 1924 occasional work as locksmith ▦ 1924-1928 studied at the Bauhaus in Weimar and Dessau: basic course, apprenticeship in the metal workshop, designed lamps with Marianne Brandt ▦ 1928 journeyman's exam, took over Wolfgang Tümpel's workshop in Halle, worked with Tümpel at times ▦ from 1929 set up a workshop in Leipzig, designed and produced appliances and lamps in coloured metals and precious metals ▦ 1932 master's exam as goldsmith and silversmith ▦ 1939-1945 military service ▦ 1945-1951 the Przyrembel workshop was run by his widow

Ab 1915 Lehre als Schlosser in Leipzig ▦ 1918 Kriegsdienst ▦ bis 1924 Gelegenheitsarbeit als Schlosser ▦ 1924-1928 Studium am Bauhaus Weimar und Dessau: Vorkurs, Lehre in der Metallwerkstatt, Entwicklung von Beleuchtungskörpern zusammen mit Marianne Brandt ▦ 1928 Gesellenprüfung, Übernahme der Werkstatt Wolfgang Tümpels in Halle, zeitweise Zusammenarbeit mit Tümpel ▦ ab 1929 Aufbau einer Werkstatt in Leipzig, Entwurf und Ausführung von Geräten und Beleuchtungskörpern in Bunt- und Edelmetallen ▦ 1932 Meisterprüfung als Gold- und Silberschmied ▦ 1939-1945 Kriegsdienst ▦ 1945-1951 die Werkstatt Przyrembel wird von seiner Witwe weitergeführt

A partir de 1915 apprentissage de serrurier à Leipzig ▦ 1918 service de guerre ▦ jusqu'en 1924 vit d'emplois occasionnels de serrurier ▦ 1924-1928 études au Bauhaus de Weimar et de Dessau: cours préliminaire d'apprentissage à l'atelier de métal, élaboration d'appareils d'éclairage avec Marianne Brandt ▦ 1928 examen de compagnonnage, reprend la direction de l'atelier de Wolfgang Tümpel à Halle, de temps en temps collaboration avec Tümpel ▦ à partir de 1929 création d'un atelier à Leipzig, conception et réalisation d'ustensiles et de lampes dans des métaux précieux et colorés ▦ 1932 examen de maîtrise comme oèvre ▦ 1939-1945 service de guerre ▦ 1945-1951 l'atelier de Przyrembel est dirigé par sa veuve

Karl Raichle 1889-1965
Apprenticeship as coppersmith in the lamp factory of Max Krüger, Berlin, journeyman in Switzerland ▦ during World War I, military service in the marines ▦ 1918-1928 lived in Urach Württemberg, worked as an author, established a literary anarcho-socialist artists' colony with like-minded friends ▦ 1928 studied at the Bauhaus in Dessau ▦ 1928-1931 returned to Urach, set up the pewtersmithy »Werkgemeinschaft Urach, K. und E. Raichle«: designed and produced hand-wrought pewterware ▦ 1931 moved to Lützenhardt in the Black Forest ▦ 1933 worked in Berlin ▦ 1933-1965 set up

the »Meersburger Zinnschmiede« pewterworks in Meersburg on Lake Constance ▦ continued the work he was doing in Urach, worked as a metal sculptor, collaborated with painter and designer Julius Bissier

Lehre als Kupferschmied bei der Lampenfabrik Max Krüger, Berlin, Gesellen- und Wanderjahre in der Schweiz ▦ während des Ersten Weltkrieges Kriegsdienst als Marinesoldat ▦ 1918-1928 in Urach/Württemberg ansässig, hier als Schriftsteller tätig, zusammen mit gleichgesinnten Freunden Bildung einer literarisch-sozialanarchistisch ausgerichteten Künstlerkolonie ▦ 1928 Studienaufenthalt am Bauhaus Dessau ▦ 1928-1931 Rückkehr nach Urach, Aufbau der Zinnschmiede »Werkgemeinschaft Urach, K. und E. Raichle«: Entwurf und Ausführung von handgeschmiedeten Zinngeräten ▦ 1931 Übersiedlung nach Lützenhardt/Hochschwarzwald ▦ 1933 in Berlin tätig ▦ 1933-1965 Aufbau der »Meersburger Zinnschmiede« in Meersburg/Bodensee: Weiterführung seiner Arbeit aus Urach, auch als Metallbildhauer tätig, Zusammenarbeit mit dem Maler und Entwerfer Julius Bissier

Apprentissage de chaudronnier à la fabrique de lampes Max Krüger à Berlin, années de compagnonnage et de voyage en Suisse ▦ sert dans la marine pendant la 1ère guerre mondiale ▦ 1918-1928 s'installe à Urach dans le Wurtemberg, s'adonne à la littérature et crée avec des amis comme lui une colonie d'artistes aux ambitions anarcho-sociolo-littéraires ▦ 1928 séjour au Bauhaus de Dessau ▦ 1928-1931 revient à Urach, ouvre un atelier de chaudronnerie «Werkgemeinschaft Urach, K. und E. Raichle»: création et réalisation d'ustensiles en étain faits à la main ▦ 1931 part s'installer à Lützenhardt en Forêt Noire ▦ 1933 travaille à Berlin ▦ 1933-1965 ouvre son atelier de chaudronnerie, les «Meersburger Zinnschmiede» à Meersburg au bord du lac de Constance, travaille en commun avec le peintre concepteur Julius Bissier

Richard Riemerschmid 1868-1957
1888-1890 studied painting at the Akademie der Bildenden Künste in Munich ▦ from 1890 freelance painter in Munich ▦ 1897 initial designs, co-founder of the »Vereinigte Werkstätten« in Munich ▦ 1900/01 interior design for the new theatre in Munich ▦ from 1902 intensive design work for the Dresden Workshops ▦ from 1905 designed »machine furniture« ▦ 1907 founder member of the Deutsche Werkbund ▦ 1907-1913 planned the first German Garden City of Hellerau ▦ 1912-1924 director of the Kunstgewerbeschule (school of Applied Arts) in Munich ▦ 1914-1918 military service ▦ 1918/19 member of the artists' council of the city of Munich ▦ 1921-1926 chairman of the Deutscher Werkbund ▦ 1926-1931 director of the Kölner Werkschulen ▦ from 1931 lived in Munich as

freelance architect and painter

1888-1890 Studium der Malerei an der Akademie der Bildenden Künste, München ▨ ab 1890 als freischaffender Maler in München tätig ▨ 1897 erste kunstgewerbliche Entwürfe, Mitbegründer der »Vereinigten Werkstätten für Kunst im Handwerk«, München ▨ 1900/01 Entwurf für die Innenausstattung des neuen Schauspielhauses in München ▨ ab 1902 intensive Entwurfstätigkeit für die »Dresdner Werkstätten für Handwerkskunst« ▨ ab 1905 Entwurf von »Maschinenmö-

beln« ▨ 1907 Gründungsmitglied des Deutschen Werkbundes ▨ 1907-1913 Gesamtplanung der ersten deutschen Gartenstadt in Hellerau ▨ 1913-1924 Direktor der Kunstgewerbeschule München ▨ 1914-1918 Kriegsdienst ▨ 1918/19 Mitglied im Künstlerrat der Stadt München ▨ 1921-1926 Vorsitzender des Deutschen Werkbundes ▨ 1926-1931 Direktor der Kölner Werkschulen ▨ ab 1931 erneut in München als freischaffender Architekt und Maler tätig

1888-1890 Etude de la peinture aux Beaux-Arts de Munich ▨ A partir de 1890 travaille comme peintre indépendant à Munich ▨ 1897 premières créations d'art décoratif, co-fondateur des «Vereinigte Werkstätten für Kunst im Handwerk» à Munich ▨ 1900/01 crée l'aménagement intérieur du nouveau théâtre de Munich ▨ A partir de 1902 grande activité créatrice pour les Ateliers d'artisanat d'art de Dresde ▨ A partir de 1902 crée des «meubles machines» ▨ 1907 membre fondateur du Werkbund Allemand ▨ 1907-1913 conception globale de la première ville-jardin allemande à Hellerau ▨ 1913-1924 nommé directeur de l'Ecole des Arts décoratifs de Munich ▨ 1914-1918 service de guerre ▨ 1918/19 membre du conseil des artistes de Munich ▨ 1921-1926 président du Deutscher Werkbund ▨ 1926-1931 directeur de Kölner Werkschulen de Cologne ▨ A partir de 1931 reprend ses activités d'architecte indépendant et de peintre à Munich

Gerrit Thomas Rietveld 1888-1964
1900-1904 trained as a cabinetmaker at his father's firm in Utrecht ▨ 1904-1913 trained and worked as a design draughtsman at the Begeer goldsmith workshop in Utrecht, attended evening classes at the Utrecht Museum of Applied Arts under the architect P.J.C.Klaarhamer ▨ from 1911/12 member of the »Kunstliefde« group of artists ▨ from 1917 established a furniture workshop in Utrecht, where he designed and produced several mod-

ernist items of furniture ▨ from 1919 contact with the De Stijl group of artists, first meeting with Theo van Doesburg and J.J.P. Oud; took part in exhibitions ▨ from 1924/25 worked as freelance architect and designer in Utrecht, while the furniture workshop was run by G. van de Groenekan ▨ 1928 co-founder of the Congrès Internationaux d'Architecture Moderne (CIAM) ▨ from 1944/45 taught at Dutch universities and academies, several architectural designs at home and abroad

1900-1904 Ausbildung als Möbel-

tischler im Betrieb seines Vaters in Utrecht ▨ 1904-1913 Ausbildung und Arbeit als Entwurfszeichner in der Goldschmiedewerkstatt Begeer, Utrecht, Besuch von Abendkursen am Utrechter Museum für Kunstgewerbe und bei dem Architekten P.J.C. Klaarhamer ▨ ab 1911/12 Mitglied der Künstlergemeinschaft »Kunstliefde« ▨ ab 1917 Aufbau einer Werkstatt für Möbelbau in Utrecht: Entwurf und Ausführung zahlreicher modernistischer Möbel ▨ ab 1919 Kontakte zu der Künstlergruppe De Stijl, erstes Zusammentreffen mit Theo van Doesburg und J.J.P. Oud, Ausstellungsbeteiligung ▨ ab 1924/25 als freischaffender Architekt und Entwerfer in Utrecht tätig, die Möbelwerkstatt wird von G. van de Groenekan weitergeführt ▨ 1928 Mitbegründer des »Congrès Internationaux d'Architecture Moderne« (CIAM) ▨ ab 1944/45 verschiedene Lehraufträge an holländischen Universitäten und Akademien, zahlreiche Architekturentwürfe für das In- und Ausland

1900-1904 formation d'ébéniste dans l'entreprise paternelle à Utrecht ▨ 1904-1913 formation et travail comme dessinateur chez Begeer, un joaillier d'Utrecht, suit les cours du soir au musée d'Arts décoratifs de la ville et chez l'architecte P.J.C. Klaarhamer ▨ A partir de 1911/12 membre de la communauté d'artistes »Kunstliefde« ▨ 1917 ouvre son propre atelier de fabrication de meubles à Utrecht: création et réalisation de meubles modernistes ▨ à partir de 1919 est en contact avec les artistes du De Stijl, première rencontre ave Theo van Doesburg et J.J.P. Oud, participation à des expositions ▨ A partir de 1924/25 travaille comme architecte concepteur indépendant, G. van de Groenekan reprend la fabrique de meubles ▨ 1928 co-fondateur des Congrès internationaux d'Architecture moderne (CIAM) ▨ 1944/45 donne des cours dans diverses universités et académies hollandaises, nombreux projets architecturaux dans le pays et à l'étranger

Emmy Roth
Until 1908 apprentice goldsmith and silversmith at the firm of Conrad Anton Beumers, Düsseldorf ▨ from 1908 self-employed goldsmith and silversmith ▨ probably moved to Berlin around 1912/13 ▨ 1916-1936 established a silversmith workshop in Berlin-Charlottenburg, designed and produced several items in precious metal and coloured metal, master's exam as silversmith, designed for the silverware factory Bruckmann & Söhne, Heilbronn ▨ 1936 emigrated to Israel ▨ 1937 exhibited her work in the Israeli Pavilion at the Paris International Exhibition ▨ 1938-1940 designed for the silverware manufacturers Van Kempen & Zoon and J. Vos, Voorschoten, near The Hague ▨ 1940 emigrated to the USA

Bis ca. 1908 Lehre als Gold- und Silberschmiedin bei der Silberschmiedefirma Conrad Anton Beumers, Düsseldorf ▨ ab ca. 1908 als selbständige Gold- und Silberschmiedin tätig ▨ vermutlich ab ca. 1912/13 in Berlin ansässig ▨ ca. 1916-1936 Aufbau einer Silberschmiedewerkstatt in Berlin-Charlottenburg, Entwurf und Ausführung zahlreicher Arbeiten in Edel- und Buntmetallen, Meisterprüfung als Silberschmiedin, Entwurfstätigkeit für die Silberwarenfabrik Bruckmann & Söhne, Heilbronn ▨ 1936 Emigration nach Israel ▨ 1937 Weltausstellung Paris: Ausstellung ihrer Arbeiten im israelischen Pavillon ▨ 1938 -1940 Entwurfstätigkeit für die Silberwarenfabrik Van Kempen & Zoon und J. Vos, Voorschoten bei Den Haag ▨ ca. 1940 Emigration in die USA

Jusqu'en 1908 apprentissage d'orfèvre chez Conrad Anton Beumers, un orfèvre de Düsseldorf ▨ à partir de 1908 environ, travaille à son compte comme orfèvre ▨ vers 1912/13 s'installe à Berlin ▨ 1916-1936 crée son propre atelier à Berlin-Charlottenbourg , création et réalisation de nombreux modèles en métal précieux et coloré, examen de maîtrise comme orfèvre sur argent , crée pour la firme Bruckmann & Fils de Heilbronn ▨ 1936 émigre en Israël ▨ 1937 Exposition universelle de Paris: ses travaux sont exposés au pavillon israélien ▨ 1938-1940 créatrice pour la fabrique Van Kempen & Zoon et J. Vos de Voorschoten près de La Haye ▨ vers 1940 émigre aux USA

Lili Schultz 1895-1970
1913/14 studied at the Kunstgewerbeschule (School of Applied Arts) in Dresden ▨ 1915-1918 studied at the Handwerkerschule (Crafts School) in Halle, serving an apprenticeship in the enamel workshop under Maria Likarz ▨ 1918/19 studied at the Kunstgewerbeschule in Munich as a master student of Fritz Helmuth Ehmcke ▨ 1919/20 self-employed in Diessen/Ammersee ▨ 1921-1924 master workshop in enamelling at the Burg Giebichenstein School of Applied Arts in Halle ▨ 1924/25 studied at the Bauhaus in Weimar (basic course) ▨ 1925-

1958 taught at the Burg Giebichenstein School of Applied Arts in Halle and directed the enamel workshop ▨ 1935 master's exam ▨ 1958-1965 taught enamelling at the Werkkunstschule (Applied Arts School) in Dusseldorf ▨ from 1965 established an enamel workshop in Seeshaupt, Starnberger See

1913/14 Studium an der Kunstgewerbeschule Dresden ▨ 1915-1918 Studium an der Handwerkerschule in Halle: Lehre im Emailwerkstatt unter der Leitung von Maria Likarz ▨ 1918/19 Studium an der

Kunstgewerbeschule München: Meisterschülerin von Fritz Helmuth Ehmcke ▨ 1919/20 selbständig in Diessen am Ammersee tätig ▨ 1921-1924 Meisteratelier für Email an der Kunstgewerbeschule Burg Giebichenstein in Halle ▨ 1924/25 Studium am Bauhaus Weimar: Vorkurs ▨ 1925-1958 Lehrauftrag an der Kunstgewerbeschule Burg Giebichenstein in Halle: Leitung der Emailwerkstatt ▨ 1935 Meisterprüfung ▨ 1958-1965 Lehrauftrag an der Werkkunstschule Düsseldorf: Klasse für Emailkunst ▨ ab 1965 Aufbau einer Emailwerkstatt in Seeshaupt/Starnberger See

1913/14 Etudes à l'Ecole des Arts décoratifs de Dresde ▨ 1915-1918 études à l'Ecole d'artisanat de Halle: apprentissage à l'atelier d'émail sous la direction de Maria Likarz ▨ 1918/19 études à l'Ecole des Arts décoratifs de Munich: examen de maîtrise dans la classe de Fritz Helmuth Ehmcke ▨ 1919/20 se met à son compte à Diessen/Ammersee ▨ 1921-1924 en classe de maîtrise de l'atelier d'émail à l'Ecole de Burg Giebichenstein à Halle ▨ 1924/25 études au Bauhaus de Weimar: cours préliminaire ▨ 1925-1958 enseigne à l'Ecole de Burg Giebichenstein : dirige l'atelier d'émail ▨ 1935 examen de maîtrise ▨ 1958-1965 chargée de cours à l'Ecole d'-Art appliqué de Düsseldorf: classe d'émail ▨ En 1965 ouvre un atelier d'émail à Seeshaupt au bord du lac de Starnberg

Paula Straus 1894-1943
Until 1921 studied at the Kunstgewerbeschule (School of Applied Arts) in Stuttgart as master student in Paul Haustein's metalwork class ▨ from 1921 she probably worked freelance, close cooperation with the Kunstgewerbeschule in Stuttgart ▨ from 1924/25 designed for the silverware manufacturers Bruckmann & Söhne, Heilbronn ▨ 1929 taught at the Staatliche Bauhochschule in Weimar ▨ from 1930 designed for the metalware manufacturers WMF in Geislingen ▨ from 1935 established a jewellery shop in

Stuttgart ▦ 1939-1942 her property was sequestered by the Nazis and she went to work in the kitchens of the Jewish retirement home in Buttenhausen/Münsingen, later becoming director of the Jewish retirement home in Haigerloch/Stuttgart ▦ in 1942 she was deported to Theresienstadt concentration camp ▦ in 1943 she was moved to Auschwitz where she died the same year

Bis 1921 Studium an der Kunstgewerbeschule Stuttgart: Meisterschülerin in der Metallklasse von Paul Haustein ▦ ab 1921 vermutlich freischaffend tätig, weiterhin enge Zusammenarbeit mit der Kunstgewerbeschule Stuttgart ▦ ab 1924/25 Entwurfstätigkeit für die Silberwarenfabrik Bruckmann & Söhne, Heilbronn ▦ 1929 Lehrauftrag an der Staatlichen Bauhochschule Weimar ▦ ab ca. 1930 Entwurfstätigkeit für die Württembergische Metallwarenfabrik, Geislingen ▦ ab 1935 Aufbau eines Schmuckwarengeschäftes in Stuttgart ▦ 1939-1942 Zwangsenteignung, als Küchenhilfe im jüdischen Altersheim Buttenhausen/Münsingen tätig, später Leiterin des jüdischen Altersheimes in Haigerloch/Stuttgart ▦ 1942 Deportation in das Konzentrationslager Theresienstadt ▦ 1943 Verlegung nach Auschwitz, hier im gleichen Jahr umgekommen

Jusqu'en 1921 étudie à l'Ecole des Arts décoratifs de Stuttgart, élève de maîtrise dans la classe d'émail de Paul Haustein ▦ à partir de 1921 probablement artiste indépendante, continue à collaborer avec l'école de Stuttgart ▦ 1924/25 crée pour la firme Bruckmann & Fils de Heilbronn ▦ 1929 chargée de cours à la Staatliche Bauhochschule de Weimar ▦ A partir de 1930 activité créatrice pour la fabrique d'objets en métal de Geislingen dans le Wurtemberg ▦ 1935 ouvre un magasin de bijoux à Stuttgart ▦ 1939-1942 expropriation forcée, travaille comme aide de cuisine dans un asile de vieillards juifs à Buttenhausen/Munsingen plus tard directrice de la maison de retraite juive de Haigerloch près de Stuttgart ▦ 1942 déportée à Auschwitz, elle mourra la même année

Eva Stricker-Zeisel 1906
1923 studied at the Royal Art Academy in Budapest ▦ 1924 pottery apprenticeship at Jakob Karapancsik, Budapest ▦ 1925/26 set up a ceramics and design workshop at the ceramics factory of Kispest, Budapest, and developed prototypes for industrial production ▦ from 1927 she worked for the ceramics firm of Hansa Kunstkeramik in Hamburg ▦ 1928-1930 designed for the firm of Majolika-Manufaktur in Schramberg, where she developed several new tableware designs and advertising designs ▦ 1930-1932 lived in Berlin and designed for the ceramics company of Christian Carstens ▦ 1932-1937 lived in the Soviet Union and designed for the state porcelain factories of Lomonosov in St. Petersburg and Dulevo in Moscow, 1935

appointed artistic director of the porcelain and glass industry of the Russian Republic, 1936 arrested on political grounds ▦ 1937 released from prison, returned to Budapest, where she once again worked for Kispest ▦ 1938 fled from the Nazi regime via Switzerland to England, emigrated to the USA ▦ from 1938/39 she designed for several American and international porcelain and ceramics manufacturers, taught ceramics at the Pratt Institute in Brooklyn, New York ▦ 1988 honorary doctorate from the Royal Academy of Art, London

1923 Studium an der Königlichen Kunstakademie in Budapest ▦ 1924 Töpferlehre bei Jakob Karapancsik, Budapest ▦ 1925/26 Aufbau einer Keramikwerkstatt, Entwurfsatelier in der Keramikmanufaktur Kispest, Budapest: Entwicklung von Prototypen für die Serienproduktion ▦ ab 1927 in Deutschland zunächst für die Hansa Kunstkeramik in Hamburg tätig ▦ 1928-1930 Entwurfstätigkeit für die Majolika-Manufaktur Schramberg: Entwicklung zahlreicher neuer Geschirrtypen, Werbegestaltung ▦ 1930-1932 in Berlin ansässig: Entwurfstätigkeit für die Keramikfirma Christian Carstens ▦ 1932-1937 in der Sowjetunion tätig: Entwürfe für die Staatliche Lomonosov-Porzellanmanufaktur, St. Petersburg, und die Dulevo-Porzellanmanufaktur, Moskau, 1935 Ernennung zur künstlerischen Direktorin für die Porzellan- und Glasindustrie in der Russischen Republik, 1936 Inhaftierung aus politischen Gründen ▦ 1937 Entlassung aus der Haft, Rückkehr nach Budapest, erneute Arbeit für die Keramikmanufaktur Kispest ▦ 1938 Flucht vor den Nationalsozialisten über die Schweiz nach England, Emigration in die USA ▦ ab 1938/39 Entwurfstätigkeit für zahlreiche amerikanische und internationale Porzellan- und Keramikproduzenten, Lehrauftrag für Keramik am Pratt Institute in Brooklyn/New York ▦ 1988 Ehrendoktor der Royal Academy of Art, London

1923 études à l'Académie royale des Beaux-Arts de Budapest ▦ 1924 apprentissage de la poterie chez Jakob Karapancsik à Budapest ▦ 1925/26 crée un atelier de céramique, atelier de création dans la manufacture de céramiques Kispest de Budapest: élaboration de prototypes destinés à la production en série ▦ 1927 commence à travailler en Allemagne, d'abord pour une fabrique de céramiques de Hambourg, la Hansa Kunstkeramik ▦ 1928-1930 collaboratrice de la manufacture Majolika de Schramberg: créations de nouveaux types de vaisselle, conception publicitaire ▦ 1930-1932 s'installe à Berlin: activité créatrice pour la maison Christian Carstens ▦ 1932-1937 travaille en Union soviétique: crée pour la manufacture nationale de porcelaine de Lomonosov à Saint-Pétersbourg et la manufacture de porcelaine de Dulevo à Moscou, 1935 nommée directrice artistique de l'industrie du verre et de

la porcelaine en République de Russie, 1936 arrêtée pour des raisons politiques ▦ 1937 libération, rentre à Budapest , travaille à nouveau pour la manufacture de céramiques Kispest ▦ 1938 fuit en Angleterre devant les nationaux-socialistes en passant par la Suisse, émigre aux USA ▦ à partir de 1938/39 grande activité de création de céramiques et de porcelaines pour des firmes américaines ou internationales, chargée de cours de céramique au Pratt Institute de Brooklyn à New York ▦ 1988 docteur honoris causa de la Royal Academy of Art de Londres

Richard Süßmuth 1900-1974
1915-1922 apprenticeship as glass cutter at Adlerhütte AG glassworks in Penzig, Silesia, where he later worked, master's exam, master at the Krinke & Jörn glasswork ▦ 1922-1924 studied under Karl Groß in the glass department of the Akademie für Kunsthandwerk in Dresden ▦ 1924-1945 established the Richard Süßmuth glass workshops in Penzig, Silesia; designed and produced numerous glasses and new experimental finishing techniques ▦ 1945 the workshops were destroyed in the war ▦ from 1946 reconstruction of the workshops in Immenhausen near Kassel, where he worked until 1970

1915-1922 Lehre als Glasschneider in der »Adlerhütte AG«, Penzig/Schlesien, später hier als Geselle tätig, Meisterprüfung, als Meister in der Glashütte Krinke & Jörn beschäftigt ▦ 1922-1924 Studium an der Akademie für Kunsthandwerk in Dresden: Fachabteilung für Glas bei Karl Groß ▦ 1924-1945 Aufbau der »Werkstätten Richard Süßmuth-Glaskunst« in Penzig/Schlesien, Entwurf und Ausführung zahlreicher Gläser und Experimente mit Veredlungstechniken ▦ 1945 Zerstörung der Werkstätten durch Kriegseinwirkungen ▦ ab 1946 Wiederaufbau der Werkstätten in Immenhausen bei Kassel, hier bis 1970 aktiv tätig

1915-1922 apprentissage de coupeur de verre à l'usine Adlerhütte AG de Penzig en Silésie, y travaille plus tard comme compagnon, devenu maître artisan, trouve un emploi à la verrerie Krinke & Jörn ▦ 1922-1924 études à la Akademie für Kunsthandwerk de Dresde: section du verre dirigée par Karl Groß ▦ 1924-1945 création des Ateliers de l'art du verre Richard Süßmuth à Penzig en Silésie, création et réalisation de nombreux verres ainsi que de nouvelles techniques d'affinage ▦ 1945 destruction des ateliers pendant la guerre ▦ à partir de 1946 reconstruction des ateliers à Immenhausen près de Kassel, restent en activité jusque vers 1970

Nikolai Mikhailovich Suetin 1897-1954
1915-1917 military service ▦ 1918-1922 studied at the Witebsk art school under Malevich ▦ 1920 founder member of the UNOWIS group of artists ▦ from 1922

worked in Petrograd ▦ from 1923 designed for the Petrograd state porcelain factory ▦ 1923-1926 worked at the state institute for artistic culture of Petrograd, where he was head of the department of general ideology ▦ 1925 took part in the Paris exhibition »Exposition internationale des arts décoratifs et industriels modernes« ▦ 1927-1930 worked in the experimental laboratories of the Art History Institute in St. Petersburg: numerous furniture and architectural designs ▦ 1932-1954 artistic director of the Lomonosov state porcelain factory in St. Petersburg ▦ 1937 designed the Soviet Pavilion for the International Exhibition in Paris ▦ 1939 designed the Soviet Pavilion for the International Exhibition in New York

1915-1917 Kriegsdienst ▦ 1918-1922 Studium an der Kunstschule Witebsk bei Malevich ▦ 1920 Gründungsmitglied der Künstlergruppe »UNOWIS« ▦ ab 1922 in Petrograd tätig ▦ ab 1923 Entwurfstätigkeit für die Staatliche Porzellanmanufaktur, Petrograd ▦ 1923-1926 Mitarbeit am Staatlichen Institut für künstlerische Kultur St. Petersburg: Leitung der Abteilung für Allgemeine Ideologie ▦ 1925 Teilnahme an der Ausstellung »Exposition internationale des arts décoratifs et industriels modernes« in Paris ▦ 1927-1930 Beschäftigung in den experimentellen Laboratorien des Instituts für Kunstgeschichte, St. Petersburg: zahlreiche Entwürfe für Möbel und Architektur ▦ 1932-1954 künstlerische Leitung der Staatlichen Lomonosov-Porzellanmanufaktur, St. Petersburg ▦ 1937 Gestaltung des sowjetischen Pavillons für die Weltausstellung in Paris ▦ 1939 Gestaltung des sowjetischen Pavillons für die Weltausstellung in New York

1915-1917 service militaire ▦ 1918 études à l'école d'art de Witebsk près de Malevitch ▦ 1920 membre fondateur du groupe «UNOWIS» ▦ à partir de 1922 travaille à Pétrograd ▦ 1923 commence à créer pour la manufacture de porcelaine de Pétrograd ▦ 1923-1926 collaborateur de l'Institut national de la culture artistique de Pétrograd: prend la direction de la section «idéologie générale» ▦ 1925 participation à l'Exposition internationale des arts décoratifs et industriels modernes à Paris ▦ 1927-1930 travaille dans les laboratoires expérimentaux de l'Institut d'histoire de l'art à Saint-Pétersbourg: nombreuses créations de meubles et d'architecture ▦ 1932-1954 direction artistique de la manufacture nationale de porcelaine de Lomonosov à Saint-Pétersbourg ▦ 1937 construit le pavillon soviétique de l'Exposition universelle de Paris ▦ 1939 réalise le pavillon soviétique de l'Exposition de New York

Wolfgang Tümpel 1903-1978
1921/22 apprentice goldsmith and silversmith at the firm of August Schlüter, Bielefeld; attended the Kunstgewerbeschule (A school of Applied Arts) in Bielefeld ▦ 1922-1925 studied at the Bauhaus in Wei-

172

mar (basic course, apprenticeship in the metal workshop) ▨ 1925/26 studied at the Burg Giebichenstein School of Applied Arts in Halle, continuing his apprenticeship in the metal workshop, journeyman's exam ▨ 1927-1929 set up a »Werkstatt für Gefäße – Schmuck – Beleuchtung« in Halle, designed for the lamp industry ▨ 1929-1932 moved to Cologne: set up a workshop, designed for metalware manufacturers WMF in Geislingen and silverware manufacturers Bruckmann & Söhne in Heilbronn ▨ 1934-1950 set up a workshop in Bielefeld ▨ 1935 master's exam ▨ 1951-1968 taught at the Landeskunstschule in Hamburg, where he headed the metalwork classes and designed products for industry ▨ from 1968 set up a workshop in Hamburg-Ahrensburg

1921/22 Lehre als Gold- und Silberschmied bei August Schlüter, Bielefeld, Besuch der Kunstgewerbeschule Bielefeld ▨ 1922-1925 Studium am Bauhaus Weimar: Vorkurs, Lehre in der Metallwerkstatt ▨ 1925/26 Studium an der Kunstgewerbeschule Burg Giebichenstein in Halle: Weiterführung der Lehre in der Metallwerkstatt, Gesellenprüfung ▨ 1927-1929 Aufbau einer »Werkstatt für Gefäße-Schmuck-Beleuchtung« in Halle, Entwurfstätigkeit für die Lampenindustrie ▨ 1929-1932 Übersiedlung nach Köln: Aufbau einer Werkstatt, Entwurfsarbeit für die Württembergische Metallwarenfabrik, Geislingen, sowie die Silberwarenfabrik Bruckmann & Söhne, Heilbronn ▨ 1934-1950 Aufbau einer Werkstatt in Bielefeld ▨ 1935 Meisterprüfung ▨ 1951-1968 Lehrauftrag an der Landeskunstschule Hamburg: Leitung der Metallklasse, Entwurfstätigkeit für Industrieprodukte ▨ ab 1968 Aufbau einer Werkstatt in Hamburg-Ahrensburg

1921/22 Apprentissage d'orfèvre chez August Schlüter à Bielefeld, étude à L'Ecole des Arts décoratifs de Bielefeld ▨ 1922-1925 étudie au Bauhaus de Weimar: cours préliminaire, apprentissage à l'atelier de métal ▨ 1925/26 étudie à l'école de Burg Giebichenstein à Halle: poursuite de son apprentissage dans l'atelier de métal, examen de compagnonnage ▨ 1927-1929 création d'un atelier «Werkstatt für Gefäße-Schmuck-Beleuchtung» à Halle, travaille pour l'industrie ▨ 1929-1932 s'installe à Cologne: ouvre un atelier, travail de création pour la fabrique d'ojets en métal de Geislingen et pour la firme Bruckmann & Fils de Heilbronn ▨ 1934-1950 création d'un atelier à Bielefeld ▨ 1935 examen de maîtrise ▨ 1951-1968 chargé de cours à la Landeskunstschule de Hambourg: dirige la classe de métal, crée des modèles de produits pour l'industrie ▨ A partir de 1968 création d'un atelier à Hambourg-Ahrensbourg

Henry van de Velde 1863-1957
1880-1885 studied painting in Antwerp and Paris ▨ 1886-1890 worked as a painter in Welcherderzande/

Antwerp; 1887 took part in the exhibition of the Salon »L'Art Indépendant«, Antwerp; from 1888 member of the »Les Vingt« group of artists ▨ 1892 gave up painting, turned to architecture and crafts ▨ 1895/96 designed and built his »Bloemenwerf« house in Uccle near Brussels, for which he designed the entire interior fittings ▨ 1897 foundation of the »Société Henry van de Velde« in Ixelles near Brussels as a workshop producing furniture designed by van de Velde ▨ 1899-1902 artistic director of Hermann Hirschwald's «Hohenzollern Kunst-

gewerbehaus« in Berlin, numerous contracts for interior decor and other designs ▨ 1902-1915 worked in Weimar as artistic advisor to Grand Duke Wilhelm Ernst, from 1902 head of the applied arts seminar, from 1907 head of the Kunstgewerbeschule in Weimar; numerous architectural and product designs ▨ from 1917 freelance architect in Switzerland and Holland ▨ 1926-1936 established and directed the »Institut Supérieur d'Architecture et des Arts décoratifs« (ISAD) in Brussels ▨ from 1947 lived in Oberägeri/ Switzerland

1880-1885 Studium der Malerei in Antwerpen und Paris ▨ 1886-1890 als Maler in Welcherderzande/Antwerpen tätig, 1887 Ausstellungsbeteiligung im Salon »L'Art Indépendant«, Antwerpen, ab 1888 Mitglied der Künstlergruppe »Les Vingt« ▨ 1892 Aufgabe der Malerei, Hinwendung zur Architektur und zum Kunstgewerbe ▨ 1895/96 Planung und Ausführung seines Hauses »Bloemenwerf« in Uccle bei Brüssel: Entwurf der gesamten Inneneinrichtung ▨ 1897 Gründung der »Société Henry van de Velde« in Ixelles bei Brüssel, einer Werkstatt zur Produktion von Möbeln nach Entwurf van de Veldes ▨ 1899-1902 künstlerische Leitung des »Hohenzollern Kunstgewerbehauses« von Hermann Hirschwald in Berlin: zahlreiche Aufträge für Inneneinrichtungen, Entwürfe für Kunstgewerbe ▨ 1902-1915 in Weimar tätig: künstlerischer Berater von Großherzog Wilhelm Ernst, ab 1902 Leiter des Kunstgewerblichen Seminars, ab 1907 Leiter der Kunstgewerbeschule Weimar, zahlreiche Entwürfe für Architektur und Kunstgewerbe ▨ ab 1917 als freischaffender Architekt in der Schweiz und in Holland tätig ▨ 1926-1936 Aufbau und Leitung des »Institut Supérieur d' Architecture et des Arts décoratifs« (ISAD) in Brüssel ▨ ab 1947 in Oberägeri/Schweiz ansässig

1880-1885 Etudie la peinture à Anvers et Paris ▨ 1886-1890 travaille comme peintre à Welcherderzande près d'Anvers, 1887 expose au Salon

de «l'Art Indépendant» à Anvers, à partir de 1888 membre du groupe «Les Vingt» ▨ 1892 se consacre à la peinture mais s'intéresse à l'architecture et à l'art appliqué ▨ 1895/96 plans et réalisation de sa maison «Bloemenwerf» construite à Uccle près de Bruxelles: conception de l'ensemble de l'aménagement intérieur ▨ 1897 fondation de la «Société Henry van de Velde» à Ixelles non loin de la capitale, atelier de production de meubles d'après des modèles de van de Velde ▨ 1899-1902 direction artistique de la «Hohenzollern Kunstgewerbehaus» de Hermann Hirschwald à Berlin: nombreuses commandes d'aménagements d'-intérieurs, créations pour les arts décoratifs ▨ 1902-1905 travaille à Weimar: conseiller artistique à la cour du grand-duc Wilhelm Ernst, en 1902 nommé directeur du séminaire d'arts décoratifs, en 1907 directeur de l'Ecole des Arts décoratifs de Weimar, nombreuses créations pour l'architecture et l'art décoratif ▨ A partir de 1917 architecte indépendant en Suisse et en Hollande ▨ 1926-1936 création et direction du nouvel «Institut supérieur d'architecture et des arts décoratifs» (ISAD) à Bruxelles ▨ 1947 s'installe en Suisse à Oberägeri

Wilhelm Wagenfeld 1900–1990
1914–1918 apprentice draughtsman to the silverware manufacturers Koch & Bergfeld, Bremen ▨ 1916–1919 studied at the Kunstgewerbeschule (School of Applied Art) in Bremen ▨ 1919-1922 studied at the Zeichenakademie (Drawing Academy) in Hanau ▨ 1922/23 studied in Bremen and Worpswede ▨ 1923–1925 studied at the Bauhaus in Weimar (basic course, apprenticeship in the metal workshop, journeyman's exam) ▨ 1926-1930 taught at the Staatliche Bauhochschule in Weimar as assistant and later director of the metal workshop ▨ 1931- 1935 designed for the Jenaer Glaswerke Schott & Gen., taught at the Grunewaldstrasse Art School in Berlin ▨ 1942-1945 military service, POW ▨ 1947-1949 taught at the Hochschule für Bildende Künste (College of Fine Arts) in Berlin ▨ 1949/50 member of the Württemberg Industrial Design Council in Stuttgart ▨ 1950-1954 design work for the metalware manufacturers WMF in Geislingen ▨ 1954-1978 set up the Wagenfeld Workshop, designing and developing industrial products in metal, glass, china and plastic

1914-1918 Lehre im Zeichenbüro der Silberwarenfabrik Koch & Bergfeld, Bremen ▨ 1916-1919 Studium an der Kunstgewerbeschule Bremen ▨ 1919-1922 Studium an der Zeichenakademie Hanau ▨ 1922/23 Studienaufenthalt in Bremen und Worpswede ▨ 1923-1925 Studium am Bauhaus Weimar: Vorkurs, Lehre in der Metallwerkstatt, Gesellenprüfung ▨ 1926-1930 Lehrauftrag an der Staatlichen Bauhochschule Weimar: Assistent und später Leiter der Metallwerkstatt ▨ 1931-1935 Entwurfstätigkeit für die Jenaer Glaswerke Schott & Gen., Lehrauftrag

an der »Staatlichen Kunsthochschule Grunewaldstraße«, Berlin ▨ 1942-1945 Kriegsdienst, Gefangenschaft ▨ 1947-1949 Lehrauftrag an der Hochschule für Bildende Künste in Berlin ▨ 1949/50 Referent für Industrielle Formgebung im Württembergischen Landesgewerbeamt, Stuttgart ▨ 1950-1954 Entwurfstätigkeit für die Württembergische Metallwarenfabrik, Geislingen ▨ 1954-1978 Aufbau der »Werkstatt Wagenfeld«: Entwurf und Entwicklung von Industrieprodukten in Metall, Glas, Porzellan und Kunststoff

1914-1918 Apprentissage dans un bureau de dessin de la fabrique d'argenterie Koch & Bergfeld à Brême ▨ 1916-1919 études à l'Ecole des Arts décoratifs de Brême ▨ 1919-1922 études à l'Académie de dessin de Hanau ▨ 1922/23 séjour d'études à Brême et à Worpswede ▨ 1923-1925 études au Bauhaus de Weimar: cours préliminaire, apprentissage à l'atelier de métal, examen de compagnonnage ▨ 1926-1930 chargé de cours à Staatliche Bauhochschule de Weimar: assistant puis directeur de l'atelier de métal ▨ 1931-1935 crée pour la verrerie Jenaer Glaswerke Schott & Gen, nommé enseignant à la Staatliche Kunsthochschule Grunewaldstraße, école d'art de Berlin ▨ 1942-1945 service de guerre, fait prisonnier ▨ 1947-1949 enseigne à l'Académie des Beaux-Arts de Berlin ▨ 1949/50 rapporteur conseiller de la forme industrielle à l'inspection du travail du Land de Wurtemberg ▨ 1950- 1954 activité créatrice pour la fabrique d'objets métalliques de Geislingen ▨ 1954-1978 création de l'atelier Wagenfeld: conception et réalisation de produits industriels en métal, en verre, en porcelaine ou en plastique

Otto Wagner 1841–1918
1857-1959 studied architecture at the Vienna Polytechnical Institute ▨ 1860-1862 studied at the Königliche Bauakademie in Berlin and the Akademie der Bildenden Künste (Academy of Fine Arts) in Vienna ▨ from 1862 entered the architecture practice of Ludwig von Förster, Vienna, which he later took over and ran under his own name ▨ 1892/93 commissioned to draw up a scheme for completely replanning Vienna ▨ 1894-1916 taught at the Akademie der Bildenden Künste in Vienna, head of a special class in architecture (Wagner Schule), where his students included Adolf Loos, Josef Hoffmann and Joseph Maria Olbrich ▨ 1899-1905 member of the Vienna Secession ▨ 1895 published his book »Moderne Architektur« ▨ by 1900 his office was employing a staff of 70 and creating

design as well as architecture ▓ 1904-1906 planned and built the Austrian Post Office Savings Bank in Vienna and designed the entire interior fittings ▓ 1904-1907 worked on the »Hohe Warte« periodical ▓ 1907 planned the church »Am Steinhof«

1857-1959 Architekturstudium am Polytechnischen Institut, Wien ▓ 1860-1862 Studium an der Königlichen Bauakademie in Berlin und der Akademie der Bildenden Künste, Wien ▓ ab 1862 Mitarbeit im Architekturbüro von Ludwig von

Förster, Wien, später selbständige Weiterführung des Architekturbüros unter seinem Namen ▓ 1892/93 Konzeption des Generalregulierungsplans der Stadt Wien ▓ 1894-1916 Lehrauftrag an der Akademie der Bildenden Künste, Wien: Leitung der Spezialschule für Architektur (Wagner-Schule), zu seinen wichtigsten Schülern zählen Adolf Loos, Josef Hoffmann und Joseph Maria Olbrich ▓ 1899-1905 Mitglied der Wiener Secession ▓ 1895 Veröffentlichung seines Buches »Moderne Architektur« ▓ um 1900 sind ca. 70 Mitarbeiter in seinem Büro beschäftigt, neben der Architektur entstehen auch kunstgewerbliche Entwürfe ▓ 1904-1906 Planung und Ausführung des Österreichischen Postsparkassenamtes in Wien: Entwurf der gesamten Inneneinrichtung ▓ 1904-1907 Mitarbeit an der Zeitschrift »Hohe Warte« ▓ 1907 Planung der Kirche »Am Steinhof«

1857-1959 Etudes d'architecture à l'Institut polytechnique de Vienne ▓ 1860-1862 études à la Königliche Bauakademie de Berlin et l'Académie des Beaux-Arts de Vienne ▓ à partir de 1862 collaborateur de l'architecte Ludwig von Förster à Vienne, plus tard reprend la direction de cette étude sous son nom ▓ 1892/93 conception de la planification urbaine de Vienne ▓ 1894-1916 enseigne à l'Académie des Beaux-Arts de Vienne dont il dirige l'école d'architecture (Wagnerschule); citons parmi ses élèves les plus connus: Adlof Loos, Joseph Hoffmann et Joseph Maria Olbrich ▓ 1899-1905 membre de la Sécession viennoise ▓ 1895 publication de son livre «Moderne Architektur» ▓ vers 1900 occupe 70 collaborateurs dans son étude, à côté de l'architecture, crée aussi des objets d'arts décoratifs ▓ 1904-1906 conception et réalisation de la caisse d'épargne de la poste autrichienne à Vienne dont il crée l'ensemble de l'aménagement intérieur ▓ 1904-1907 collabore à la revue «Hohe Warte» ▓ 1907 plans de l'église «Am Steinhof»

Hans Warnecke 1900
1914-1928 apprenticeship, probably as goldsmith and silversmith ▓ 1919-1922 studied at the Kunstgewerbeschule (School of Applied Art) in Magdeburg ▓ 1922-1925 set up an enamelling workshop ▓ 1925-1933 taught at the Kunstschule (Art School) in Frankfurt, where he directed the workshop for enamelling, jewellery and appliances ▓ 1930-1944 set up a workshop for enamelling and precious metalwork with Erhard Warnecke ▓ 1946-1948 taught at the Trade College of the Precious Metals Industry in Schwäbisch Gmünd ▓ 1948-1966 taught at the Akademie der Bildenden Künste (Academy of Fine Arts) in Stuttgart as director of the metalworking class

1914-1928 Lehre, vermutlich als Gold- und Silberschmied ▓ 1919-1922 Studium an der Kunstgewerbeschule Magdeburg ▓ 1922-1925 Aufbau einer Werkstatt für Emailarbeiten ▓ 1925-1933 Lehrauftrag an der Kunstschule Frankfurt: Leitung der Werkstatt für Email, Schmuck und Gerät ▓ 1930-1944 Aufbau einer Werkstatt für Email- und Edelmetallarbeiten zusammen mit Erhard Warnecke ▓ 1946-1948 Lehrauftrag an der Höheren Fachschule für die Edelmetallindustrie in Schwäbisch Gmünd ▓ 1948-1966 Lehrauftrag an der Staatlichen Akademie der Bildenden Künste, Stuttgart: Leitung der Metallklasse

1914-1928 apprentissage d'orfèvre probablement ▓ 1919-1922 études à l'Ecole des Arts décoratifs de Magdebourg ▓ 1922-1925 création d'un atelier d'émail ▓ 1925-1933 chargé de cours à l'Ecole des Beaux-Arts de Francfort: dirige l'atelier d'émail, de bijou et d'ustensiles ▓ 1930-1944 ouvre avec Erhard Warnecke un atelier d'émail et de métal précieux ▓ 1946-1948 enseignant à l'Institut professionnel de l'Industrie du métal précieux à Schwäbisch Gmünd ▓ 1948-1966 chargé de cours à la Staatliche Akademie der Bildenden Künste de Stuttgart, dirige la classe de métal

Gustav Weidanz 1889-1970
1905–1908 apprenticed as a metal enchaser to Alexander Schönauer, Hamburg ▓ 1908-1910 studied at the Kunstgewerbeschule (School of Applied Art) in Hamburg ▓ 1910/11 worked in the studio of Franz Metzner and Ignatius Taschner in Berlin ▓ 1911-1916 studied at the Kunstgewerbeschule in Berlin ▓ 1916-1959 taught at the Handwerkerschule (Crafts School) in Halle, which later became the Burg Giebichenstein School of Applied Arts, where he was head of the sculpture classes for stone, wood and metal; set up a ceramics workshop, designed ceramics and porcelain ▓ from 1959 freelance sculptor

1905-1908 Lehre als Ziseleur bei Alexander Schönauer, Hamburg ▓ 1908-1910 Studium an der Kunstgewerbeschule Hamburg ▓ 1910/11 im Atelier von Franz Metzner und

Ignatius Taschner in Berlin tätig ▓ 1911-1916 Studium an der Kunstgewerbeschule Berlin ▓ 1916-1959 Lehrauftrag an der Handwerkerschule (später Kunstgewerbeschule Burg Giebichenstein) in Halle: Leitung der Fachklassen für Plastik in Stein, Holz und Metall, Aufbau einer Keramikwerkstatt, Entwurfstätigkeit im Bereich Keramik und Porzellan ▓ ab 1959 als freischaffender Bildhauer tätig

1905-1908 Apprentissage de ciseleur chez Alexander Schönauer à Hambourg ▓ 1908-1910 étudie à

l'Ecole des Arts décoratifs de Hambourg ▓ 1910/11 travaille dans l'atelier de Franz Metzner et d'Ignatius Taschner à Berlin ▓ 1911-1916 étudie à l'Ecole des Arts décoratifs de Berlin ▓ 1916-1959 nommé enseignant à l'Ecole artisanale (deviendra plus tard l'Ecole des Arts décoratifs de Burg Giebichenstein) de Halle: dirige les classes professionnelles du plastique dans la pierre, le bois et le métal, création d'un atelier de céramique, activité créatrice dans le domaine de la céramique et de la porcelaine ▓ A partir de 1959 travaille comme sculpteur indépendant

Svend Weihrauch 1899-1962
Trained as a silversmith ▓ worked for the silversmith Georg Jensen in Copenhagen until 1928 ▓ 1928-1956/58 worked in the silverware factory of Frantz Hingelberg in Arhus, designing and producing silverware ▓ his designs for Frantz Hingelberg were shown at the 1935 International Exhibition in Brussels and the 1937 International Arts and Crafts Exhibition in Paris

Ausbildung zum Silberschmied ▓ bis 1928 Mitarbeiter der Silberschmiede Georg Jensen, Kopenhagen ▓ 1928-1956/58 in der Silberwarenfabrik Frantz Hingelberg in Arhus tätig: Entwurf und Ausführung von Silberwaren ▓ seine Silberentwürfe für Frantz Hingelberg waren 1935 auf der Weltausstellung in Brüssel und 1937 auf der Internationalen Kunstgewerbeausstellung in Paris vertreten

Formation d'orfèvre ▓ collaborateur de l'orfèvre Georg Jensen à Copenhague jusqu'en 1928 ▓ 1928-1956/58 travaille dans la fabrique d'objets en argent de Frantz Hingelberg à Arhus: conception et réalisation d'argenterie ▓ ses créations pour Frantz Hingelberg sont présentées à l'Exposition universelle de Bruxelles en 1935 et à l'Exposition internationale des Arts décoratifs de Paris en 1937

Theodor Wende 1883-1968
1898-1903 apprenticeship as gold-

smith and silversmith at the firm of Sy & Wagner in Berlin ▓ 1903-1905 journeyman at Sy & Wagner, attended the Kunstgewerbe- und Handwerkerschule (Applied Arts and Crafts School) in Berlin-Charlottenburg ▓ 1905 worked for Heinze jewellers in Dresden ▓ 1905-1907 studied at the Kunstgewerbeschule (School of Applied Arts) in Berlin ▓ 1908-1912 studied at the Zeichenakademie in Hanau ▓ 1912-1913 worked as independent goldsmith and silversmith in Berlin, and was involved in designing the Royal cutlery ▓ 1913-1920 member of the

Darmstadt artists' colony ▓ 1921-1951 taught at the Badische Kunstgewerbeschule in Pforzheim where he gave goldsmith and silversmith master classes ▓ 1925 appointed master of the Zunft Jungkunst (Young Art Guild) in Pforzheim

1898-1903 Lehre als Gold- und Silberschmied bei der Goldschmiedefirma Sy & Wagner, Berlin ▓ 1903-1905 als Geselle bei Sy & Wagner tätig, Besuch der Kunstgewerbe- und Handwerkerschule in Berlin-Charlottenburg ▓ 1905 bei dem Juwelier Heinze in Dresden tätig ▓ 1905-1907 Studium an der Zeichenakademie Hanau ▓ 1908-1912 Studium an der Kunstgewerbeschule Berlin ▓ 1912-1913 als Gold- und Silberschmied selbständig in Berlin tätig, Mitarbeit am Kronprinzensilber: Entwurf und Ausführung der Besteckmodelle ▓ 1913-1920 Mitglied der Darmstädter Künstlerkolonie ▓ 1921-1951 Lehrauftrag an der Badischen Kunstgewerbeschule Pforzheim, Leitung der Meisterklassen für Gold- und Silberschmieden ▓ 1925 Ernennung zum Obermeister der Zunft Jungkunst in Pforzheim

1898-1903 Apprentissage d'orfèvre dans l'orfèvrerie Sy & Wagner à Berlin ▓ 1903-1905 compagnon chez Sy & Wagner, études à la Kunstgewerbe- und Handwerkerschule de Berlin-Charlottenburg ▓ 1905 travaille chez le joaillier Heinze à Dresde ▓ 1905-1907 étudie à l'Académie du dessin de Hanau ▓ 1908-1912 étudie à l'Ecole des Arts décoratifs de Berlin, collabore à l'élaboration de l'argenterie du Kronprinz: création et fabrication des modèles des couverts ▓ 1913-1920 membre de la colonie d'artistes de Darmstadt ▓ 1921-1951 enseigne à la Badische Kunstgewerbeschule de Pforzheim: dirige la classe d'orfèvrerie, année de maîtrise ▓ 1925 reçoit le titre honorifique de grand maître de la confrérie du Jungkunst (Art jeune) à Pforzheim

Franz Rudolf Wildenhain 1905-1980
1919-1924 trained as lithographer

at the art-publishing house of Eckert & Pflug in Leipzig ▨ 1924/25 studied at the Bauhaus in Weimar (basic course, apprenticeship in the Dornburg ceramics workshop) ▨ 1925-1929 studied at the Burg Giebichenstein School of Applied Arts in Halle, continued his pottery apprenticeship, journeyman's exam, master's exam ▨ 1930 taught at the Margarethenhöhe pottery workshop in Essen, married Marguerite Friedlaender ▨ 1930-1933 taught at the Burg Giebichenstein School of Applied Arts in Halle, where he was director of the pottery ▨ 1933-

174

1940 removed from the teaching staff by the Nazi regime, emigrated to Holland, set up the »Het Kruikje« pottery in Putten ▨ 1940-1942 set up a ceramics workshop in Amsterdam ▨ 1943-1947 military service, POW ▨ 1947-1949 emigrated to the USA, worked in the ceramics workshop of Marguerite Friedlaender in Guerneville/Cal. ▨ 1950-1956 taught at the School for American Craftsmen, Rochester Institute of Technology in Rochester, New York (classes in pottery and sculpture) ▨ 1956 set up a workshop for ceramics and sculpture in Rochester/New York

1919-1924 Ausbildung als Lithograf im Kunstverlag Eckert & Pflug, Leipzig ▨ 1924/25 Studium am Bauhaus Weimar: Vorkurs, Lehre in der Keramikwerkstatt in Dornburg ▨ 1925-1929 Studium an der Kunstgewerbeschule Burg Giebichenstein in Halle: Fortsetzung der Töpferlehre, Gesellenprüfung, Meisterprüfung ▨ 1930 Lehrtätigkeit in der Töpferwerkstatt der Margarethenhöhe in Essen, Heirat mit Marguerite Friedlaender ▨ 1930-1933 Lehrauftrag an der Kunstgewerbeschule Burg Giebichenstein in Halle: Leitung der Töpferei ▨ 1933-1940 Entlassung als Lehrkraft durch die Nationalsozialisten, Emigration nach Holland, Aufbau der Keramikwerkstatt »Het Kruikje« in Putten ▨ 1940-1942 Aufbau einer Keramikwerkstatt in Amsterdam, Lehrauftrag an der Schule für Angewandte Kunst in Amsterdam ▨ 1943-1947 Kriegsdienst, Gefangenschaft ▨ 1947-1949 Emigration in die USA, Arbeit in der Keramikwerkstatt seiner Ehefrau Marguerite Friedlaender in Guerneville/Cal. ▨ 1950-1956 Lehrauftrag an der School for American Craftsmen, Rochester Institute of Technology in Rochester/New York: Klassen für Töpferei und Bildhauerei ▨ 1956 Aufbau einer Werkstatt für Keramik und Skulptur in Rochester/New York

1919-1924 Formation de lithographe à la maison d'édition d'art Eckert & Pflug de Leipzig ▨ 1924/25 étudie au Bauhaus de Weimar:

cours préliminaire, apprentissage dans l'atelier de céramique à Dornburg ▨ 1925-1929 étudie à l'Ecole des Arts décoratifs de Burg Giebichenstein à Halle: poursuite de son apprentissage de potier, examen de compagnonnage et de maîtrise ▨ 1930 enseigne à l'atelier de poterie de la colline Sainte-Marguerite à Essen, épouse Marguerite Friedlaender ▨ 1930-1933 enseignant à l'école de Burg Giebichenstein : dirige la poterie ▨ 1933-1940 révoqué par les nationaux-socialistes, émigre en Hollande, crée l'atelier de céramique «Het Kruikje» à Putten ▨ 1940-1942 création d'un atelier de céramique à Amsterdam, enseigne à l'Ecole d'Art appliqué d'Amsterdam ▨ 1943-1947 service de guerre, détention comme prisonnier de guerre ▨ 1947-1949 émigre aux USA, travaille dans l'atelier de céramique de sa femme à Guerneville en Californie ▨ 1950-1956 chargé de cours à la School for American Craftsmen au Rochester Institute of Technology de Rochester/New York: classes de poterie et de sculpture ▨ 1956 création d'un atelier de céramique et de sculpture à Rochester

Carl Witzmann 1883-1952

Apprenticed as a carpenter to Adolf Legerer in Vienna ▨ attended the Carpenters' Trade School in Vienna ▨ 1900-1906 studied at the Kunstgewerbeschule (School of Applied Art) in Vienna, worked at the Wiener Werkstätte (Vienna Workshop), designed jewellery ▨ 1906-1910 taught at the Carpenters' Trade School in Vienna ▨ 1910-1949 taught at the Kunstgwerbeschule in Vienna, where he gave classes in draughtsmanship, cabinet-making and design, from 1912 he produced several architectural designs ▨ 1914-1918 military service ▨ 1910-1925 designed virtually all the exhibitions of the Austrian Museum of Art and Industry

Lehre als Tischler bei Adolf Legerer, Wien ▨ Besuch der Fachschule für Tischler, Wien ▨ 1900-1906 Studium an der Kunstgewerbeschule Wien, Mitarbeit in der Wiener Werkstätte: Entwürfe für Schmuck ▨ 1906-1910 Lehrauftrag an der Fachschule für Tischler, Wien ▨ 1910-1949 Lehrauftrag an der Kunstgewerbeschule Wien: Fachklassen für Entwurfszeichnen, Möbelbau und Innenarchitektur, intensive Entwurfstätigkeit im Bereich Innenarchitektur, Möbelbau und Kunstgewerbe, ab 1912 zahlreiche Architekturentwürfe ▨ 1914-1918 Kriegsdienst ▨ 1910-1925 Gestaltung nahezu aller Ausstellungen des Österreichischen Museums für Kunst und Industrie

Apprentissage d'ébéniste chez Adolf Legerer à Vienne ▨ Suit les cours de l'Ecole professionnelle d'ébénisterie à Vienne ▨ 1900-1906 étudie à l'Ecole des Arts décoratifs de la ville, collaboration aux Ateliers viennois: créations de bijoux ▨ 1906-1910 enseigne à l'Ecole professionnelle d'ébénisterie ▨ 1910-1949 chargé de cours à l'Ecole des Arts décoratifs de Vienne: classes

professionnelles de dessin de création, construction de meubles et de décoration intérieure; grande activité créatrice dans le domaine de l'aménagement d'intérieurs, conception de meubles et art décoratif, à partir de 1912 nombreuses créations d'architecture ▨ 1914-1918 service de guerre ▨ 1910-1925 conception de presque toutes les expositions du Musée autrichien de l'Art et de l'Industrie

Frank Lloyd Wright 1867-1959

1885-1887 studied engineering at the University of Wisconsin, Ma-

dison ▨ 1887-1892 architect in the practices of Lymann Silsbee and Adler & Sullivan in Chicago/Ill. ▨ 1893-1897 set up his own design and architecture office in Chicago, later moving to Oak Park near Chicago, where he designed and built houses and interiors ▨ 1897 moved his architecture practice to Steinway Hall, Chicago ▨ 1905 first trip to Japan, where he studied Japanese architecture and began collecting and dealing in Japanese prints ▨ 1909-1911 extensive travels in Germany and Italy ▨ 1911-1914 set up a new studio and house (which he named »Taliesin« – the shimmering hill) at Spring Green/Wisc. – several major architectural contracts at home and abroad ▨ 1914 »Taliesin« burned down in an arson attack and rebuilt ▨ 1915 opened an architecture office in Tokyo, planned and supervised the »Imperial Hotel« building in Tokyo ▨ 1922 opened an architecture office in Los Angeles and went on to work internationally as an architect, town planner and writer

1885-1887 Studium der Ingenieurwissenschaften an der Universität von Wisconsin, Madison ▨ 1887-1892 als Architekt in den Architekturbüros von Lymann Silsbee und Adler & Sullivan in Chicago/Ill. tätig ▨ 1893-1897 Aufbau eines eigenen Architektur- und Entwurfsbüros in Chicago, später in Oak Park bei Chicago, Planung und Ausführung von Wohnbauten, intensive Entwurfstätigkeit für Inneneinrichtungen ▨ 1897 Verlegung seines Architekturbüros in die Steinway Hall, Chicago ▨ 1905 erste Japan-Reise, intensive Beschäftigung mit der japanischen Architektur, Beginn seiner Sammler- und Händlertätigkeit von japanischen Drucken ▨ 1909-1911 ausgedehnte Reise nach Deutschland und Italien ▨ 1911-1914 Aufbau eines neuen Ateliers und Wohnhauses (die Anlage nennt er »Taliesin«, schimmernder Hügel) bei Spring Green/Wisc.: zahlreiche Entwürfe und Ausführung von bedeutenden Bauten im In- und Ausland ▨ 1914 fällt der »Taliesin« einem

Brandstifter zum Opfer, Wiederaufbau ▨ 1915 Eröffnung eines Architekturbüros in Tokio: Planung und Betreuung der Bautätigkeiten des »Imperial Hotel« in Tokio ▨ 1922 Eröffnung eines Architekturbüros in Los Angeles, in der Folgezeit international als Architekt, Städteplaner und Schriftsteller tätig

1885-1887 Etudes d'ingénieur à l'université du Wisconsin à Madison ▨ 1887-1892 collabore à l'étude d'architectes de Lymann Silsbee et à celle d'Adler & Sullivan à Chicago/Ill. ▨ 1893-1897 création de sa propre étude d'architecte et de création à Chicago, transférée plus tard à Oak Park près de Chicago, plans et construction de maisons, grande activité créatrice dans le domaine de l'aménagement d'intérieurs ▨ 1897 transfert de son étude dans le Steinway Hall de Chicago ▨ 1905 premier voyage au Japon, étude approfondie de l'architecture japonaise, début de son activité de commerçant et de collectionneur d'estampes japonaises ▨ 1909-1911 voyage en Allemagne et en Italie ▨ 1911-1914 création d'un nouvel atelier et d'une nouvelle maison (qu'il nomme «Taliesin», la colline étincelante) dans les environs de Spring Green dans le Wisconsin, création et réalisation de nombreuses maisons dans le pays et à l'étranger ▨ 1914 la «Taliesin» est incendiée, reconstruction ▨ 1915 ouverture d'un bureau d'architecte à Tokyo: plans et supervision des travaux de «l'hôtel Imperial» de Tokyo ▨ 1922 création d'une étude d'architecte à Los Angeles, activités internationales d'architecte, d'urbaniste et d'écrivain.

Bibliography
Bibliographie
Bibliographie

Anscombe, Isabelle & Gere, Charlotte: Arts & Crafts in Britain and America. London 1978

Bröhan, Torsten (ed.): Glaskunst der Moderne. Von Josef Hoffmann bis Wilhelm Wagenfeld. München 1992

Buddensieg, Tilmann & Rogge, Henning: Industriekultur. Peter Behrens und die AEG 1907-1914. Berlin 1990

Burckhardt, Lucius (ed.): The Werkbund. Studies in the history and ideology of the Deutscher Werkbund 1907-1933. London 1980

Fiell, Charlotte & Fiell, Peter: Modern Chairs. Köln 1993

Garner, Philippe (ed.): The Encyclopedia of Decorative Arts. 1890-1940. London 1978

Droste, Magdalena: Bauhaus 1919-1933. Köln 1990

Droste, Magdalena & Ludewig, Manfred: Marcel Breuer Design. Köln 1992

Halén, Widar: Christopher Dresser. London 1990

Junghans, Kurt: Der Deutsche Werkbund. Sein erstes Jahrzehnt. Berlin 1982

Klein, Dan & Bishop, Margaret: Decorative Art 1880-1980. London 1989

Krekel-Aalberse, Annelies: Art Nouveau and Art Déco Silver. London 1989

Pevsner, Nikolaus: Wegbereiter moderner Formgebung von Morris bis Gropius. Köln 1983

Schneider, Katja: Burg Giebichenstein. Die Kunstgewerbeschule unter Leitung von Paul Thiersch und Gerhard Marcks 1915 bis 1933. Weinheim 1992

Schweiger, Werner J.: Die Wiener Werkstätte. Kunst und Kunsthandwerk 1903-1932. Wien 1982

Selle, Gerd: Design-Geschichte in Deutschland. Produktkultur als Entwurf und Erfahrung. Köln 1987

Sembach, Klaus-Jürgen, Leuthäuser, Gabriele & Gössel, Peter: Twentieth-Century Furniture Design. Köln, 1988

Sembach, Klaus-Jürgen & Schulte, Birgit (eds.): Henry van de Velde. Ein europäischer Künstler seiner Zeit. Köln 1992

Tolstoj, Vladimir (ed.): Art Décoratif Sovietique 1917-1937. Paris 1989

Varnedoe, Kirk: Wien 1900. Kunst, Architektur & Design. Köln 1987

Wichmann, Hans: Design contra Art Déco. 1927-1932 Jahrfünft der Wende. München 1993

Wingler, Hans M.: Das Bauhaus. 1919-1933 Weimar, Dessau, Berlin und die Nachfolge in Chicago seit 1937. Bramsche 1962

Catalogues
Kataloge
Catalogues

Das deutsche Kunstgewerbe 1906. München 1906

Industrial Design. Unikate – Serienerzeugnisse. Die Neue Sammlung. Ein neuer Museumstyp des 20. Jahrhunderts. München 1985

The Machine Age in America 1918-1941. Brooklyn Museum. New York 1986

Bent Wood and Metal Furniture 1850-1946. The American Federation of Arts. New York 1987

Berlin 1900-1933. Architecture and Design. Cooper-Hewitt Museum of Decorative Arts and Design. Berlin 1987

Josef Hoffmann 1870-1956. Ornament zwischen Hoffnung und Verbrechen. Die Sammlungen des Österreichischen Museums für Angewandte Kunst, der Hochschule für Angewandte Kunst, Wien, mit Objekten aus dem Historischen Museum der Stadt Wien. Wien 1987

Wiener Werkstätte. Atelier Viennois 1903-1932. Europalia 1987. Galerie CGER. Bruxelles 1987

Art Nouveau in Munich. Masters of Jugendstil. Philadelphia Museum of Art. München 1988

L'Art Deco en Europe. Tendances décoratives dans les arts appliqués vers 1925. Europalia 1989. Société des Expositions du Palais des Beaux-Arts Bruxelles 1989

Metallkunst, Kunst vom Jugendstil zur Moderne (1889-1939). Sammlung Karl H. Bröhan. Bd. IV. Bröhan Museum. Berlin 1990

Modern Design in the Metropolitan Museum of Art 1890-1990. Metropolitan Museum of Art. New York 1990

Museum Künstlerkolonie Darmstadt. Darmstadt 1990

Decorative Arts 1850-1950. A Catalogue of the British Museum Collection. British Museum. London 1991

Die Metallwerkstatt am Bauhaus. Bauhaus Archiv. Berlin 1992

Burg Giebichenstein. Die Hallesche Kunstschule von den Anfängen bis zur Gegenwart. Staatliche Galerie Moritzburg. Halle 1993

Index